Historical Perspectives on Modern Economics

Economic theories in a non-Walrasian tradition

Historical Perspectives on Modern Economics

General Editor: Professor Craufurd D. Goodwin, Duke University

This series contains original works that challenge and enlighten historians of economics. For the profession as a whole it promotes a better understanding of the origin and content of modern economics.

Economic theories in a non-Walrasian tradition

Takashi Negishi
University of Tokyo

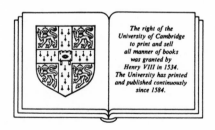

The right of the
University of Cambridge
to print and sell
all manner of books
was granted by
Henry VIII in 1534.
The University has printed
and published continuously
since 1584.

CAMBRIDGE UNIVERSITY PRESS

Cambridge
New York   New Rochelle
Melbourne   Sydney

Published by the Press Syndicate of the University of Cambridge
The Pitt Building, Trumpington Street, Cambridge CB2 1RP
32 East 57th Street, New York, NY 10022, USA
10 Stamford Road, Oakleigh, Melbourne 3166, Australia

First published 1985
First paperback edition 1989

Printed in the United States of America

Library of Congress cataloging in Publication Data

Negishi, Takashi, 1933–
Economic theories in non-Walrasian tradition.
(Historical perspectives on modern economics)
Bibliography: p.
Includes indexes.
1. Economics – History. I. Title.   II. Series.
HB75.N42   1985   330'.09   21467

ISBN 0-521-25967-3 hard covers
ISBN 0-521-37860-5 paperback

To my Aiko for our china wedding anniversary

Contents

Contents

Preface

This book is a collection of essays on topics in the history of economics which were selected from the point of view of their relation to current mainstream economics. One aim of studying this history of economics is to learn of thoughts and theories quite different from those of mainstream Walrasian economics. Thus we may develop the science further in new directions and new areas. Topics like division of labor, economy of scale, wages, profit, international trade, the market mechanism, and money are considered from the point of view of non-Walrasian economic theories – those of the classical, Marxist, Austrian, Jevonian, and Cambridge schools – as well as from the point of view of Walrasian economic theory. This book is, therefore, a natural sequel to my previous studies of Walrasian economics (*General equilibrium theory and international trade*, 1972) and non-Walrasian economics (*Microeconomic foundations of Keynesian macroeconomics*, 1979).

I owe thanks for valuable comments and warm encouragement to my colleagues in the University of Tokyo, members of the Japanese History of Political Economy (HOPE) Association, and participants of seminars where some of the essays were read. Although some of them are mentioned in relevant chapters below, I regret that I cannot mention names of the many other persons to whom I am greatly indebted. My research activities have been supported financially by the Foundation for Promoting Economics of the University of Tokyo. The *Zeitschrift für Nationalökonomie* and the *Manchester School of Economic and Social Studies* kindly permitted me to use my articles published in their pages: "Wickwell's missing equation and Böhm-Bawerk's three causes of interest in a stationary state," in Chapter 9, and "A note on Jevons's law of indifference and competitive equilibrium," in Chapter 12. Last, but not least, I would like to thank Professor Craufurd D. W. Goodwin, anonymous readers of the manuscript, and Cambridge University Press editors for valuable suggestions and editorial efforts, and Mrs. Tamami Kawamura and Miss Tomoko Kiyama for excellent typing and other secretarial services.

T. N.

CHAPTER 1

Anti-neoclassical or non-Walrasian economic theories

The neoclassical economic theory that is currently predominant should, to be precise, be referred to as Walrasian or neo-Walrasian economic theory, to distinguish it from the Marshallian tradition that was originally designated neoclassical economics (Latsis 1976, p. 86). The aim of this book is to study economic theories of the past that are not directly related to this Walrasian mainstream, so that we can develop boldly new economic theories that are heretical to the currently prevailing theory.

The theories to be studied were once predominant or were influential in some stages of the development of economic science but are now either regarded as having played out their historical roles or else are supported only by a minority of the present economics profession. But this study is not antiquarian, since the theories to be considered raise interesting questions that can be solved with modern techniques. What is of interest is not only what previous economists did do, but also what they did *not* do. We should not, however, indulge ourselves in an easy victory like a modern army, slipped through time, to overcome a band of medieval knights. We can find in the works of previous economists clues to questions of present interest or techniques of analysis that might be applied to modern problems. It is this possibility that is the motivation for studying the history of economic thought.

Studies of the works of previous economists are useful for the development of new theories, particularly if those economists to be studied belong to schools different from the currently dominating one. More generally, the history of science is studied to develop new theories that are heretical to the current ones. In the next section, I discuss two examples in the history of science, one the case of Copernicus in the history of astronomy, and the other the case of Keynes in the history of economic thought. I then try to justify my position by reviewing some recent developments in the philosophy of the history of science.

The organization of this book is not historical and the chapters are not ordered chronologically. The focus is not so much on what some previous economists really meant and what they contributed to the development of economics as on what suggestions for the new theories on our own problems we can obtain by reworking problems the previous economists

1

could not solve completely. Hence the chapters are grouped according to their topics: Increasing returns and diminishing cost, Wages and profit, International trade and investment, and Markets and money.

Revolutions in the history of science

The early writings of Adam Smith (1967) contain "Principles which lead and direct Philosophical Enquiries, illustrated by the History of Astronomy."[1] When Smith discussed, in the history of astronomy, the revolutionary contribution to the astronomy made by Copernicus, he duly emphasized the role of the past history of astronomy in the development of Copernican theory. Copernicus began to consider that the heavenly bodies should be arranged in a different order from that in which Aristotle and Hipparchus had placed them, so as to give a solution to the problem of the planets that is simultaneously simpler and more precise than that of Ptolemy.

To discover this arrangement, he examined all the obscure traditions delivered down to us, concerning every other hypothesis which the ancients had invented, for the same purpose. He found, in Plutarch, that some old Pythagoreans had represented the Earth as revolving in the center of the universe, like a wheel round its own axis, and that others, of the same sect, had removed it from the center, and represented it as revolving in the Ecliptic like a star round the central fire. By this central fire, he supposed they meant the Sun, and though in this he was very widely mistaken, it was, it seems upon this interpretation, that he began to consider how such a hypothesis might be made to correspond to the appearances. The supposed authority of those old philosophers, if it did not originally suggest to him his system, seems, at least, to have confirmed him in an opinion, which, it is not improbable, that he had before-hand other reasons for embracing, not withstanding what he himself would affirm to the contrary. (Smith 1967, pp. 71–72)[2]

Even a widely mistaken interpretation of past theories, however obscure and immature they might have been, was important, if not to suggest originally, at least to confirm the development of new revolutionary theories. What is important is not whether a particular interpretation of a past theory is correct, but whether it is useful in developing a new theory in the present. Perhaps in the days of Copernicus the authority of old philosophers was necessary in order to say something new and different from established doctrine. It may be the case, furthermore, that the history of economics differs from the history of astronomy, because in the former the object of the study, the economy, changes rapidly through history so that old theories do not apply to the new situation. To clear up these possible objections, therefore, let us move from the astronomy of the

Renaissance and the case of Copernicus to the economics in the twentieth century and the case of Keynes.

The crux of the Keynesian economics is the possibility of an equilibrium with involuntary unemployment in a monetary economy due to over-saving that cannot be cleared by automatic adjustment in the rate of interest. The economics of Keynes was a revolution against the classical economics of Ricardo and of Marshall (Shove 1942). If we compare Keynes with Copernicus, therefore, it seems that the mercantilists are to classical economists what the Pythagoreans are to Ptolemy. While writing the *General theory*, Keynes tried to show that he was "not really being so great an innovator, except as against the classical school," but had "important predecessors and [was] returning to an age-long tradition of common sense" (Keynes 1973, p. 552). In the final version of the *General theory*, Keynes argued as follows:

It is impossible to study the notions to which the mercantilists were led by their actual experiences, without perceiving that there has been a chronic tendency throughout human history for the propensity to save to be stronger than the inducement to invest. The weakness of the inducement to invest has been at all times the key to the economic problem. Today the explanation of the weakness of this inducement may chiefly lie in the extent of existing accumulations, whereas, formerly, risks and hazards of all kinds may have played a larger part. But the result is the same. (Keynes 1936, pp. 347–48)

The mercantilist and Keynesian reasons for over-saving are different, just as the economy in the days of mercantilism is different from that of Keynes.[3] It cannot be said, therefore, that the mercantilists anticipated Keynes. There is no doubt, however, that they influenced Keynes, for Keynes recognized them as predecessors and believed over-saving to have been a chronic tendency through human history.

Keynes's view on Malthus is also interesting. Keynes claimed, with sympathy and admiration, that Malthus was the first of the Cambridge economists. This is, of course, not so much because of Malthus's immortalized principle of population as because of the brilliant intuitions in his more far-reaching principle of effective demand. Malthus's theory was, of course, not complete. His criticism against Say's law can be removed by the loanable funds theory of interest (Eagly 1974, p. 101). This point is recognized by Keynes himself:

Malthus's defect lay in his overlooking entirely the part played by the rate of interest. Twenty years ago I should have retorted to Malthus that the state of affairs he envisages could not occur unless the rate of interest had first fallen to zero. Malthus perceived, as often, what was true, but it is essential to a complete comprehension of why it is true, to explain how an excess of frugality does not bring with it a decline to zero in the rate of interest. (Keynes 1972, p. 102)

In other words, unemployment is not explained by over-saving unless the nonzero rate of interest is prevented from falling by preference for liquidity. Therefore, Malthus may not be called a precursor of Keynes. Nevertheless, like Keynes, we cannot deny the influence of Malthus on Keynes. Past theories are important, not because they happened to anticipate the current theory, but because they influenced the development of the current theory. We are not interested in uncovering some buried past theories that turn out to have already developed quite unnoticedly some aspect of the currently prevailing theory. What is important is not that mercantilists and Malthus are precursors of Keynes but that they influenced Keynes so that he was made to consider whether the classical economics of Ricardo and Marshall was correct (Mehta 1977, p. 93). This is true independent of whether Keynes's interpretation of mercantilists and Malthus is correct from the point of view of "what they really meant."

One might argue that the case of Keynes is, after all, the very special case of a great economist and that knowledge of past theories is not necessary for economists in general, who do not attempt to make a revolution in economics but wish to make modest contributions to the progress of economic science. This suggests that we consider the nature of the general law that governs the progress of sciences.

Paradigms and research programs

The Keynesian revolution reminds us the theory of scientific revolution developed by Thomas Kuhn from his study of the Copernican revolution (Kuhn 1957, 1970). The history of science is not the history of continuous conjectures and refutations à la Popper (1959). It is marked by long periods of steady refinement, normal science or problem-solving activity in the context of an accepted theoretical framework, a paradigm, interrupted on occasion by scientific revolutions, discontinuous jumps from one ruling paradigm to another with no bridge for communicating between them. It should be emphasized that a paradigm cannot be overthrown by a single empirical refutation. It is overthrown in consequence of repeated refutations and mounting anomalies only when a competing, alternative paradigm is ready.

A typical reaction of economists to Kuhn's theory can be seen in Bronfenbrenner's (1971) interpretation that Kuhn's theory is a catastrophic theory. Bronfenbrenner does not deny the existence of scientific revolutions in the sense of Kuhn, but thinks that the catastrophic theory of Kuhn does not explain the facts very well in the history of economics because some special features distinguish the history of economics from that of other disciplines. First, the catastrophic theory maintains that paradigms, once displaced, are displaced definitely. But, according to Bronfenbrenner, outmoded ideas are never definitely displaced in economics. Second, advances in economics tend to be major accretions without a rejection of existing pardigms, which Bronfenbrenner argues is inconsistent with catastrophic theory. Two examples given by Bronfenbrenner of outmoded and displaced ideas that still continue to exist in economics are elements of the medieval notion of just price, on which modern income policy proposals are based, and mercantilist notions, which continue to exist in spite of their displacement by classical economics.

Mehta (1977, pp. 198–201) defends Kuhn and criticizes Bronfenbrenner to the effect that Kuhn's theory is not the catastrophic theory that Bronfenbrenner claims it to be. Kuhn's theory is not a theory of scientific revolutions that are complete and unaccountable breaks with the past, since Kuhn himself admits that new paradigms usually preserve a great deal of the most concrete parts of past achievement. In other words, in the later and weaker version of Kuhn's theory, any period of scientific development is marked by a larger number of overlapping and interpenetrating paradigms, some of which may be incommensurable but certainly not all of which are (Kuhn 1970, pp. 199–200). Paradigms are not considered to be replaced by each other immediately. In economics as well as in other sciences, then, outmoded ideas continue to exist, since outmodedness can be defined, as was emphasized by Mehta, only relative to a given paradigm. From this point of view, the study of the history of economics is very important to promote the progress of economics, since an idea that is outmoded relative to one of the currently dominating paradigms may be useful for the development of another, possibly new, paradigm.

Such a view of scientific progress can be, however, explained more nicely by the theory of Lakatos (1970), which is a halfway point between Popper and Kuhn. Lakatos considered that the history of science has been and should be a history of competing research programs (paradigms) but that it has not been and not become a succession of periods of normal science, the monopoly of a research program. All scientific research programs may be characterized as having an immutable hard core that is irrefutable and that is surrounded by a changeable, protective belt of auxiliary, refutable hypotheses that has to bear the brunt of tests. Let us note that scientific research programs are not competing theories but competing series of changing theories. If changes increase content, they are called progressive, whereas if they are ad hoc and decrease content, they are called degenerating.

When two research programs, R_1 and R_2, compete, their first models usually deal with different aspects of the domain. As the rival research programs expand, however, they gradually encroach on each other's territory. In other words, they are commensurable. This overlapping of R_1 and R_2 eventually results in the first battle between the two programs in which, say, the nth version of R_1 will be bluntly, dramatically inconsistent with the mth version of R_2. Suppose the battle is won by R_1, as a result of an experiment. But the war is not yet over, since any research program is allowed a few such defeats. All it needs for a comeback is to produce an $m + 1$ content-increasing version and a verification of some of its novel content (Easlea 1973, pp. 21–22). It is difficult to see why an apparently defeated research program cannot make a triumphal return with its hard core the same as before but with a better articulated and different protective belt.[4] But, to make a triumphal return, there must be some scientists seeking to develop it while it was in a state of hibernation. In other words, it is necessary to study theories that are regarded as past one from the point of view of other research programs.

It may be too early to decide whether Kuhn's or Lakatos's theory of history of science can be mechanically applied to the history of economics (Blaug 1980, Goodwin 1980, and Latsis 1976). It is certain, however, that the historical development of economic theories is not a unidirectional progression toward the truth and that the currently influential theory is not necessarily superior, in every respect, to past theories, which have been neglected so far (Cesarano 1983). In this book we shall show that the relation between the current economic theory and history of economics is by no means one way. It is, of course, impressive to see how important problems unsolved by past, crude theories are elegantly analyzed by the modern, improved techniques (Samuelson 1966, pp. 339–422). It is more important, however, to know that outmoded ideas hidden in the past theories are useful, suggestive, or encouraging when one tries to add something new to the current economic theory, irrespective of whether it is a revolutionary change or a minor modification.

Organization of the book

Part I of this book consists of four chapters on increasing returns and diminishing cost, which Walrasian theory of competitive equilibrium has not succeeded in dealing with effectively. Chapter 2, "Adam Smith and increasing returns in a competitive situation," considers how increasing returns due to the division of labor, which is limited by the extent of the market, is compatible with competition in *The wealth of nations* and compares Smith's theory with some recent non-Walrasian theories of the kinked demand curve. The relation between the division of labor and required accumulation of capital is discussed in Chapter 3, "A reconstruction of Smith's doctrine on the natural order of investment," and a new theory of international trade between homogeneous countries is suggested by the reconstruction of Smith's theory of the order of investment. Marx's law of the falling rate of profit was denied by Shibata and Okishio by the application of a static Walrasian model of perfect competition and constant returns to scale. Chapter 4, "The possibility of a falling rate of profit under diminishing cost," argues that the Marxist law should be considered dynamically by a model of imperfect competition under diminishing cost. Finally, in Chapter 5, "Rehabilitation of Marshall's life-cycle theory to explain diminishing cost," I try to apply the basic idea of Marshall's life-cycle theory of firms to explain diminishing cost in modern firms whose life span is not limited.

We learn from non-Walrasian theories of distribution, studied in four chapters of Part II, "Wages and profit," the significance of the time structure of capital[5] and of subsistence wages. Chapter 6, "Conditions for the wages fund doctrine and Mill's recantation of it," considers the classical wages fund doctrine, which has already played its role as a wage theory but still has some use as a capital theory. We consider Marx's *Das Kapital* as a theory of distribution in Chapter 7, "Marx and exploitations in production and in circulation," and in Chapter 8, "Marx's dichotomy between exploitation and redistribution of surplus products." In the former, the exploitation theory based on subsistence wages is criticized because Marx did not consider properly the role of capital in the time-consuming process of production. Pointed out in the latter is the difficulty of Marx's dichotomy between volumes I and III of *Das Kapital*, which is due to his neglect of land in the process of production. Finally in Chapter 9, "Böhm-Bawerk and the positive rate of interest in a stationary state," the Austrian theory of capital is considered and a model is constructed to explain the positive rate of interest by the first and third causes, which Böhm-Bawerk himself intended to do.

Results of studies in Part II are applied in the two chapters of Part III, "International trade and investment," to consider non-Walrasian theories of international trade and investment. In Chapter 10, "The role of exporters and importers in classical and Keynesian theories," the classical price-specie-flow mechanism, Ricardian theory of terms of trade, and foreign exchange gains in a Keynesian situation are discussed with emphasis on the role of exporters and importers, which is derived from non-Walrasian capital theory based on the time structure of production. Implications of subsistence wages determined exogenously as necessary to reproduce labor are clarified in Chapter 11, "Ricardo, the natural wage, and international unequal exchange," with respect to Ricardian and neo-Marxist theories of international economics. Interesting results, not expected in Walrasian (that is, Heckscher–Ohlin) theory, can be obtained by taking into consideration the time structure of capital to be advanced to cover the cost during the period of production and wages determined exogenously by socioeconomic factors.

Finally, Part IV, "Markets and money," contains three chapters on the theory of markets and money, developed by non-Walrasian economists of the marginal revolution. Chapter 12, "Jevons, Edgeworth, and the competitive equilibrium of exchange," argues that Jevons, followed by Edgeworth, tried to explain what Walras simply assumed – the existence of market prices, not necessarily equilibrium ones – and that what Jevons had in mind has not yet been fully developed by Edgeworth and his modern followers. Menger's marketability or salability of commodities and money is compared with the short-side principle of recent non-Walrasian disequilibrium theories in Chapter 13, "Menger's *Absatzfähigkeit*, a non-Walrasian theory of markets and money." The final chapter, 14, "The Marshallian foundation of macroeconomic theories," insists that Walrasian *tâtonnement* economics cannot be a microeconomic foundation of monetary macroeconomics and that Marshallian non-*tâtonnement* theory of the market suggests a theory of kinked demand curve, which can be a microeconomic foundation of Keynesian economics, while the Marshallian theory of the trade cycle is very similar to recent monetarist macroeconomics.

PART I

Increasing returns and diminishing cost

CHAPTER 2

Adam Smith and increasing returns in a competitive situation

A great classic often has many different aspects that permit many different and mutually inconsistent interpretations by later scholars. *The wealth of nations* of Adam Smith is a good example of such a classic. Karl Marx, for example, highly valued the fact that Smith made a great advance beyond the Physiocrats in the analysis of the nature and origin of surplus values on the basis of the determination of the exchange value of commodities by the quantity of labor expended on them, though he at the same time criticized that Smith's conception of natural price as the sum of wages, profit, and rent falls into a vicious circle (Marx 1963, pp. 70, 83, 93–94). Schumpeter, on the other hand, argued that the rudimentary equilibrium theory in Chapter 7, Book I of *The wealth of nations* based on the concept of natural price is by far the best piece of economic theory turned out by Adam Smith and it in fact points toward Say and, through Say's work, to Walras (Schumpeter 1954, p. 189).

The division of labor that improves labor productivity is the key characteristic and driving force in *The wealth of nations*. Smith gave two propositions concerning the division of labor, "that the division of labour is limited by the extent of the market," and that "as the accumulation of stock must, in the nature of things, be previous to the division of labour, so labour can be more and more subdivided in proportion only as stock is previously more and more accumulated" (Smith 1976, pp. 31, 277). The first proposition is particularly interesting from the point of view of the reconciliation of competition and increasing returns, which are caused by the subdivision of labor within a firm. The second proposition is, on the other hand, important when we consider the natural course of economic development, which is, as Young (1928) emphasized, caused by the progressive division and specialization of industries. In this chapter we consider the implications of the first proposition; those of the second will be treated in the next chapter.

To add a new interpretation to the already rich variety of interpretations of different aspects of *The wealth of nations* is certainly troublesome for those who wish to know what Smith really meant. But our purpose here is to examine the history of economics as the rich source from which we can obtain hints, suggestions, and encouragement to develop boldly

11

new economic theories that are heretical to the currently prevailing theories. Thus we are asking Adam Smith to support our attempt to reconcile perfect competition and increasing returns in the sense of an internal economy of individual firms.

According to our interpretation of the equilibrium model of Adam Smith, a competitive firm is faced with a kinked demand curve that is formally similar to the kinked demand curve in oligopoly theory, though its implications are quite different. The kinked demand curve model in the oligopoly theory has been criticized because the location of the kink is indeterminate. In the case of the competitive model of Adam Smith, however, this criticism is irrelevant, the location of the kink being determined by appealing to Smith's idea of the natural price. In other words, Smith's equilibrium concept of competitive pricing is more flexible than that of neoclassical economics, and is very similar to some recent models of non-Walrasian or Keynesian economics. It is flexible enough to cover the case of a firm for which there is a demand deficiency. Increasing returns in the sense of an internal economy of individual firms need not, therefore, produce concentration and monopoly, since a firm with an internal economy of scale to produce a given product is always subject to demand deficiency; that is, division of labor within a firm is limited by the extent of the market. Competition and increasing returns are not inconsistent in Smith's theoretical model.

The following section documents the concepts of competition and the natural price in *The wealth of nations* and argues that they can be interpreted to the effect that a competitive firm is faced with a demand curve with a kink at the natural price and effectual demand. Similarly, documented in the subsequent section, "Division of labor limited by the market," is the presence in *The wealth of nations* of the idea of increasing returns due to the internal economy of a firm, which is made possible by division of labor, the extent of which is limited by the market. The section, "Demand deficiency and increasing returns," has two purposes. First, Smith's model of a competitive firm is compared with the recent Keynesian model of a firm under demand deficiency and both of them are shown to differ in an important way from the Walrasian model of an ideally well-organized market. Second, I argue that competition and increasing returns are reconciled in Smith's model, in which increasing returns are limited by the extent of the market; that is, demand cannot be increased without a drastic reduction of the price.

Competition and natural price

The essential characteristic of competition in neoclassical economics is that the individual producer cannot modify the prices prevailing in the market. This means the producer faces a demand curve for its product that is infinitely elastic. For Adam Smith, however, as well as for other classical economists, competition is characterized by free entry. This can be seen, for example, in the following arguments of Smith.

The whole of the advantages and disadvantages of the different employments of labour and stock must, in the same neighbourhood, be either perfectly equal or continually tending to equality. If in the same neighbourhood, there was any employment evidently either more or less advantageous than the rest, so many people would crowd into it in the one case, and so many would desert it in the other, that its advantages would soon return to the level of other employments. This at least would be the case in a society where things were left to follow their natural course, where there was perfect liberty, and where every man was perfectly free both to chuse what occupation he thought proper, and to change it as often as he thought proper. (Smith 1976, p. 116)

This is certainly a very important difference between classical economics and neoclassical economics. It raises questions rather than solves them, however. One may argue that even in neoclassical economics, free entry is a part of conditions of competition in the long run. Even for Smith, furthermore, there must be some arguments on whether an individual firm can modify the conditions of the market, including price in the competition.[1]

In his famous Chapter 7 of Book I of *The wealth of nations*, which is an early, pioneering attempt to develop a market equilibrium theory (Schumpeter 1954, p. 189), Smith made the following statement.

When the quantity brought to market is just sufficient to supply the effectual demand, and no more, the market price naturally comes to be either exactly, or as nearly as can be judged of, the same with the natural price.[2] The whole quantity upon hand can be disposed of for this price, and cannot be disposed of for more. The competition of the different dealers obliges them all to accept of this price, but does not oblige them to accept of less. (Smith 1976, p. 74)

Though this statement is concerned with the case of a given quantity, the key sentence, that the whole quantity upon hand can be disposed of at this price and the competition of the different dealers obliges them all to accept this price, can be interpreted to mean that an individual supplier perceives an infinitely elastic demand curve for quantities less than the given one – that is, the effectual demand. This interpretation is made in view of Smith's statement on monopoly that "the monopolists, by keeping the market constantly under-stocked, by never fully supplying the effectual demand, sell their commodities much above the natural price" (Smith 1976, p. 78), a statement showing that Smith realized that higher price can be obtained only by reducing the quantity. Free entry would make such monopolistic behavior impossible.

As it does for neoclassical economists, therefore, competition seems to mean for Smith, not only free entry, but also the given unchangeable price and the infinitely elastic demand curve perceived by individual suppliers. The similarity is, however, only partial. The statement that the "competition of the different dealers obliges them all to accept of this price but does not oblige them to accept of less" implies that an individual supplier firm cannot modify the price upward but that it can if it wishes, and though it need not, reduce it. When the quantity brought to market is just sufficient to supply the effectual demand, the whole quantity on hand can certainly be disposed of for the natural price. However, "when the quantity brought to market exceeds the effectual demand, it cannot be all sold to those who are willing to pay the whole value of the rent, wages, and profit, which must be paid in order to bring it thither.[3] Some part must be sold to those who are willing to pay less" (Smith 1976, p. 74). Hence, an individual supplier, at the natural price-effective demand equilibrium, cannot expect to increase sales without reducing price below the natural price. Perhaps we should mention that the number of actual competitors in the industry is assumed to be not infinitely large so that a supplier cannot expect an infinitely large increase in sale by an infinitesimally small reduction in price, though the number of potential competitors is infinitely large from the assumption of the free entry. Unlike the neoclassical system, therefore, the demand curve perceived by an individual supplier in Smith's system cannot be infinitely elastic and must be downwardly sloping for a quantity larger than effectual demand.

In other words, a competitive supplier in Smith's system perceives a demand curve that has a kink at the point of effectual demand and the natural price, with the right-hand part downward sloping and the left-hand part infinitely elastic. Because the effectual demand is simply defined as demand at the natural price (Smith 1976, p. 73), the location of the kink is determined by the natural price. Adam Smith defined the natural price as follows: "When the price of any commodity is neither more nor less what is sufficient to pay the rent of land, the wages of the labour, and the profits of the stock employed in raising, preparing, and bringing it to market, according to their natural rates, the commodity is then sold for what may be called its natural price" (Smith 1976, p. 72). The natural rates of wages, profit, and rent are their ordinary or average rates, when the stages of development – advancing, stationary, or declining – are specified.

As for the relationship between the natural price and cost, we can say that the natural price corresponds to Marshallian long-run unit cost (normal expenses of production), which includes normal profit (normal earnings), if the term *cost* is interpreted as something that must be covered for the production to be maintained (Frisch 1950). This can be clearly seen in Smith's arguments following his definition of natural price.

The commodity is then sold precisely for what it is worth, or for what it really costs the person who brings it to market; for though in common language what is called the prime cost of any commodity does not comprehend the profit of the person who is to sell it again, yet if he sells it at a price which does not allow him the ordinary rate of profit in his neighbourhood, he is evidently a loser by the trade; since by employing his stock in some other way he might have made that profit. His profit, besides, is his revenue, the proper fund of his subsistence. As, while he is preparing and bringing the goods to market, he advances to his workmen their wages, or their subsistence; so he advances to himself, in the same manner, his own subsistence, which is generally suitable to the profit which he may reasonably expect from the sale of his goods. Unless they yield him this profit, therefore, they do not repay him what they may very properly be said to have really cost him. (Smith 1976, pp. 72–73)

Since modern interpretations of Adam Smith are quite divided, some of them naturally support the interpretation I have just given, or at least are not inconsistent with it, while some others are against it. It is Sylos-Labini (1976) who emphasized that there exists a very large distance between the neoclassical static conception of competition and that of Smith, and that for Smith competition implies free entry but monopoly is characterized by obstacles to entry. Samuelson (1977a) insisted, however, by the use of programming, dual variables, shadow prices, and other means, that the price theory of Smith is very modern. Schumpeter (1954, p. 606) argued that in classical literature the concept of demand schedules or curves of willingness to buy specified quantities of a commodity at specified prices proved unbelievably hard to discover and to distinguish from the concept of quantity demanded. Stigler (1965, p. 69), fortunately, made a more favorable interpretation of the case of Smith, and Hollander (1973, p. 118) concluded that Smith had in mind the concept of a negatively sloped demand schedule.

Division of labor limited by the market

In the Smithian system, the equilibrium of a firm is characterized by a kink in the demand curve it perceives, and the location of such a kink is explained by appealing to Smith's concept of the natural price. The natural price, which corresponds to Marshallian normal unit cost including normal profit, is in turn explained by the natural rate of wages, profits, and rent in different stages of development (progressive, stationary, and declining). Even if a stage of development is given, and therefore

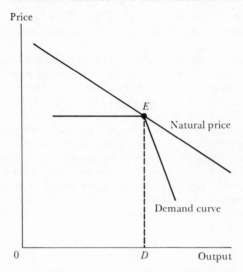

Figure 2.1

the natural rate of wages, profits, and rent are constant, however, the natural price may change with the size of the firm, if the normal cost changes with the level of output of the firm. Assuming that it diminishes with the level of output, a Smithian equilibrium for a firm at the natural price and effectual demand is shown as the point E in Figure 2.1.

If the demand for the industry increases, the firm's equilibrium point temporarily shifts horizontally to the right, or even upward to the right, with the market price higher than the natural price. Because this implies wages, profits, and rent all higher than natural rates, the entry of new suppliers who, to obtain markets, undersell old suppliers, reduces the market price toward the natural price. Because old suppliers have already realized lower natural price before the entry of new ones, it is unlikely, particularly when the reduction of natural price is irreversible, that the eventual level of output is smaller than $0D$ in Figure 2.1.[4] An increase in effectual demand slides the equilibrium E down along the natural price curve. Smith explained this as follows: "The increase of demand, though in the beginning it may sometimes raise the price of goods, never fails to lower it in the long run. It encourages production, and thereby increases the competition of the producers, who in order to undersell one another, have resource to new divisions of labour and new improvements of art which might never otherwise have been thought of" (Smith 1976, p. 748).[5]

The natural price, which is diminishing with respect to the size of the firm as is shown in Figure 2.1, implies the existence of the increasing returns to scale or diminishing cost due to the internal economy of the scale of the firm. Smith's explanation of such increasing returns or diminishing cost is that "producers have recource to new divisions of labour." As a matter of fact, Smith gave two different kinds of illustrations of the division of labor. One is concerned with an interfirm division of labor or the specialization of firms in the same industry, the extent of which is limited by the industrial demand, while the other is concerned with the subdivision of different operations to produce a given product, the extent of which is limited by the demand for the output of the plant. It is, of course, the latter kind of division of labor, the subdivision of labor within the firm, with which we are concerned here.

The illustration of the former kind of division of labor is drawn from nail making in *The wealth of nations*.

A smith who has been accustomed to make nails, but whose sole or principal business has not been that of a nailer, can seldom with his utmost diligence make more than eight hundred or a thousand nails in a day. I have seen several boys under twenty years of age who had never exercised any other trade but that of making nails, and who, when they exerted themselves, could make, each of them, upwards of two thousand three hundred nails in a day. The making of a nail, however, is by no means one of the simplest operations. The same person blows the bellows, stirs or mends the fire as there is occasion, heats the iron, and forges every part of the nail: In forging the head too he is obliged to change his tools. The different operations into which the making of a pin, or of a metal button, is subdivided, are all of them much more simple, and the dexterity of the person, of whose life it has been the sole business to perform them, is usually much greater. (Smith 1976, p. 18)

The difference between nail making and pin and button making, which is Smith's illustration of the latter kind of division of labor, can be explained by the principle that the division of labor is limited by the extent of the market. Demand for the output of the plant was sufficiently large in the case of pins and buttons to justify a labor force adequate for *sub*division (see Hollander 1973, pp. 208, 239). Smith described the effect of this latter kind of division of labor in the following.

The trade of the pin-maker; a workman not educated to this business, nor acquainted with the use of the machinery employed in it, could scarce, perhaps, with his utmost industry, make one pin in a day, and certainly could not make twenty. But in the way in which this business is now carried on, not only the whole work is a peculiar trade, but it is divided into a number of branches, of which the greater part are likewise peculiar trades. One man draws out the wire, another straights it, a third cuts it, a fourth points it, a fifth grinds it at the top for receiving the head; to make the head requires two or three distinct operations; to put it on, is a peculiar business, to whiten the pins, is another; it is even a trade by itself to put them into the paper; and the important business of making a pin is, in this manner, divided into about eighteen distinct operations, which, in some manu-factories, are all performed by distinct hands, though in others the same man will sometimes perform two or three of them. I have seen a small manufactory of this kind where ten men only were employed, ... Those ten persons could make among them upwards of forty-eight thousands pins in a day. Each person, there-fore, ... might be considered as making four thousand eight hundred pins in a day. (Smith 1976, pp. 14–15).

Adam Smith pointed out clearly that the latter division of labor, the case of pin making and button making, is a more advanced stage than the former division of labor, the case of nail making.

Samuelson (1977a) assumed constant returns in his mathematical model of Adam Smith's economics, which is not inconsistent with interpretations by Blaug (1978, p. 42) and Bladen (1974, p. 31). For Young (1928), however, Smith's theorem that the division of labor, which causes increa-sing returns, depends upon the extent of the market is one of the most illuminating and fruitful generalizations in the whole literature of eco-nomics. The concept of such increasing returns is, however, by no means unique among those who see it in Adam Smith. Hollander (1973, p. 239) insists on the originality of Smith in the attempt to account for the sub-division of labor *in terms of plant size*, while Richardson (1975) states that an interfirm division of labor, the extent of which is limited by the size of the market, does correspond closely to Smith's vision. Young (1928) went further to conclude that increasing returns are not to be discerned adequately by observing the effects of variations in the size of an indivi-dual firm or a particular industry and that the progressive division and specialization of industries is an essential part of the process by which increasing returns are realized.

Demand deficiency and increasing returns

The kinked demand curve was originally developed by Sweezy (1939) to explain price rigidity in oligopolistic industries. An oligopolistic firm perceives a kinked demand curve, since rival firms react asymmetrically according to whether a price change is upward or downward. If the firm raises its price, it must expect to lose business to its rivals, who will not raise their prices, while if the firm cuts its price it has no reason to believe it will succeed in taking business away from its rivals, who will retaliate by cutting their prices so as to avoid the loss. Although it has often been

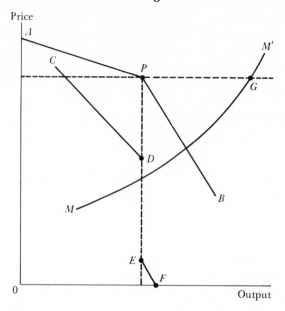

Figure 2.2

criticized that the location of the kink is indeterminate, Sweezy insisted that the perceived demand curve can only be thought of with reference to a given starting point, a price–output combination that depends upon the history of the case and that it has a kink at this starting point.

In Figure 2.2, the marginal revenue curve *CDEF* is derived from the perceived demand curve *APB* and has a discontinuity at the level of output where the perceived demand curve has a kink. If the marginal cost curve *MM'* passes between the two parts of the discontinuous marginal revenue curve, the starting point *P* is also the point of profit maximization. Sweezy pointed out that a disturbance that affects only the position of the marginal cost curve may leave the equilibrium price and output entirely unaffected. More important for oligopolistic price rigidity, however, is the fact that, as Sweezy stated, any shift in demand will clearly first make itself felt in a change in the quantity sold at the current price. In other words, a shift in demand shifts the position of the starting point *P*, at which the kink occurs, to the right or left without affecting the price. If the marginal cost is not increasing rapidly, the equilibrium price remains unchanged while shifts in demand are absorbed by changes in the level of output.

Literature on the theory of the kinked demand curve is still growing, though empirical tests in oligopolistic markets have not yet been unambiguous (Reid 1981, p. 99). From the point of view of the comparison with the case of Adam Smith, however, a recent application of the kinked demand curve to give a microeconomic foundation to Keynesian macroeconomics is most interesting, since it is concerned with, not an oligopolistic, but a competitive firm under demand deficiency.

Whereas a kinked demand curve in Sweezy's theory of oligopoly is due to the asymmetric reaction of rival firms, it is considered to be a result of asymmetric reaction of customers in the case of competitive firms in the Keynesian situation. Lower prices asked by a supplier may not be fully advertised to customers currently buying from other suppliers who are maintaining their current prices, while a higher price charged by the same supplier necessarily induces present customers to leave in search of lower price suppliers, whom they easily find, since in the Keynesian situation there are many other firms that wish to supply more at the current price unchanged (Negishi 1979a, pp. 36, 87; Reid 1981, pp. 96–99; Scitovsky 1978; Stiglitz 1979.)

In Figure 2.2, therefore, AP is horizontal and CD coincides with AP for a competitive firm in the Keynesian case. In Keynesian terminology, we may call the determination of the level of output at which the expected profit is maximized with given marginal revenue and marginal cost cur the problem of short-term expectation. Short-term expectation is assumed by Keynes to be realized (Negishi 1979a, pp. 28–29, 90); thus such a level of output must coincide with the level of output corresponding to the given starting point P in Figure 2.2, which the firm knows from its current experiences in the marketing. Although it wishes to supply at the current price up to the level of output corresponding to point G, where the current price and the marginal cost are equalized, the firm is trapped at the level of output corresponding to P, with no incentive to reduce price to increase demand. There exists an implicit excess supply or idle capacity GP due to the deficiency of the aggregate effective demand. The first postulate of classical economics – that price is equalized with marginal cost – is discarded, because it is not the rising marginal cost but the difficulty of selling larger quantities without reducing the price which limits the size of the firm. Any shift in the aggregate effective demand changes the position of P horizontally, with price unchanged. If the marginal cost is not increasing rapidly, shifts in the aggregate demand are entirely absorbed by changes in the level of output (Negishi 1979a, pp. 89–90; Reid 1981, pp. 65–66; Woglom 1982).

There is, of course, an important difference between the Smithian equilibrium of the firm in the long run and the Keynesian equilibrium of the firm in the short run. In the latter, the price at the starting point (the location of the kink) is explained by a hangover from the past, modified by changes in expectation, inflationary or deflationary inertia, and other factors. In the former, on the other hand, the price is given as the natural price, which is in turn explained as the long-run normal cost by the given natural rate of wages, profits, and rent.

The similarity is more important than the difference, however. In both cases, the size of the firm is limited, not by the rising cost, but by the extent of the market. In other words, unlike the case of neoclassical economics, competitive firms cannot perceive infinitely elastic demand curves. Why in the case of neoclassical competitive suppliers are demand curves perceived as infinitely elastic for any quantity, so that any quantity can be sold at the given price? The neoclassical model of competitive pricing is, like Walrasian *tâtonnement*, that of the organized exchanges in which quoted prices are quickly changed so as to equate demands and supplies almost continuously, with the result that individual suppliers can safely assume, without much loss, that they can sell whatever quantity they like at the current quoted price. It is true that there is no role as a medium of exchange to be played by money if all the economy is organized in such a way, which leads to the reason why the neoclassical economics can be dichotomized into the real, barter price theory and the aggregate monetary theory (see Chapter 14). Such is not, however, the world of Smith, who considered both prices and money in the same place (Book I of *The wealth of nations*), let alone the monetary world of Keynes.

In the Walrasian model of *tâtonnement* in organized exchanges, prices are changed by the auctioneer according to the size of the excess demand or excess supply. In the Smithian model of competitive but not well-organized markets, prices are changed by the negotiations among demanders and suppliers, which are strictly subject to the power of competition. Not only the size of excess demand and supply, therefore, but also the situations in which demanders and suppliers find themselves are reflected in price changes, which is duly noted by Smith.

When the quantity of any commodity which is brought to market falls short of the effectual demand, ... the market price will rise more or less above the natural price, according as either the greatness of the deficiency, or the wealth and wanton luxury of the competitors, happen to animate more or less the eagerness of the competition. Among competitors of equal wealth and luxury the same deficiency will generally occasion a more or less eager competition, according as the acquisition of the commodity happens to be of more or less important to them.... When the quantity brought to market exceeds the effectual demand, ... prices will sink more or less below the natural price, according as the greatness of the excess increases more or less the competition of the sellers, or according as it happens to be more or less important to them to get immediately rid of the commodity. (Smith 1976, pp. 73–74)

Although Smith pointed out clearly that subdivision of labor within a firm occurs at a more advanced stage than the specialization of firms and industries, contemporary scholars like Young and Richardson who emphasize the importance of Smithian increasing returns based on division of labor put more emphasis on the latter than the former. One of the reasons for this seems to be the historically celebrated inconsistency between competition and increasing returns due to the internal economy of scale of a firm. Richardson, for example, observed: "If we consider a group of firms making identical products for the same market, then it is clear that, so long as any of them experiences increasing returns, competition must produce concentration and, in the end, monopoly"; he seems to conclude that increasing returns should be considered as leading to specialization and interdependence of firms in the same industry rather than to straightforward concentration, in order to go along with "Adam Smith, who did not appear to be in the least troubled by the thought that competition and increasing returns might not be able to coexist" (Richardson 1975, p. 354).

We can say, however, that Adam Smith need not "be in the least troubled by the thought that competition and increasing returns might not be able to coexist," since increasing returns are limited by the extent of the market, which firms know cannot be increased without reducing price. If an infinitely elastic demand curve is perceived through E in Figure 2.1 for the level of output larger than OD, the optimal size of the firm is certainly infinitely large. The equilibrium point E remains unchanged, however, if the elasticity of demand curve perceived in the right of E is properly small so that it is located below the downward sloping curve of the long-run normal cost (the natural price).[6]

In this way, we can reply, at least partly, to Kaldor's criticism on equilibrium theory that

it is evident that the coexistence of increasing returns and competition is a very prominent feature of de-centralized economic system but the manner of functioning of which is still a largely uncharted territory for the economist, ... [and] we have no clear idea of how competition works in circumstances where each producer faces a limited market as regards sales and yet a highly competitive market as regards price. (Kaldor 1972, pp. 1251–52)

In spite of Kaldor, we can still see the relevance of equilibrium economics for the important phenomena of increasing returns due to division of labor, indivisibility, the three-dimensional nature of space.[7]

CHAPTER 3

A reconstruction of Smith's doctrine on the natural order of investment

Smith's thesis concerning the different productivities of capital and the associated argument concerning the natural order of investment developed in Books II and III of *The wealth of nations* are sometimes regarded as being among the less successful parts of the edifice, in comparison with the theory of division of labor and the rudimentary equilibrium theory, both developed in Book I.[1] Smithian arguments to support the hierarchy of productivity of industries, headed by agriculture, followed by manufacture, inland trade, and foreign trade have been subject to severe criticism from many eminent scholars, including Ricardo and J. S. Mill. They are, as a matter of fact, not systematic, not persuasive; rather, they are ambiguous, confusing, and mutually inconsistent (see Kobayashi 1977, ch. 7). Note, furthermore, the fact that the conclusion about the different employment of capital and the natural progress of opulence is reached independently of the division of labor, which, Smith emphasized, has so much to do with the accumulation of capital.[2]

Though it is not successfully proven, however, the theory of the productivity hierarchy is an important and indispensable part of *The wealth of nations,* since it is employed, in Books III and IV, against the mercantilist policy of favoring foreign commerce and manufacturing, to argue that mercantile policy had diverted capital to less productive uses, with slower returns, than would otherwise have been the case. It is, therefore, not unreasonable to try to reconstruct Smith's arguments rationally by picking up correct fragments and putting them in order. In a sense this has already been done by Hollander (1973, pp. 281, 287) from the neoclassical point of view by emphasizing that Smith correctly considered the different profitability of industries in terms of factor endowments and relative factor prices. Although I am the last to deprecate Hollander's attempt, in this chapter I shall try an alternative reconstruction by emphasizing the increasing returns caused by division of labor, which are made possible by the accumulation of capital. The reason for this exercise is that a reconstruction from a particularly Smithian point of view, which has not been fully developed in neoclassical tradition, is more interesting, at least to me, than a reconstruction from the viewpoint that Smith is

23

essentially not different from neoclassicals and therefore offers little for us modern economists to learn.

The perspective on international trade afforded by this reconstructed theory of the order of investment suggests a new theory of international trade between homogeneous rather than heterogeneous countries. Ricardian and Heckscher–Ohlin theories of comparative cost presuppose the existence of international differences in climate, technology, and factor endowments, so that they cannot explain trades among homogeneous countries that dominate current world trades. Comparative advantages, however, need not be assumed exogenously. They can be created endogenously among homogeneous countries along Smithian lines based on the principle of increasing returns, which itself is based on the principle of the division of labor.

The plan of chapter is as follows. Smith's arguments on the natural order of investments in *The wealth of nations* are documented first and critically considered with reference to criticism of some modern scholars. The first half of the section titled "Division of labor and capital accumulation" is devoted to documenting Smith's theorem that capital accumulation is necessary for the division of labor; the second half presents and analyzes a simple formal model of the relationship between the division of labor and the required level of capital accumulation. Natural order of investment is then reconstructed, to the effect that investment should be made so as to develop the division of labor, for which the current level of capital accumulation is sufficiently high. Finally, I point out some implications of a new line of the theory of international trade suggested by Smith's arguments on foreign trade.

Smith on the different employment of capital

In Chapter 5, Book II of *The wealth of nations*, Smith argued on the different productivities of capital in agriculture, manufacture, and trade.

When the capital of any country is not sufficient for all . . . purposes, in proportion as a greater share of it is employed in agriculture, the greater will be the quantity of productive labour which it puts into motion within the country; as will likewise be the value which its employment adds to the annual produce of the land and labour of the society. After agriculture, the capital employed in manufacture puts into motion the greatest quantity of productive labour, and adds the greatest value to the annual produce. That which is employed in the trade of exportation, has the least effect of any of the three. (Smith 1976, p. 366)

Ricardo criticized this argument as a confusion of gross and net revenues, but Hollander seems to defend it by arguing that it is immaterial whether one speaks of maximizing gross or net revenue, when the population is given (Ricardo 1951, p. 347; Hollander 1973, p. 279). What is important, however, is that the maximization of the quantity of the productive labor is generally different from the maximization of the revenue, unless productive labor is equally productive everywhere.[3] Smith correctly considered that the only way of increasing the annual value of the national income is to increase the quantity of productive labor employed, or to increase its productivity. Productive labor only being employed by capital, however, it is easy to slip over to the conclusion that the quantity of productive labor employed by capital provides a test of the addition to the annual wealth of the community by that capital (see Bowley 1975).

For Smith, however, the concept of productive labor is sometimes flexible enough so that cattle and even nature herself are productive. In his somewhat Physiocratic statement,

No equal capital puts into motion a greater quantity of productive labour than that of the farmer. Not only his labouring servants, but his labouring cattle, are productive labours. In agriculture too nature labours along with man; and though her labour costs no expence, its produce has its value, as well as that of the most expensive workmen.... The labourers and labouring cattle, therefore, employed in agriculture, not only occasion, like the workmen in manufactures, the reproduction of a value equal to their own consumption, or to the capital which employs them, together with its owners [sic] profits; but of a much greater value. Over and above the capital of the farmer and all its profits, they regularly occasion the reproduction of the rent of landlord. This rent may be considered as the product of those powers of nature, the use of which the landlord lends to the farmer.... The capital employed in agriculture, therefore, not only puts into motion a greater quantity of productive labour than any equal capital employed in manufactures, but in proportion too to the quantity of productive labour which it employs, it adds a much greater value to the annual produce of the land and labour of the country, to the real wealth and revenue of its inhabitants. Of all the ways in which a capital can be employed, it is by far the most advantageous to the society. (Smith 1976, pp. 363–64)

To argue that agriculture is more productive than manufacture because there is land rent only in agriculture is confusing and is criticized by Ricardo and J. S. Mill to the effect that the reason the use of land bears a price is simply the limitation of its quantity (Ricardo 1951, p. 76; Mill 1965, pp. 28–29). In other words, positive land rent is, though a sufficient, not a necessary condition for agriculture being more productive than manufacture.

Being quite inconsistent with the argument just quoted, however, Smith also insisted that investment should be, and actually was, made first in agriculture when rent is low, while investment should, and actually was, shifted into manufacture as rent increased.

It has been the principal cause of the rapid progress of our American colonies towards wealth and greatness, that almost their whole capitals have hitherto been employed in agriculture.... Were the Americans either by combination or by any other sort of violence, to stop the importation of European manufactures, and, by thus giving a monopoly to such of their own countrymen as could manufacture the likely goods, divert any considerable part of their capital into this employment, they would retard instead of accelerating the further increase in the value of their annual produce, and would obstruct instead of promoting the progress of their country towards real wealth and greatness. (Smith 1976, pp. 366–67)

In our North-American colonies, where uncultivated land is still to be had upon easy terms, no manufactures for distant sale have ever yet been established in any of their towns. When an artificer has acquired a little more stock than is necessary for carrying on his own business in supplying the neighbouring country, he does not, in North America, attempt to establish with it a manufacture for more distant sale, but employs it in the purchase and improvement of uncultivated land.... In countries, on the contrary, where there is either no uncultivated land, or none that can be had upon easy terms, every artificer who has acquired more stock than he can employ in the occasional jobs of the neighbourhood, endeavours to prepare work for more distant sale. The smith erects some sort of iron, the weaver some sort of linen or woollen manufactory. (pp. 378–379)

According to Hollander (1973, p. 287), Smith's emphasis on agricultural investment as the most advantageous to society on the grounds that rents are thereby generated is a serious error in logic. But Smith's emphasis on agricultural investment itself is correct, Hollander asserts, since Smith also had in mind the question of factor endowments and relative factor prices that determine the relative profitability of agriculture and manufacturing. If we assume neoclassical production functions with constant returns to scale and diminishing marginal rate of substitution, less-land-using manufacture will expand relative to more-land-using agriculture, as capital and labor increase and land remains unchanged.

The capital employed in home trade purchases "in one part of the country in order to sell in another the produce of the industry of that country, generally replaces by every such operation two distinct capitals that had both been employed in the agriculture or manufactures of that country, and thereby enables them to continue that employment" (Smith 1976, p. 368). Domestic trade is, therefore, no more productive than agriculture and manufacture. The foreign trade of consumption purchases, on the other hand, foreign goods for home consumption with the product of home industry, and "replaces too, by every such operation, two distinct capitals; but one of them only is employed in supporting domestic industry." It will, therefore, "give but one-half of the encouragement to the industry or productive labour of the country." This is true as far as immediate effects on employment are concerned. If foreign industries are more profitable, however, foreign trade will yield more and may eventually be more favourable to the labor of the country (see Chapter 10). Smith argued further that "the returns of the foreign trade of consumption are very seldom so quick as those of the home-trade" and therefore the capital employed in home trade will give "more encouragement and support to the industry of the country than" the capital employed in foreign trade. In a note to this passage in his edition of *The wealth of nations*, Cannan pointed out that "if this doctrine as to the advantage of quick returns had been applied earlier in the chapter, it would have made havoc of the argument as to the superiority of agriculture" (Smith 1973, p. 349; 1976, p. 369).

In view of these quotations from *The wealth of nations* and considerations on them, we can hardly say that Smith's expositions of doctrine of the natural order of investment are systematic, consistent, and persuasive, though some parts of them can be interpreted in terms of neoclassical theory of production. What seems strange, though, is that Smith does not take into consideration the role of the division of labor sufficiently in his exposition of different productivities of capital and the natural course of accumulation of capital.

Division of labor and capital accumulation

Smith's famous theorem that the division of labor depends upon the extent of the market, which Young (1928) called one of the most illuminating and fruitful generalizations in the whole literature of economics, appeared as early as his Glasgow lectures in the early 1760s (Smith 1978, p. 494). Similarly, a theorem that capital accumulation is necessary for the division of labor is also suggested in the Glasgow lectures in the section dealing with the cause of slow progress of affluence.

A rude and barbarous people are ignorant of the effects of the division of labour, and it is long before one person, by continualy working at different things, can produce any more than is necessary for his daily subsistence. Before labour can be divided some accumulation of stock is necessary. A poor man with no stock can never begin a manufacture. Before a man can commence farmer [sic] he must at least have laid in a years provision, because he does not receive the fruits of his labour till the end of the season. . . . This is one great cause of the slow progress of opulence in every country; till some stock be produced there can be no division of labour, and before a division of labour take place there can be very little accumulation of stock. (Smith 1978, pp. 521–22)

It is remarkable, as pointed out by Bowley (1975), that Smith realized that the division of labor is the prime technical means of increasing productivity before he developed profit and capital theory fully in *The wealth of nations*, a first in the history of economics. It is important, therefore, to see his approach to capital from the point of view of his theory of the division of labor.

Smith's theory of the division of labor itself is apparently not changed between the Glasgow lectures and *The wealth of nations*. In particular, the relation between the accumulation of capital and the division of labor is clearly stated in the Introduction of Book II.

In that rude state of society in which there is no division of labour, in which exchanges are seldom made, and in which every man provides everything for himself, it is not necessary that any stock should be accumulated or stored up beforehand in order to carry on the business of the society.... But when the division of labour has once been thoroughly introduced, the produce of a man's own labour can supply but a very small part of his occasional wants. The far greater part of them are supplied by the produce of other men's labour, which he purchases with the produce, or, what is the same thing, with the price of the produce of his own. But this purchase cannot be made till such time as the produce of his own labour has not only been completed, but sold. A stock of goods of different kinds, therefore, must be stored up somewhere sufficient to maintain him, and to supply him with the materials and tools of his work till such time, at least, as both these events can be brought about. (Smith 1976, p. 276)

As the accumulation of stock must, in the nature of things, be previous to the division of labour, so labour can be more and more subdivided in proportion only as stock is previously more and more accumulated. The quantity of materials which the same number of people can work up, increases in a great proportion as labour comes to be more and more subdivided; and as the operations of each workman are gradually reduced to a greater degree of simplicity, a variety of new machines come to be invented for facilitating and abridging those operations. As the division of labour advances, therefore, in order to give constant employment to an equal number of workmen, an equal stock of provisions, and a greater stock of materials and tools than what would have been necessary in a ruder state of things, must be accumulated beforehand. (p. 277)

In view of Smith's arguments quoted in the preceding pages, we may construct a simple model to show the relation between the division of labor and the capital accumulation. Consider a stationary economy producing two goods with a given supply of labor. Conditions for the balance of demand and supply of two goods and labor in a given unit period are

$$c_1 + a_{11}x_1 + a_{12}x_2 = b_1x_1 \tag{3.1}$$
$$c_2 + a_{21}x_1 + a_{22}x_2 = b_2x_2 \tag{3.2}$$
$$x_1 + x_2 = L \tag{3.3}$$

where L is the given supply of labor, x_1 is the labor input for the production of the ith good ($i = 1, 2$), $b_i x_i$ is the output of the ith good, $a_{ij} x_j$ is the input of the ith good (materials and provisions for laborers) for the production of the jth good ($i, j = 1, 2$), and c_i is the surplus of the ith good to be consumed by capitalists. Because L, b_i's, and a_{ij}'s are assumed to be given constants, Equations (3.1)–(3.3) are solved for c_1, c_2, x_1, and x_2, provided the ratio of c_1 to c_2 is given by the preference of consumers.

Let us compare the required capital accumulation for two different situations. Consider first the situation with no division of labor, where each production unit produces two goods, so that firms are not specialized and there is a single industry. In the second situation there is division of labor, where each production unit produces only one good, so that firms are specialized and there are two industries. In the latter situation, of course, b_i's are larger than in the former, since the productivity of labor is increased by the division of labor. For the sake of later discussions, it is convenient to distinguish three cases.

1. Suppose the turnover of capital in the production of the second good is n (>1) times as quick as in the production of the first good. In other words, the period of production of the first good is identical to the given unit period assumed in Equations (3.1)–(3.3) whereas that of the second good is only one-nth of it. In the situation with no division of labor, a stock of $a_{11} x_1 + a_{12} x_2$ of the first good and $(a_{21}/n) x_1 + (a_{22}/n) x_2$ of the second good is necessary at the beginning of the period. This is because the new output of the first good is not available until the period is over, whereas that of the second good is available after only one-nth of the period is passed. In the situation with the division of labor, however, the necessary stock of the second good is changed into $a_{21} x_1 + (a_{22}/n) x_2$, because the first industry producing the first good cannot purchase the new output of the second good until its own new output is available. If the allocation of labor between two goods is not changed very much (that is, x_1 and x_2 are not changed very much), between two situations, therefore, division of labor requires a larger stock of the second good, in the production of which turnover of capital is quicker, to be accumulated from the very beginning of the period in the hands of the producers of the first good, in the production of which turnover of capital is slower.[4]

2. Even if there is no difference in the period of production between two goods ($n = 1$), furthermore, the required capital $a_{11} x_1 + a_{12} x_2$ and $a_{21} x_1 + a_{22} x_2$ to be accumulated from the beginning of the period may be larger in the situation with division of labor than in the situation with no division of labor. This is the case Smith emphasized, where not only b_i's but also a_{ij}'s are increased by the division of labor. The use of materials is certainly increased if the speed of operation is increased by the division of labor,

though there is a counteracting tendency to save the waste of materials through more careful operations made possible by the division of labor.

3. Even if there is no difference in the period of production between two goods ($n = 1$), and a_{ij}'s remain unchanged in spite of the division of labor, finally, one may argue that turnover of capital is slower in the situation with division of labor than in the situation with no division of labor. This is because not only the period of production but also the period of circulation must pass before a producer can purchase products of others in the former situation. If the turnover of capital in the latter situation is k (>1) times as quick as in the former situation, so that the period of production is only one-kth of the given unit period assumed in Equations $(3.1)-(3.3)$ while the sum of the period of production and the period of circulation is identical to the given unit period in the former situation, the division of labor requires k times as large capital accumulation for any given allocation of labor input.

Natural order of investment reconsidered

The "accumulation of stock is previously necessary for carrying on this great improvement in the productive powers of labor, so that accumulation naturally leads to this improvement" (Smith 1976, p. 277). Because the natural order of investment is concerned exactly with how the capital accumulation leads to improvement in productivity due to the division of labor, it is clear that investment must start in a most unspecialized, self-sufficing industry and gradually proceed so that industries are more and more subdivided and specialized.[5]

Agriculture can be regarded as such a most inclusive and most unspecialized industry if we include household and coarser manufactures into agriculture. This may not be so foreign to Smith's view of agriculture.

It has been the principal cause of the progress of our American colonies towards wealth and greatness, that almost their whole capitals have hitherto been employed in agriculture. They have no manufactures, those household and coarser manufactures excepted which necessarily accompany the progress of agriculture, and which are the work of the women and children in every private family. (Smith 1976, p. 366)

At other times manufactures for distant sale grow up naturally, and as it were of their own accord, by the gradual refinement of those household and coarser manufactures which must at all times be carried on even in the poorest and rudest countries. (p. 408)

Without the assistance of some artificers, indeed, the cultivation of land cannot be carried on, but with great inconveniency and continual interruption.... When an artificer has acquired a little more stock than is necessary for carrying on his own business in supplying the neighbouring country, he does not, in North America, attempt to establish with it a manufacture for more distant sale, but employs it in the purchase and improvement of uncultivated land. From artificer he becomes planter, ... (pp. 378–79)

Though Smith and Hollander tried to explain this priority of agriculture by the relative cheapness of land, the possibility of which I do not deny, we may alternatively explain that the capital accumulation is not large enough to support "a manufacture for more distant sale," which is profitable only if operated in a large scale, and that the division of labor is not advanced. All the three cases considered in the preceding section apply to argue that an all-inclusive agriculture cannot be divided into an independent manufacture and agriculture unless a certain stock of capital is accumulated.

When enough capital is accumulated to support a manufacture as an independent, specialized industry, however, investment should be and actually is made so as to develop the occasional jobs in the neighborhood of artificers into a regular manufacture for more distant sale. As Smith explained: "every artificer who has acquired more stock than he can employ in the occasional jobs of the neighbourhood, endeavours to pre-pare work for more distant sale. The smith erects some sort of iron, the weaver some sort of linen or woollen manufactory" (Smith 1976, p. 379). Of course, Smith and Hollander explained this on the ground of dimin-ishing returns in agriculture – that is, high land rent. We can explain it, instead, on the ground of increasing returns in manufactures, due to the division of labor made possible by a large market and accumulation of capital. As capital accumulates more, the division of labor advances to interdistrict specialization of local manufactures.

The manufactures first supply the neighbourhood, and afterwards, as their work improves and refines, more distant markets. For though neither the rude produce, nor even the coarse manufacture, could, without the greatest difficulty, support the expence of a considerable land carriage, the refined and improved manu-facture easily may. In a small bulk it frequently contains the price of a great quantity of rude produce. (Smith 1976, p. 409)

Interdistrict specialization requires still larger capital accumulation, since, first, returns from such specialized manufactures for distant sale are very slow so that the consideration given in the case 3 in the preceding section applies. Since the specialization here is due, second, not so much to such local differences as climate and factor endowments, as to the increasing returns caused by the division of labor between manufactures, considerations on the required accumulation of capital in cases 1 and 2 in the preceding section are also relevant. Investment in home trade should be done, therefore, only when the accumulation of capital has already reached the stage when interdistrict specialization is possible.[6]

The highest stage of the division of labor is that of international trade based on the international division of labor. Only in this last stage is investment in foreign trade relevant. Since "the returns of foreign trade of consumption are very seldom so quick as those of the home-trade" (Smith 1976, p. 368), the considerations given in the case 3 of the preceding section apply and the required domestic capital accumulation is larger than in the case of home trade. International division of labor differs, however, from interdistrict division of labor in that labor does not move easily between nations. We have to consider, therefore, two sets of Equations (3.1)–(3.3), one for each identical country, and suppose that two goods are very similar so that $c_1 = c_2$, $a_{11} = a_{12}$, $a_{21} = a_{22}$, and $b_1 = b_2$. This is because the international specialization to be considered here is not due to preexisting international differences in taste, climate, technology, or factor endowments, but is to be created by subdivisions of industries. Either the two sets of equations are solved separately with c_i's and x_i's identical for both sets (autarky), or they are jointly solved with $x_1 = L$, $x_2 = 0$ for the first set and $x_1 = 0$, $x_2 = L$ for the second set (international specialization). In the case of the latter solution, two sets of equations are merged into

$$c_1 + a_{11}x_{11} + a_{12}x_{22} = b_1 x_{11} \tag{3.4}$$
$$c_2 + a_{21}x_{11} + a_{22}x_{22} = b_2 x_{22} \tag{3.5}$$
$$x_{11} = L \tag{3.6}$$
$$x_{22} = L \tag{3.7}$$

where x_{11} is the labor input of the first country in the production of the first good and x_{22} is the labor input of the second country in the production of the second good.[7] If turnover of capital in the case of autarky is k (>1) times as quick as in the case of international specialization, the required capital accumulation for each country in the latter case (that is, $a_{11}L$ of the first good and $a_{21}L$ of the second good), is k times larger than the required capital accumulation in the former case, since $a_{11} = a_{12}$ and $a_{21} = a_{22}$.

Thus, Smith's theory of international trade should be interpreted as a theory based on increasing returns due to large markets caused by international division of labor, which is made possible by sufficient accumulation of capital.

When the produce of any particular branch of industry exceeds what the demand of the country requires, the surplus must be sent abroad, and exchanged for something for which there is a demand at home. Without such exportation, a part of the productive labor of the country must cease, and the value of its annual produce diminish. The land and labour of Great Britain produce generally more corn, woollens, and hard ware, than the demand of the home-market requires. The surplus part of them, therefore, must be sent abroad, and exchanged for something for which there is a demand at home. It is only by means of such exportation, that this surplus can acquire a value sufficient to compensate the labour and expence of producing it. (Smith 1976, p. 372)

If this is simply taken as the vent for surplus argument, a host of questions arise from the point of view of neoclassical theory of production. Why do these surpluses tend to be produced in the first place? And why, if foreign markets for them are not available, are the resources involved not transferred to the production of other goods at home for which there is a demand, and especially goods of a kind imported from abroad? "Smith speaks often of the internal mobility of factors" points out Bloomfield (1975), and he observes that the problem does not, "at least in the case of Great Britain, seem to arise from any serious lack of employment opportunities."

Assuming factor mobility and full employment, however, we can reply to these questions as follows. "The division of labor is limited by the extent of the market" according to Smith, and hence increasing returns are not exploited in autarky even if domestic factors are fully employed and the value of the annual produce is smaller than it is when foreign trade is possible. The required level of capital accumulation is lower and the resulting quantity of productive labor is smaller in autarky.

The process of the division of labor described is the process of subdivision of industries and of specialization of each of such subdivisions. Smith's theory of international trade based on this process is, therefore, a theory of intraindustrial specialization rather than a neoclassical theory of interindustrial specialization. It can be applied to international trade among identical, homogeneous countries, as was done in this section; the neoclassical theory, on the other hand, explains trade among different, heterogeneous countries. The case of Britain's trade with its colony, America, to which Smith often referred and which was quoted earlier, is the trade that should be explained in the neoclassical way as was done by Hollander on the basis of the difference in factor endowments. It is no wonder, then, that natural order of investment is not followed in colony and foreign trade preceding the development of manufactures (see Kobayashi 1977, p. 227). While comparative advantage is presupposed (given exogenously) in neoclassical theory of trade, as the one due to difference in climate, technology, taste, factor endowments, and the like, Smith's theory explains it endogenously by increasing returns caused by the division of labor. It seems to be basic to Smith's philosophy to explain, rather than assume, the existing difference by the division of labor. (See also Arrow 1979.)

The difference of natural talent in different men is, in reality, much less than we are aware of; and the very different genius which appears to distinguish men of different professions, when grown up to maturity, is not upon many occasions so much the cause, as the effect of the division of labour. The difference between the most dissimilar characters, between a philosopher and a common street porter, for example, seems to arise not so much from nature, as from habit, custom, and education. (Smith 1976, pp. 28–29)

Smith's theory of international trade suggests a new line of theory of international trade which has many important implications in view of the gap existing between the theoretical model of the traditional theory of international trade and the reality of world trade today. First, it is well known that almost two-thirds of world trade is carried on among large industrial areas that are very similar. Traditional theory presupposes the existence of international differences in climate, resources, technology, and factor endowments to explain the comparative advantages. International trade between dissimilar countries, or trade in primary products, can surely be explained in terms of differences in climate, natural resources, and factor endowments. Trade between similar countries, or trade in manufactures, however, cannot be so explained. Smithian theory, on the other hand, can explain trade heavily carried on among similar industrial areas, since it considers comparative advantages to be created by subdivision of industries and international division of labor to be intraindustrial rather than interindustrial.

If comparative advantages can be explained in a Smithian way, the second implication is that the current pattern of world trade is not statically determinate, but dynamically changeable and quite unstable. Because there is some degree of freedom concerning which countries specialize in which subdivisions of industries, there exists room for policy interference and international negotiations to change the present pattern of world trade. This is the world of agreed international specialization that Kojima (1971, pp. 58–67) has defined. Although it is somewhat ironic in light of Adam Smith's insistence upon the merits of laissez faire and severe criticism of mercantilism, Smithian theory of trade may also lead to a new perspective on mercantilism and protectionism which tries to change the current pattern of world trade (see Schmitt 1979). Since the current conflicts in international trade cannot be solved by merely insisting on the optimality of free trade derived from the traditional theory of international trade, there is an important role to be played by Smithian theory, which suggests possibilities both for international cooperation and for mercantilism and protectionism.

CHAPTER 4

The possibility of a falling rate of profit under diminishing cost

The truth of Marx's law of the falling rate of profit due to a rising organic composition of capital seems to be denied by the Shibata–Okishio theorem, which states that the technical innovations to be adopted by the capitalists do not reduce the general rate of profit.[1] Even if it is true that a technical invention with rising organic composition implies falling rate of profit, it is impossible to see it realized, because such an invention would never be adopted by profit-maximizing capitalists. Okishio tried to salvage Marx's law by arguing that the organic composition rises and the rate of profit falls if the rate of real wage rises. As is pointed out by Shaikh and was, of course, admitted by Okishio, however, Marx presented a rising organic composition as a technical cause of a falling rate of profit, rather than as an economic effect of an already fallen rate of profit occasioned by rising wages.[2] If wages first rose, the effect of the adoption of a technique with higher organic composition would not be to reduce the rate of profit further, but to mitigate the effect of a higher rate of wages.

The Shibata–Okishio theorem, like other recent Marxist theorems after Sraffa, was developed under the assumption of constant cost (returns to scale) and perfect competition in the neoclassical sense, according to which firms face infinitely elastic demand curves.[3] However, Marx's description of the process of the falling rate of profit reminds us, rather, of a world of diminishing cost (internal economy of scale) and firms facing demand curves sloping downward – that is, Chamberlin's DD and dd demand curves.[4]

A capitalist working with [an] improved but not as yet generally adopted method of production sells below the market-price, but above his individual price of production; his rate of profit rises until competition levels it out. (Marx 1959, p. 231)

Under competition, the increasing minimum of capital required with the increases in productivity for the successful operation of an independent industrial establishment, ... No capitalist ever voluntarily introduces a new method of production, no matter how much more productive it may be, and how much it may increase the rate of surplus value, so long as it reduces the rate of profit. Yet every such new method of production cheapens the commodities. Hence, the capitalist sells them originally above their price of production, ... His method of production stands above social average. But competition makes it general and subject to the general law. There follows a fall in the rate of profit which is, therefore, wholly independent of the will of the capitalist. (pp. 262, 264–65)

My purpose in this chapter is to argue that the Shibata–Okishio theorem is too straight a jacket for Marx by showing that the falling rate of profit is possible, though not necessary, if diminishing cost is assumed only in the industry where organic composition of capital is rising. In the next section I document in Marx's *Das Kapital* the concept of competition with downward sloping demand curve and diminishing cost due to the existence of fixed or overhead cost that increases as an aspect of rising organic composition of capital. The Shibata–Okishio theorem for the two-good case is explained in the subsequent section by a simple formal model, where constant returns are assumed. Then, by changing assumptions slightly, to introduce diminishing cost in the industry where organic composition of capital is to be raised, I show the possibility of a falling rate of profit. The fourth section, titled "Dynamics of the rate of profit," first describes informally a process of falling rate of profit, where a pioneering firm can make extra profit by adopting a technique with higher organic composition and larger fixed cost but competition makes extra profit eventually disappear and the resulting general rate of profit can be lower than before technical invention. Second, the implications of the behavior of relative price are discussed and the limited purpose of our argument – to show the possibility of falling rate of profit against the Shibata–Okishio theorem – is emphasized. A mathematical appendix is given in the final section for the general multiple-good case.

Marx on competition and diminishing cost

It is true that free competition is assumed throughout Marx's *Das Kapital*. As Sylos-Labini (1976) emphasized in the case of classical economics, however, here competition implies merely free entry and, unlike the case of neoclassical perfect competition, not necessarily an infinitely elastic demand curve for an individual supplier. This can be clearly seen from Marx's arguments on extra surplus value and market price or value:

the working-day of 12 hours is, as regards him, now represented by 24 articles instead of 12. Hence, in order to get rid of the product of one working-day, the demand must be double what it was, i.e., the market must become twice as extensive. Other things being equal, his commodities can command a more extended market only by a diminution of their prices. (Marx 1954, p. 301)

If one produces more cheaply and can sell more goods, thus possessing himself of a greater place in the market by selling below the current market-price, or market-value, he will do so, and will thereby begin a movement which gradually compels the others to introduce the cheaper mode of production, . . . (Marx 1959, p. 194)

If the demand curve for an individual firm that is a supplier is infinitely elastic, the firm can sell whatever amount it likes without reducing price. What Marx had in mind, therefore, must be a demand curve for an individual supplier under free entry, which is infinitely elastic for the quantities smaller than the current sale, but downward sloping for the quantities larger than it.[5] This is exactly the case of Adam Smith, which was discussed in the second section of Chapter 2.

Internal economy of scale is also not foreign to Marx:

The battle of competition is fought by cheapening of commodities. The cheapness of commodities depends, ceteris paribus, on the productiveness of labour, and this again on the scale of production. Therefore, the larger capitals beat the smaller. It will further be remembered that, with the development of the capitalist mode of production, there is an increase in the minimum amount of individual capital necessary to carry on a business under its normal conditions. (Marx 1954, pp. 586–87).[6]

The productiveness of labor depends on the scale of production, which is at least partly due to the diminishing overhead cost. Marx emphasized the role of fixed capital in the process of falling rate of profit due to higher organic composition:

owing to the distinctive methods of production developing in the capitalistic system the same number of labourers, i.e., the same quantity of labour-power set in motion by a variable capital of a given value, operate, work up and productively consume in the same time span an ever-increasing quantity of means of labour, machinery and fixed capital of all sorts, raw and auxiliary materials – and consequently a constant capital of ever-increasing value. (Marx 1959, p. 212)

In addition to its durability, we have to notice the overhead cost of fixed capital, which Marx did clearly:

the simultaneous employment of a large number of labourers effects a revolution in the material conditions of the labour-process. The buildings in which they work, the store-houses for the raw material, the implements and utensils used simultaneously or in turn by the workmen; in short, a portion of the means of production, are now consumed in common. . . . When consumed in common, they give up a smaller part of their value to each single product; partly because the total value they part with is spread over a greater quantity of products, . . . (Marx 1954, p. 307)

Another rise in the rate of profit is produced, not by savings in the labour creating the constant capital, but by savings in the application of this capital itself. On the one hand, the concentration of labourers, and their large-scale co-operation, saves constant capital. The same buildings, and heating and lighting appliances, etc., cost relatively less for the large-scale than for small-scale production. The same is true of power and working machinery. Although their absolute value increases, it falls in comparison to the increasing extension of production ... (Marx 1959, p. 82)

This reading of *Das Kapital* suggests the following model of a falling rate of profit due to increasing fixed or overhead capital. Because Chamberlin's *dd* curve is less steep, those who first adopt a new technique can enjoy economy of scale and extra profit by selling a large amount. It turns out eventually, however, that the new technique prevails and the economy of scale is less than expected, Chamberlin's *DD* curve being very steep. The result is a lower rate of profit.

Relative price and the rate of profit

The so-called Shibata–Okishio theorem can be seen, in the case of two goods, as a special case of a theorem obtained in the following system.[7] Suppose goods are produced from goods and labor, while a unit labor power is reproduced by consuming given quantities of goods. Since the subsistence wage to be paid is a linear function of prices of goods, the price–cost relations are

$$p = (1 + r) F(p, q) \tag{4.1}$$

$$q = (1 + r) G(p, q, t) \tag{4.2}$$

where p and q are prices of goods, r is the rate of profit, F and G are (minimum) unit-cost functions, strictly increasing and linearly homogeneous with respect to p and q, and t is the shift parameter of the cost function of the second good. In other words, a change in t indicates adoption of a different technique. By making the first good *numeraire* ($p = 1$), we can determine the price of the second good q and the rate of profit r in (4.1) and (4.2), when t is given.

When t is changed, we can see first from (4.1) that r and q cannot move in the same direction. Supposing that G is an increasing function of t, second, we can see from (4.2) that r can be reduced if and only if t is increased. Suppose r is reduced. We know from (4.1) that q must be increased. Since G is strictly increasing and linearly homogeneous with respect to p and q, and p is now given constant, however, (4.2) cannot be satisfied unless t is increased.[8] Conversely, suppose t is increased. If r is increased as a result of it, we have to increase q so as to keep (4.2) unchanged, which is a contradiction from (4.1). Therefore, r must be reduced by an increase in t. In other words, the falling rate of profits is possible if and only if a new technique is adopted so as to make the cost of production higher for the given prices. An attempt to reduce the cost of production for given prices always increases the rate of profit.

In the Shibata–Okishio theorem, where the neoclassical perfect competition and the constant returns to scale are assumed, input coefficients are regarded as given constants and both F and G are considered as linear with respect to p and q. Changes in t imply changes in these given input coefficients. A new technique (a change in t) with higher organic composition is adopted only when the cost calculated with current prices is reduced, that is, when G is decreased. This implies, however, a higher rate of profit when new prices are established. Because techniques that increase current cost and lead to lower rate of profit under current prices are not adopted by profit-maximizing capitalists, a falling rate of profit due to higher organic composition is impossible unless the real rate of wage increases.

Let us now assume, slightly generalizing Shibata–Okishio's assumptions, that input coefficients in F are zero degree homogeneous functions of prices; that is,

$$F = a_{11}p + a_{21}q \tag{4.3}$$

where a_{11} and a_{21} are functions of p and q but remain unchanged when p and q are changed proportionally, and that input coefficients in G are not only zero degree homogeneous functions of prices but also decreasing functions of the level of output; that is,

$$G = a_{12}p + a_{22}q + ((b_{12}p + b_{22}q)/x_2) \tag{4.4}$$

where a_{12}, a_{22}, b_{21}, and b_{22} are functions of p and q but remain unchanged for a proportional change in them, and x_2 signifies the level of output of the representative firm. In other words, there is no fixed capital and only circulating capital exists so that constant cost prevails in the production of the first good, while there is fixed capital in addition to circulating capital and diminishing cost prevails in the production of the second good. Of course, we neglect the durability aspect of fixed capital for the sake of simplicity and concentrate on the problem of the diminishing cost due to the existence of fixed cost.[9]

If we consider a_{i2}'s and b_{ij}'s as functions of t and substitute (4.3) and (4.4) into (4.1) and (4.2), we find that now (4.1) and (4.2) cannot determine q and r for a given value of t, unless the value of x_2 is also specified. In other words, when the technique to be adopted is specified, price–cost relations alone cannot determine the relative price and the rate of profit, unless the level of output of the representative firm is given in the second industry, where cost is diminishing. The relative price q, the rate of profit r, and the level of output x_2 have to be determined simultaneously for the given technique t in a general-equilibrium system that includes not only price–cost relations but also demand and supply equilibrium conditions for two goods. In this sense, we can first consider x_2 as a function of t and then solve (4.1) and (4.2), considered as relations among q, r, and t only, for q and r when t is given.

Our theorem still applies. First, as t changes, r and q move in the opposite directions, and, second, r can be reduced if and only if t is changed in such a way that G is increased for the given initial value of q. Unlike the case of the Shibata–Okishio theorem, however, this does not necessarily imply that a falling rate of profit is impossible. The second half of the theorem requires an increase in the unit cost at the level of output at which the representative firm arrives eventually, after all the firms have adopted the new technology and all the equilibrium conditions for the economy are reestablished. This unit cost is different, however, from the one that the firm takes into consideration when it decides to adopt a new technique, the unit cost at the level of output that it expects to achieve, assuming that the old technique prevails among other firms.

Dynamics of the rate of profit

An equilibrium of the representative firm in the second industry is described in Figure 4.1, where $(1 + r) G$ is shown as a function of x_2, when r and q are given (i.e., $q = \bar{q}$). $0A$ signifies $(1 + r) (a_{12}p + a_{22}q)$ in Equation (4.4) and Ed is Chamberlin's dd demand curve drawn under the assumption that other firms in the same industry keep the price at $\bar{q}$. Consider the introduction of a new technique with higher organic composition of capital such that total fixed capital is increased but circulating capital per unit of output is decreased[10] – that is, a change in t such that a_{12} and a_{22} are decreased while b_{12} and b_{22} are increased in Equation (4.4). In Figure 4.1, when Ed is not steep, the curve $(1 + r) G$ can be shifted below Ed for sufficiently large x_2, even though it is above Ed at $\bar{x}_2$, since $0A$ is reduced. In other words, a profit-maximizing firm adopts such a technique if it considers that a sufficiently large amount of output can be sold without much price reduction.

When many firms adopt a new technique and try to sell a larger amount, however, the necessary price reduction turns out to be much larger than expected. Chamberlin's DD curve is drawn as ED under the assumption that all the firms charge the same price; ED is much steeper than the Ed curve. A $(1 + r) G$ curve fails to shift below the ED curve. The result is that the price of the second good falls and the rate of profit of all the firms in the second industry must be lower than the general rate of

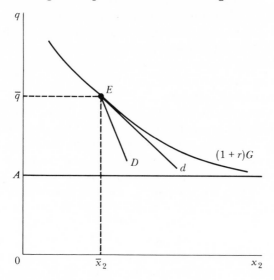

Figure 4.1

profit. For those firms that have not followed the adoption of the new technology yet, it is profitable to move to the first industry, where the rate of profit is higher. When the number of firms in the second industry is reduced, however, the demand for the representative firm is increased and E can be shifted upward and to the right. An equilibrium with x_2 larger than $\bar{x}_2$ and q higher than $\bar{q}$ is possible. In other words, "with the development of the capitalist mode of production, there is an increase in the minimum amount of individual capital necessary to carry on a business under its normal conditions" (Marx 1954, p. 587). When an economywide equilibrium is reestablished, the general rate of profit r can be lower if q is higher than $\bar{q}$ in this way.

One may argue, like Steedman, that "unless the previously adopted technique is no longer available, ... Even if new invention should lead many capitalists mistakenly to adopt it, as soon as it is found to be less profitable than the previously used technique, all capitalists will revert to the latter.... Since technical knowledge has seldom, if ever, been lost beyond recovery within the capitalist era..." (Steedman 1977, pp. 128–29). This is certainly true in a static problem of choice of two techniques, since q is higher than $\bar{q}$. In a dynamic capitalist economic process, however, there eventually appears another technique with still higher organic composition of capital than the currently prevailing one. Then, the choice is not between the previously used technique, with organic composition lower than the currently prevailing one, and the currently prevailing technique. The choice should be between the previously used technique and the newest technique, which has not yet been used and has the highest organic composition. For a single firm it may be possible that the adoption of the newest technique is more profitable than reversion to the previously used one.

Nor can one blame the short-sightedness or myopic behavior of individual firms that adopt such a technique as resulting eventually in a falling rate of profit. Since future profits have to be discounted to be compared with current profit, for a pioneering firm lower rate of profit in the future can be compensated by the current extra profit. It is logically possible, therefore, to have a never-ending, repeating process of adopting a technique with higher organic composition which causes the rate of profit to fall.

Finally, one may feel uneasy with the first half of the theorem proposed in the previous section. One may not trust the result that a falling rate of profit implies an increase in relative price of the good for the production of which a new technique has been introduced (lower r implies higher q, given p, in Equation (4.1)). It is unlikely, one may argue, that the introduction of a technique with large fixed capital would fail to reduce the price of the product. Marx himself was well aware of this when he mentioned that "the fall in commodity-prices and the rise in the mass of profit on the argumented mass of these cheapened commodities is but another expression for the law of the falling rate of profit" (Marx 1959, p. 231). The first half of the theorem is robust provided that we, like many others, assume constant returns for the first industry, the industry where a new technique is not introduced. Hence one may conclude that the Marxist case of a falling rate of profit due to higher organic composition of capital is, though logically possible, unrealistic and remains an exceptional and unsuccessful case for capitalists in situations where either increase in demand caused by reduced price is less than expected or the reduction of the number of firms is insufficient.

It can be argued, however, that such a change in the relative price is not entirely implausible and should be considered, at least, as an empirically refutable conjecture.[11] Marx himself argued that "with the development of the capitalist mode of production, there is an increase in the minimum amount of individual capital necessary to carry on a business under its normal conditions. The smaller capitals, therefore, crowd into spheres of production which Modern Industry has only sporadically or incompletely got hold of" (Marx 1954, p. 587). If we consider that the first industry with Equation (4.1) is such an industry into which smaller capitals crowd, it is likely that the relative price of the first good falls through excess supply, since relative price is now, unlike in the case of the Shibata–Okishio theorem, not independent of demand and supply through the specification of G in Equation (4.4).

Most generally, of course, we can discard the assumption of constant returns for the first industry and consider the possibility of falling rate of profit and falling or rising relative price of the good in the production of which a new technique with higher organic composition of capital is introduced. Everything can happen, however, in such a model, depending on different specifications on demand (taste, distribution, and so forth) as well as specifications on production (increasing or diminishing cost). Such a model is too far removed from the world of the Shibata–Okishio theorem, a critical examination of which is the limited purpose of this chapter. For this purpose, the model presented here was made as close as possible to the models used by Shibata, Okishio, and many other Marxist economists after Sraffa.

The case of multiple goods

As a mathematical appendix, let us consider an extension of the theorem proposed earlier into the general case of n goods. Let p_i be the price of the ith good, r be the rate of profit, and t_i be a shift parameter of the unit-cost function of the ith good F_i which is a strictly increasing and linearly homogeneous function of $p_1, \ldots, p_n$. Price–cost relations are

$$p_i = (1 + r) F_i (p_1, \ldots, p_n, t_i) \quad i = 1, \ldots, n \qquad (4.5)$$

If all the F_i's are linear with respect to $p_1, \ldots, p_n$, as in the case of the Shibata–Okishio theorem, we can show that the rate of profit falls (rises) if costs of some goods increase (decrease) through increases (decreases) in input coefficients induced by changes in t_i's, by using the famous Frobenius theorem on positive square matrices, since $(1 + r)$ is the reciprocal of the Frobenius root, the largest positive eigenvalue of the input-coefficient matrix, which increases when input coefficients increase. The Frobenius theorem cannot by itself determine the direction of changes in the rate of profit, however, if some input coefficients are increased and some others are decreased, as in the case of changes in organic composition of capital.

The Frobenius theorem was generalized by Morishima into the case of nonlinear eigenvector problems

$$m V_i = H_i (V_i, \ldots, V_n, e) \quad i = 1, \ldots, n \qquad (4.6)$$

where H_i is, like F_i, positive, strictly increasing, and linearly homogeneous function of nonnegative V_i's, and some H_i's increase, but no one decreases if e is increased. Morishima proved a nonlinear version of the Frobenius theorem, which includes, among other results, that the unique m corresponding to unique positive $(V_1, \ldots, V_n)$ increases if e is increased. It is clear that we can show that r decreases (increases) when some F_i's increase (decrease) for given p_i's as t_i's change in (4.5) even if F_i's are nonlinear, by using Morishima's result as a lemma.[12]

Let us next consider the changes in relative price of a good whose cost is increased (decreased) to other goods in general n good case (4.5). Without loss of generality, we can consider that F_n is increased under given p_i's as a result of a change in t_n and make the nth good *numeraire* (i.e., $p_n = 1$). It was already shown that r is decreased in such a case. Suppose prices of some goods whose cost functions do not shift rise and p_k ($k \neq n$) rises proportionally most among such prices. In the kth equation of (4.5),

$$p_k = (1 + r) F_k (p_1, \ldots, p_k, \ldots, p_{n-1}, p_n, t_k) \tag{4.7}$$

p_n and t_k remain unchanged while r is reduced, p_k increased proportionally most, and other p_i's ($i \neq k, n$) either increase less than p_k or decrease. In view of linear homogeneity of F_k with respect to $p_1, \ldots, p_n$, F_k does not increase proportionally to p_k and therefore the right-hand side is now smaller than the left-hand side in (4.7). We have to conclude, therefore, that no p_i ($i \neq n$) can rise and that all p_i ($i \neq n$) have to fall, since they cannot remain unchanged to satisfy (4.5) when r is reduced. Similarly, we can show that all p_i ($i = \neq n$) have to rise relative to p_n, if F_n is reduced under given p_i's as a result of a change in t_n and therefore r is increased.

CHAPTER 5

Rehabilitation of Marshall's life-cycle theory to explain diminishing cost

Marshall offered several different solutions for the compatibility of increasing returns or diminishing cost and competitive equilibrium (see Robertson 1930 and Hague 1958).[1]

1. Individual firms face a downward sloping demand curve even in a competitive market, unless the market is ideally organized like a Walrasian one.

When we are considering an individual producer, we must couple his supply curve – not with the general demand curve for his commodity in a wide market, but – with the particular demand curve of his own special market. And this particular demand curve will generally be very steep; perhaps as steep as his own supply curve is likely to be, even when an increased output will give him an important increase of internal economies. (Marshall 1961, p. 458. See also Marshall 1961, pp. 457 and 459 and Chapter 14 of this book.)

In this sense, it is also possible to argue that Marshall was a pioneer of modern theory of imperfect competition after Sraffa.

2. Increasing returns may be due to the external economies rather than to the internal economies. As Robinson (1933, pp. 337–43) argued, of course, this does not solve the problem, if external economies of an industry are due to increasing returns in other industries which are based on economies either internal or external to individual firms there. Nor can we rely on a Smith–Young specialization of firms in an industry, the extent of which is dependent on the general development of the industry, since there is no reason why such specialization is impossible from the beginning, when the scale of the industry is small, unless there are internal economies in individual firms. Increasing returns due to division of labor cannot be compatible with competition, unless individual demand curves are, at least partially, downward sloping, as is argued in Chapter 2. The only remaining possibility, therefore, for external economies seems to be the supply of public factors of production or public intermediate goods, which is favorable to larger industries.

3. Internal economies may not be fully exploited by an individual firm since its life span is limited. Like an individual tree in a forest, an

45

individual firm in an industry grows and decays, though forest and industry remain stationary.

> Rapid growth of firms in some trades which offer great economies to production on a large scale.... But long before this end [monopoly] is reached, his [a new businessman's] progress is likely to be arrested by the decay, if not of his faculties, yet of his liking for energetic work. (Marshall 1961, pp. 285–86)

> A tendency to Increasing Return prevails: that is, an increasing output can generally be produced at a diminishing rate of cost. It is obvious that, under this tendency a firm, which had once obtained the start of its rivals, would be in a position to undersell them progressively, provided its own vigour remained unimpaired, and it could obtain all the capital it need.... under the law of Increasing Return, there might have seemd to be nothing to prevent the concentration in the hands of single firm of the whole production of the world, ... The reason why this result did not follow was simply that no firm ever had a sufficient long life of unabated energy and power of initiative for the purpose. (Marshall 1921, pp. 315–16)

Although this life-cycle theory of firm gives a realistic picture of the nineteenth-century industry, however, the question is its relevancy after the great development of joint-stock companies. Marshall himself was well aware of this problem.

> As with the growth of trees, so was it with the growth of business as a general rule before the great recent development of vast joint-stock companies, which often stagnate, but do not readily die. (Marshall 1961, p. 316)[2]

> A private firm without great vigour is sure to die; a large joint stock company has special advantages, many of which do not materially dwindle with age. (Marshall 1921, p. 316)

Since Marshall put the main burden in solving the problem of the compatibility of increasing returns and competitive equilibrium on his life-cycle theory of the firm, however, it is worthwhile to consider whether the theory can be revived in somewhat-modified form even without the assumption that the life span of an individual firm is limited.

Instead of a regular cycle of the birth, growth, decay, and death of individual firms, Shove (1930), Wolfe (1954) Newman (1960), and Newman and Wolfe (1961) introduce random influences that "work on the firm's cost curve, shifting it bodily upwards or downwards" (Newman 1960). To prevent the firm from expanding output unlimitedly when the cost curve shifts downward, furthermore, they emphasize an important empirical fact – namely, that the expansion of a firm is slow and takes time, so that its "luck may have deserted" it (Shove 1930) by the time it has enlarged its capacity and output. Though "even if everything else is all in Marshall, transition matrices certainly are not" (Newman and

Wolfe 1961), I would be the last to deny the significance of Newman and Wolfe's study of stochastic adjustment process and the resulting statistical long-run equilibrium of the industry – that is, the size distribution of firms.

In this chapter, however, we shall consider an alternative, more pedestrian modification of Marshall's life-cycle theory of a firm, which keeps the original idea of the life cycle more firmly. Unlike Marshall, I do not assume that the life span of an individual firm is limited. The life span of a factory, a section, or a branch of a firm is made limited, however, by the introduction of technical progress, with the result that internal economies remain unexhausted. More specifically, a capital asset with embodied technology has a limited life, since wages rise as a result of technical progress. In the next section, I confirm the incompatibility of competition and internal economy in a Marshallian stationary state where the life span of firms is not limited and suggest consideration of technical progress and a steady balanced growth equilibrium, which may bring us nearer to real life than does the notion of stationary equilibrium. Compatibility of competition and internal economy is argued next under the assumption that wages continue to rise owing to technical progress and the life span of capital with embodied technology is limited. The final section is devoted to further consideration of the nature of internal economy compatible with competition under less restrictive conditions.

Stationary state and balanced growth

To make the story simple, let us assume that capital goods do not depreciate physically. Given a set of capital goods k, the average variable cost of output y produced by the use of k and some primary factor of production like labor is denoted by $c(y, k)$. The marginal cost of y is increasing, since k is given. The average cost curve is U shaped, therefore, first diminishing with respect to y owing to the diminishing average constant cost, and then increasing with respect to y owing to the increasing marginal cost. Marshallian internal economies are, however, not concerned with short-run diminishing average cost under the given capital k. Marshallian internal economies imply that the average cost is diminishing, not with y, but with k.

"The tendency to increasing return does not act quickly," wrote Marshall (1961, p. 455). "We expect the short-period supply price to increase with increasing output. But we also expect a gradual increase in demand to increase gradually the size and efficiency of this representative firm, and to increase the economies both internal and external which are at its disposal (p. 460)."

As Marshall's first step, "towards studying the influences exerted by the element of time on the relations between cost of production and value," (Marshall 1961, p. 366), he considered the stationary state of an industry. So we also start with the stationary state where technical progress does not exist and all the prices remain unchanged through time. Unlike Marshall, however, we consider that the life span of a firm is not limited. Since capital goods do not depreciate physically as well as morally, investment is carried out so that the condition that the rate of profit is indefinitely normal; that is,

$$py - c(y, k) y = rqk \tag{5.1}$$

is satisfied, where p, q, and r denote, respectively, the price of the output, the price of a set of capital goods, and the normal rate of profit. By dividing with the level of output y, we have

$$p = c(y, k) + (rqk/y) \tag{5.2}$$

which implies that the price is equalized to the average cost including normal profit in the long-run equilibrium.

"The normal supply price of any amount of that commodity may be taken to be its normal expenses of production (including gross earnings of management)" according to Marshall (1961, pp. 342–43) (see also Frisch 1950).

In a long-run equilibrium defined by the condition (5.1), however, the excess profit

$$E = py - c(y, k)y - rqk \tag{5.3}$$

which vanishes at the equilibrium, must be maximized with respect to the level of output y and the amount of capital k. The following conditions are, therefore, necessary.

$$\partial E/\partial y = p - c(y, k) - y\, \partial c(y, k)/\partial y = 0 \tag{5.4}$$

and

$$\partial E/\partial k = -y\, \partial c(y, k)/\partial k - rq = 0 \tag{5.5}$$

Condition (5.4) is nothing but the condition that the marginal cost of output, $c + y\partial c/\partial y$, is equalized to the price, and can be satisfied easily from our supposition that the competitive price is constant and the marginal cost is increasing. Condition (5.5) requires, on the other hand, that there should be no unexhausted internal economies remaining at the equilibrium, in the sense that the average cost including normal profit, $c + (rqk/y)$, can no longer be decreased by increasing k.

Provided that the long-run average cost including normal profit is falling, in other words, there cannot be a long-run competitive equilibrium, since investment in capital assets is expanded indefinitely. Internal economies are not compatible with competition in a stationary equilibrium, if the life span of the firm and its capital is unlimited.

While Marshall solved the problem by limiting the life span of the firm, let us do it by introducing technical progress and limiting the life span of its capital. Though Marshall "exclude[s] from view any economies that may result from substantive new inventions" (Marshall 1961, p. 460), we can argue that the balanced growth equilibrium with the technical progress is not so foreign from his "modification of the fiction of a stationary state" which will "bring us nearer to real life and help to break up a complex problem."[3]

The stationary state has just been taken to be one in which population is stationary. But nearly all its distinctive features may be exhibited in a place where population and wealth are both growing, provided they are growing at about the same rate, ... For in such a state by far the most important conditions of production and consumption, of exchange and distribution will remain of the same quality, and in the same general relations to one another, though they are all increasing in volume. (Marshall 1961, p. 368)[4]

The possibility of a steady-state growth equilibrium with technical progresss can be seen by considering the following simplified aggregate model of a growing economy where technical progress is embodied in capital. Suppose the investment-saving relation is simply

$$K(t) = sY(t) \tag{5.6}$$

where $Y(t)$ denotes the aggregate level of malleable output at time t, which can be either consumed or invested, $K(t)$ denotes the aggregate level of investment at t, and s is a positive constant less than 1. Because capital does not depreciate physically, $K(t)$ denotes also the amount of existing capital produced at t. The capital–output ratio is assumed to be such a technical constant that one unit of capital always produces one unit of output. If capitals up to T years old are actually utilized in the production, then, aggregate output available is

$$Y(t) = K(t) + K(t-1) + \cdots + K(t-T) \tag{5.7}$$

The capital–labor ratio is also assumed technically constant in such a way that a unit of $K(t)$ requires a^t units of labor to be operated, where a is a positive constant less than 1. Technical progress can be seen in the fact that less labor is required by newer capital to produce the same output. Since labor market must be cleared,

$$L = K(t)\, a^t + K(t-1)\, a^{(t-1)} + \cdots + K(t-T)\, a^{(t-T)} \qquad (5.8)$$

where L denotes the stationary supply of labor.

By substituting $K(t) = Ax^t$, where A and x are unknown constants, into (5.8), we can see easily that the steady-state growth rate x is $(1/a)$ in this vintage capital model with fixed coefficients (Allen 1967, p. 301). Both aggregate output and newly produced capital grow at the rate of $(1/a)$, always with capitals up to T years old being in use. By eliminating $Y(t)$ in (5.6) and (5.7), then, we can see that T and s vary inversely. While the supply of labor remains stationary, the level of real wage $w(t)$ rises also at the rate of $(1/a)$, since the condition

$$1 = a^{(t-T)}\, w(t) \qquad (5.9)$$

must be nearly satisfied if t changes almost continually. In other words, one cannot expect profit from the use of capital oldest among actually used. In view of (5.9), profits obtained from the use of capitals less old than T,

$$1 - a^{(t-s)}\, w(t) = 1 - a^{(T-s)}, \quad s < T \qquad (5.10)$$

are independent of t.

As a result of technical progress, therefore, we may conclude that in general wages and prices of primary factors of production whose supplies are given continue to rise at the rate of growth of the economy while the rate of profit remains unchanged. Even though the capital assets do not depreciate physically, they depreciate morally, since the cost of product resulting from them, combined with the labor and other primary factor input, increases as time goes on. The economic life span of capital assets is limited and there is a life cycle, not of a firm, but of technology embodied in capital, or of a branch or sector of a firm – that is, a set of capital assets. A set of newly produced capital assets, being the most efficient ones, make a profit larger than the normal one, though in the next period, being old and less efficient, they make a profit less than normal, even negative, but still replace the variable cost. Finally in the third period and on, being unable to replace even the variable cost, they cease to be utilized. In the long-run equilibrium, we can say not only the industry but also firms (unlike Marshall 1961, p. 367) are in equilibrium, though different sections of a firm are constantly changing through the process of birth, growth, decay, and death.

Internal economy due to technical progress

Let us consider whether an internal economy remains unexhausted in a section of a firm when the economy grows with technical progress and wages and prices of primary factors of production continue to rise but other prices and the normal rate of profit are stationary. Though capital goods do not depreciate physically, they now depreciate morally, since they have to compete with newer, more efficient capital goods. Suppose a section of a firm is newly created and investment is done there in the period 0, so that capital assets k can be used in the period 1 and on. In period 1 a profit larger than the normal one can be made by the use of k, since, k being the most efficient capital, the average variable cost $c(y, k)$ of output y is much lower than the given price p of output y. In period 2, however, only a profit lower than the normal level can be made by the use of k, since the average cost $c'(y, k)$ is much higher than $c(y, k)$, owing to higher wages of labor and prices of primary factors of production caused by the use of more efficient capital goods in the other parts of the economy. Since the capital cost is sunk, nevertheless, k is still used in period 2, provided that c' is somewhat lower than the unchanged p. Finally, in period 3, k ceases to be used at all and this section of the firm has to be dissolved, since the average cost $c''(y, k)$ is now higher than p, owing to still higher wages and prices of primary factors of production.

Since capital goods now depreciate morally, we have to take the depreciation into consideration in the calculation of average cost to be compared to price in each period. To simplify the story by avoiding this problem, however, let us assume that capital goods are also useful for consumption and can be sold in period 2 with the same price with which they were bought in the period 0, even though they are useless as capital goods in the production. This simplifying assumption is to be replaced by a more reasonable one in the next section.

The condition for the optimal level of investment in the period 0 is clearly

$$(py - c(y, k) y)/(1 + r) + (py' - c'(y', k) y' + qk)/(1 + r)^2 = qk$$
(5.11)

where p, y, y', q, and r denote, respectively, the unchanged price of output, the level of output in period 1 and that in period 2, the unchanged price of capital assets k, and the unchanged rate of normal profit. Condition (5.11) states that the sum of the discounted revenues expected is equalized with the cost of k in the period 0. It is changed into

$$E = (py - c(y, k)y - rqk) + (py' - c'(y', k)y' - rqk)/(1 + r) = 0$$
(5.12)

which corresponds to (5.1) and (5.3) if there is no technical progress and the average cost remains unchanged, so that k can be used for production indefinitely. Condition (5.12) states that the excess profit is zero or the total profit is normal, with the profit in period 1 higher and the profit in period 2 lower than the normal level.

In an equilibrium defined by the condition (5.12), furthermore, the excess profit E, whcih actually vanishes there, must be maximized with respect to y, y', and k. The following conditions are, therefore, necessary.

$$\partial E/\partial y = p - c(y, k) - y\, \partial c(y, k)/\partial y = 0 \tag{5.13}$$

$$\partial E/\partial y' = (p - c'\,(y', k) - y'\, \partial c'(y', k)/\partial y')/(1 + r) = 0 \tag{5.14}$$

and

$$\partial E/\partial k = (-y\, \partial c(y, k)/\partial k - rq) \\ + (-y'\, \partial c'(y', k)/\partial k - rq)/(1 + r) = 0 \tag{5.15}$$

Condition (5.13) and (5.14) are nothing but the condition that the marginal cost of output is equalized to the price in the each period.

In Figure 5.1, the level of output in period 1 is measured horizontally and the cost and price, vertically. The curve AC shows the average cost including normal profit, $c(y, k) + (rqk/y)$; and curve MC, the marginal cost, $c(y, k) + y\partial c(y, k)/\partial y$. The profit here being higher than normal, AC must be increasing at y, which satisfies (5.13). The dashed curve is the envelope for AC curves with different $k's$ and AC curve is shifted to rightward when k is increased. Since the envelope is downward sloping, there exists an internal economy and the average cost at y can be reduced by increasing k, since AC curve is higher than the envelope at y, satisfying (5.13) which is located to the right of the tangential point T of two curves. This implies that the first term of $\partial E/\partial k$ in (5.15) is positive.

Figure 5.2, on the other hand, shows the situation in period 2. The level of output is measured horizontally, and the cost and price, vertically. Since the profit here is lower than normal, AC must be decreasing at y', which satisfies (5.14). The average cost at y' must be decreased by increasing k, and y' must be located to the left of the tangential point T of two curves, since the second term of $\partial E/\partial k$ in (5.15) must be negative.

Unlike in the case of Equation (5.5) which corresponds to condition (5.15) when there is no technical progress, condition (5.15) can be satisfied with finite k, with the first term in (5.15) being positive and the second, negative, even though the minimum (with respect to y and y') of average cost including normal profit $c(y, k) + (rqk/y)$ and $c'(y', k) + (rqk/y')$ decrease as k is increased. This is because a further increase in k diminishes the average cost in period 1 but increases the average cost in period 2. In other words, the competitive equilibrium is possible, even if an internal economy remains unexhausted and the average cost including normal profit diminishes as the amount of capital is increased.

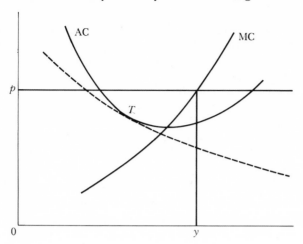

Figure 5.1

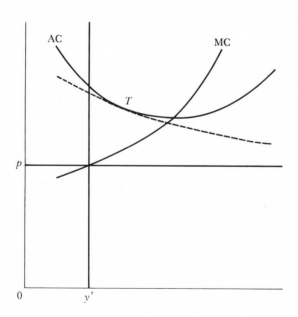

Figure 5.2

In his life-cycle theory of the firm, Marshall argued that internal economies exist and cost diminishes as the scale of production is enlarged, under given prices, provided the firm's vigor remains unimpaired, but that such internal economies remain unexploited in the competitive situation since actually "no firm ever had a sufficient long life of unabated energy and power of initiative." In our life-cycle theory of technology embodied in capital, we argue that internal economies exist and cost diminishes as the scale of production is enlarged, under given prices, but that such internal economies remain unexploited in the competitive situation, since actual prices (wages and prices of primary factors of production) change and capital is morally depreciated. Competition and internal economies are compatible even if firms' vigor remain unimpaired and they can obtain all the capital they need, and unlike Shove and unlike Wolfe and Newman, I do not assume that the expansion of a firm is slow and takes time.

Marshall considered a balanced composition of an industry where young firms are growing and old firms are decaying, some firms are making higher profit and some others are making lower profit, but industry as a whole is making normal profit. Similarly, we consider a balanced composition of a firm where sections that embody new technology are making higher profit and those with old technology are making lower profit, but the firm as a whole is just making normal profit. Though Marshall had to invent a representative firm that is the miniature of a balanced industry in order to consider a firm in equilibrium, we need not do so, since our firm is already in equilibrium.

Further considerations

To see the nature of the diminishing cost that we found compatible with competition, let us consider it, not in terms of cost function, but more fundamentally in terms of production function. Since capital does not depreciate, we can use the same production function F in both period 1 and in period 2.

$$y = F(L, k), \quad y' = F(L', k) \tag{5.16}$$

where y, y' and k denote the output of period 1, that of period 2 and the amount of capital as in the previous section while L and L' denote the labor input in period 1 and that in period 2. Then, the condition for the zero excess profit, (5.12), is now

$$E = (pF(L, k) - wL - rqk) \\ + (pF(L', k) - w'L' - rqk)/(1 + r) = 0 \tag{5.17}$$

where w and w' denote the wage rate in period 1 and that in period 2, while p, r, and q are, as before, unchanged price of output, normal rate of profit, and price of the capital goods.

The maximization of E with respect to L and L' requires

$$pF_1(L, k) - w = 0 \tag{5.18}$$

and

$$pF_1(L', k) - w' = 0 \tag{5.19}$$

where F_1 denotes the partial derivative of F with respect to the first variable, that is, L or L', which implies the marginal productivity of labor. Because $w' > w$, and the marginal productivity of labor diminishes (the second order partial derivative of F with respect to the first variable is negative, i.e., $F_{11} < 0$), conditions (5.18) and (5.19), which correspond to (5.13) and (5.14), imply that $L > L'$. It is also evident that the first term of E is positive and the second term negative in (5.17), which means the profit in period 1 is higher and that in period 2 lower than normal.

The maximization of E with respect to k requires

$$(pF_2(L, k) - rq) + (pF_2(L', k) - rq)/(1 + r) = 0 \tag{5.20}$$

where F_2 denotes the partial derivative of F with respect to the second variable, k, the marginal productivity of capital. Since $L > L'$, the first term in the left-hand side of (5.20) is positive and the second term, negative. As shown in Figures 5.1 and 5.2, the profit in period 1 can be increased further if k is increased, while that in period 2 must be decreased if k is increased. If we assume that the marginal produtivity of capital is diminishing (the second order partial derivative of F with respect to k is negative; i.e., $F_{22} < 0$), the second order condition of maximization of E with respect to k is satisfied.

The condition for the compatibility of competition and internal economy can also be seen as follows. Consider the average cost including normal profit

$$(wL + rqk)/F(L, k) \tag{5.21}$$

and minimize it with respect to L. By the so-called envelope theorem, then, the minimum average cost is decreased and the long-run average cost curve or the envelope of short-run average cost curves (the dotted curve in Figures 5.1 and 5.2) is downward sloping if (5.21) is diminishing with respect to k at the minimum with respect to L. The condition for this is

$$rqF(L, k) - (wL + rqk)\,F_2(L, k) < 0 \tag{5.22}$$

Since $pF(L, k) > wL + rqk$ in period 1 as shown in Figure 5.1, this requires that $rq < pF_2(L, k)$ at the minimum of the AC curve there.

It should be noted that our production function F is neoclassically well behaved with F_{11} and F_{22} negative. The reason for the diminishing cost is, therefore, not the increasing marginal productivity of capital, which makes the feasibility set corresponding to production function nonconvex, but the fact that the amount of capital is too little for the normal rate of profit so that the value marginal productivity of capital is still higher than the normal rate of profit. Even if the minimum average cost can be reduced by increasing capital, however, the profit in period 2 is also reduced by it, since labor input is smaller, and therefore the level of output is lower, than the one corresponding to the minimum average cost in period 2.

Internal economy remains unexhausted, therefore, simply because capital input cannot be changed, unlike the case of labor, in each period. In the section titled "Internal economy due to technical progress," it was assumed that capital goods bought in period 0 cannot be sold in period 1, but can be sold in period 2 at the same price at which they were bought in period 0. If they can be sold in period 1, capital will be increased so far as the value marginal productivity is higher than the normal rate of profit and internal economy cannot be compatible with competition. By definition, however, capital goods are something which, once installed, cannot be disposed of so soon. If they cannot be sold, furthermore, they are used rather than thrown away in period 2.

If capital goods cannot be sold, we have to take depreciation into consideration. Condition (5.11) should be replaced by

$$(py - c(y, k)y)/(1 + r) + (py' - c'(y', k)y')/(1 + r)^2 = qk \qquad (5.23)$$

from which we derive for some depreciation quotas D_1 and D_2 such that $D_1(1 + r) + D_2 = 1$,

$$E = (py - c(y, k)y - rqk - D_1qk)$$
$$+ (py' - c'(y', k)y' - rqk - D_2qk)/(1 + r) = 0 \qquad (5.24)$$

which corresponds to (5.12). Depreciation quotas may be constants or some function of y, y', k, r, etc. For any such depreciation quotas, similar arguments as those given in this chapter can be done. Particularly if depreciation quotas are constants, we have only to replace rqk by $(r + D_1)qk$ in the first term of E and by $(r + D_2)qk$ in the second term of E in (5.12). Provided that the first term of E is positive and the second term of it is negative in (5.24) – in other words, the profit net of depreciation is higher in period 1 than period 2 – internal economy can be compatible with competition.

Wages and profit

Conditions for the wages fund doctrine and Mill's recantation of it

Conditions for the relevancy of the wages fund doctrine, prerequisites for the predetermined wages fund, are not very unrealistic in a certain stage of economy where agriculture is predominant and the rate of wage is at a level not far from that of subsistence. These assumptions lost their realism as the economy developed, so that manufactures predominate over agriculture, agriculture itself is highly artificialized, and distinct consumption patterns between classes are not observed. Wages fund doctrine surely played some historical roles, but now it has almost played them out.

Recall that according to Bronfenbrenner (1971), however, outmoded ideas are never definitely displaced in economics. "To throw out the wages fund theory *in toto* is to cut oneself off from the key to the meaning of real capital that it furnished. It was a bad theory of wages, but it had the ingredients of a good theory of capital" (Blaug 1978, p. 196). Hicks (1977, pp. 149–65) emphasized the importance of the fundist theory of capital (capital is a fund, a sum of values) of Jevons and Böhm-Bawerk against the neoclassical materialist theory (capital consists of physical goods) with respect to social accounting and economic planning. It is worth considering, therefore, under what conditions we can find "the wage-fund doctrine, properly stated, not 'wrong' logically" (Schumpeter 1954, p. 669). In some recent literature on Mill's famous recantation of the wages fund doctrine, unfortunately, there is some confusion on what conditions are *necessary* for the unitary elasticity of the demand curve for labor in the naive version of the wages fund doctrine, as well as confusion on what conditions are sufficient for the zero elasticity of demand curve for labor which Mill admitted in his recantation.[1]

A set of assumptions that are *sufficient* conditions for the unitary elasticity of the demand curve for labor is given in Ekelund's (1976) short-run model of a wages fund. Among such assumptions, two are most important; we may call them, respectively, the annual harvest assumption and the wage good assumption.

The annual harvest assumption in the simplest version implies point input–point output in the sense that the time interval between an input and the resultant output is a technologically given constant and identical to the time elapsed between an input and the subsequent input, or be-tween an output and the next output. Ekelund claimed, however, that the annual harvest assumption is not necessary for the determinacy of the wages fund and unitary elasticity of demand for labor, while Schwartz (1972) emphasized that the rejection of this assumption lies at the origin of Mill's recantation. As will be shown in this chapter, the confusion arises out of the reason that the full implication of the assumption was not recognized. The assumption implies not only that the period of production (the interval between input and output) is a given constant, but also that it is identical to the market interval (the interval between successive inputs and the interval between such outputs). We can show that the wages fund actually offered is not predetermined if the period of produc-tion differs from the market interval, and the demand for labor cannot be of the unitary elasticity.

The wage good assumption means, on the other hand, that laborers consume only wage goods while capitalists do not. This assumption is necessary for the wages fund doctrine, since with this assumption Ekelund treated Mill's recantation as a matter of analytical error while without this assumption Hollander (1968) can interpret the recantation as a simple and correct argument. Without the wage good assumption, however, investment in and disinvestment out of circulating capital are relevant even within a single period in a short-run model. In addition to the fixed technical coefficients in production required by Hollander, therefore, the fixed intertemporal coefficients in consumptions are necessary for the zero elasticity of demand for labor, as we shall see, so that saving or dissaving takes place properly in the face of changing rate of wage, and therefore changing rate of profit.

In this chapter I first follow Ekelund (1976), to consider the implica-tions of the annual harvest assumption and the wage good assumption and to document them in Mill (1965 and 1967). I then devote a section to the argument that the annual harvest assumption is necessary for the unitary elasticity of demand for labor, in spite of Ekelund's argument to the contrary. Finally, I construct a model of Mill's recantation of the wages fund doctrine, in which zero elasticity of demand for labor is endogenously explained.

Annual harvest assumption and wage good assumption

Ekelund (1976) considered a short-run model of the wages fund with the following assumptions: (1) an aggregate point input–point output pro-duction function for all goods produced; (2) an economy's real output

```
------·x------x·------x ------ x------ x---------- t
      t₁      t'      t₂      t"      t₃
```

Figure 6.1

composed solely of machinery (fixed capital), wage goods, and the capitalist (non−wage-earner) consumables; (3) a constant ratio of fixed to circulating capital in the economy; (4) perfect competition (at constant cost) in all markets; (5) a fixed money stock; and (6) constant population and productivity over the period or periods under discussion. We may call assumption 1 the annual harvest assumption and assumption 2 the wage good assumption.

If we neglect, as Ekelund did following Mill in the recantation, invest-ment in fixed capital and consider a naive version, the annual harvest assumption may be described in Figure 6.1 as follows. At time t_1, a given stock of wage goods exists, which is invested in the circulating capital to sustain labor over the period of production $t_1 t_2$, which is a technologically given constant as in the case of traditional agriculture. Then, a stock of ripened wage goods is available at time t_2, which is again invested to tide labor over $t_2 t_3$ $(= t_1 t_2)$.

"Self-evident as the thing is, it is often forgotten that the people of a country are maintained and have their wants supplied, not by the produce of present labour, but of the past," Mill pointed out (1965, p. 64). The wage good assumption implies that laborers consume only wage goods, while capitalists consume only nonwage goods. A textual support for dif-ferential consumption patterns for labor and capitalist classes may be as follows.

It may be said, perhaps that wines, equipages, and furnitures, are not subsistence, tools, and materials, and could not in any case have been applied to the support of labour; that they are adapted for no other than unproductive consumption, and that the detriment to the wealth of the community was when they were produced, not when they were consumed. (Mill 1965, p. 72)

Since the stock of wage goods available at t_1 is given, and laborers cannot be supported by nonwage goods, the aggregate real capital to be used to employ labor at t_1 is determined by this predetermined wages fund, and the demand for labor has unitary elasticity with respect to real wage. Higher real wage is possible only at the sacrifice of employment, or only if the population given in the assumption 6 is small. Allocation of labor for the production of different goods in the period of production $t_1 t_2$ is determined by the demand for different goods expected at t_2. The demand for labor is determined, however, by the predetermined wages fund existing at t_1.

What supports and employs productive labour, is the capital expended in setting it to work, and not the demand of purchasers for the produce of the labour when completed. Demand for commodities is not demand for labour. The demand for commodities determines in what particular branch of production the labour and capital shall be employed; it determines the direction of the labour; but not the more or less of the labour itself, or of the maintenance or payment of the labour. These depend on the amount of the capital, or other funds directly devoted to the sustenance and remuneration of labour. (Mill 1965, p. 78)

Ekeleud emphasized that the predetermined wages fund is real, not monetary. Mill argued, however, in terms of monetary funds in his recantation, as the following quotation can be so interpreted.

The capitalist's pecuniary means consist of two parts – his capital, and his profits or income. . . . If he has to pay more for labour, the additional payment comes out of his own income; perhaps from the part which he would have saved and added to capital; . . . perhaps from what he would have expended on his private wants or pleasures. There is no law of nature making it inherently impossible for wages to rise to the point of absorbing not only the funds which he had intended to devote to carrying on his business, but the whole of what he allows for his private expenses, beyond the necessaries of life. (Mill 1967, pp. 644–45)

It was easy, therefore, for Ekelund to show, by using his short-run model of wages fund, that Mill was wrong in the recantation. Since stocks of both wage goods and nonwage goods are predetermined, and money stock is also fixed by assumption 5, capitalists' larger expenditure on labor in terms of money due to higher nominal wage simply results in a proportionally higher money price of wage goods and a lower money price of nonwage goods. Even though the level of nominal wage is indeterminate, changeable by capitalists' decisions on the allocation between monetary wages fund and their private expenses, the real wage is determined by the wages fund and the population. The real wage fund remains unchanged under the wage good assumption, since the stock of wage goods is predetermined. Without the wage good assumption, however, change in the allocation of monetary fund may cause changes in the real wages fund, money being merely a veil in the classical dichotomy of real and monetary economics. To support the wage good assumption, therefore, Ekelund referred to Pasinetti's (1974) model of Ricardian economics, where a crucial role is played by the assumption of differential consumption patterns for different classes.

Hollander's interpretation of Ricardian economics is different from that of Pasinetti in many important aspects, including the present one.

Ekelund's position follows from a rigid distinction, attributed to Mill and the classics generally and Ricardo in particular, between wage goods and profit goods which rules out increases in labor's real earnings during the production period in consequence of increased demand for labour in money terms. It is precisely this assumption which we have seen cannot be attributed to Ricardo. (Hollander 1979, p. 332)

It is natural, therefore, that Hollander (1968) is favorable to Mill's recantation and tried to consider under what conditions Mill's arguments in the recantation are justified, with, of course, the wage good assumption discarded.

Unitary elasticity of demand for labor

Schwartz (1972) argued that the rejection of the yearly period of production, the annual harvest assumption, lies at the origin of the recantation. "It seems that Mill came to think that the only basis for speaking of a rigid wages fund lay in this very artificial assumption of income accruing at yearly intervals" (Schwartz 1972, pp. 95, 275). This interpretation that Mill considered income accruing more often than at yearly intervals in the recantation seems to be supported by Mill's text, since he insisted that capitalist's "profit is made as his transactions go on, and not at Christmas or Midsummer, when he balances his books" (Mill 1967, p. 645). As Schwartz himself admitted, however, Mill did not explain properly how the wages fund doctrine can be rejected by the new assumption of income accruing more often than at yearly intervals. Nor is Schwartz himself clear on this. Though he suggests considering "what motivates an employer to hire more or less labor at any given moment" (Schwartz 1972, p. 96), in terms of the comparison of the rate of wage with the marginal product of labor, he did not explain why the rate of wage is not determined by the predetermined stock of the wage goods and the population at any given moment.

Naturally, Ekelund (1976) is critical of Schwartz and correctly pointed out that the wages fund remains predetermined provided that a positive period of production, however short, exists and circulating capital has to be advanced (unless input and output are perfectly and instantaneously synchronized). Though Ekelund argues that Schwartz seems to assume this perfect and instantaneous synchronization, however, this accusation is not warranted since the latter stated "that the wages fund was advanced and replaced continually" (Schwartz 1972, p. 96). Ekelund further insisted that the annual harvest assumption is not required for the short-run determinacy of a wages fund: "Even in a continuous-flow model a real wages fund exists if the flow of any particular day is determined by decisions made some time before" (Ekelund 1976). By this, Ekelund seems to mean, however, merely a continuous shortening of the period of production t_1t_2, since otherwise he could not, as we shall see, so argue.

It seems to me that all these ambiguities and confusions are due to imperfect recognition of the full significance of the annual harvest assumption. It implies not only that the period of production, the time interval t_1t_2 between an input and the resultant output is given, but also that the period of production is identical to the time interval between successive inputs and also to the time interval between successive output. In other words, an input can be made either at time t_1 or at time t_2 and the resultant output is available, respectively, either at t_2 or at t_3 such that the period t_1t_2 is equal to the period t_2t_3, and no input can be made at any time between t_1 and t_2, and no output is available at any time between t_2 and t_3. Because making an input means to purchasing labor (with wage goods) and output has to be sold, markets are open only at t_1, t_2, t_3 and are closed at any time between t_1 and t_2 and between t_2 and t_3. Therefore, the annual harvest assumption implies that the period of production is identical to the market interval.

It is because of this implication of the annual harvest assumption that capitalists can "never [allow] capital to be idle" (Schumpeter 1954, p. 666). Suppose at time t_1 the rate of wage is higher than the level a capitalist firm expects as normal. Even though the rate of profit is lower than the level the capitalist firm expects as normal, however, it is not wise for the firm to postpone the start of production and to let capital to be idle. Since the next market to be opened is at t_2, and by that time the production started at t_1 will be completed and the capital advanced at t_1 will be replaced, it never pays to let capital to be idle in the period of production t_1t_2, even though the rate of profit in this period is lower than the level expected in the subsequent period of production t_2t_3. All the stock of wage goods existing at t_1 has, therefore, to be expended to employ labor at t_1. This is why the wages fund at t_1 is predetermined.

This suggests that the implication of the annual harvest assumption essential to the wages fund doctrine is not that the period of production is a year but that the market interval is identical to the period of production. Abandonment of the annual harvest assumption is, therefore, not to make the period of production shorter, but to make the market interval shorter than the period of production. The annual harvest assumption is best satisfied in the case of traditional agriculture, where production takes time and seasonal variations of input and output cannot be removed at will. In the case of manufactures and highly artificialized agriculture, on the other hand, production still takes time but it can start at any time, so that market interval is much shorter, almost nil, in comparison with the period of production.

Suppose the period of production is still t_1t_2 (and t_2t_3) but it is twice as long as the market interval. Let the midpoint of t_1 and t_2 be t' and that of t_2 and t_3 be t'' in Figure 6.1. Markets are open at t_1, t', t_2, t'', and t_3. Let the rate of real wage (in terms of wage goods) at time t_1 be w_1 and the normal rate of real wage expected by a capitalist in the wage good industry to prevail at time t' and on be w.

Having a stock of wage goods at hand, the capitalist firm has two alternatives at t_1, either to exchange its wages fund with labor at t_1 and start production immediately so that output is available at t_2, or to wait until t' and then to exchange its wages fund with labor to start production, with the result that output is not available until t''. The internal rate of return for unit market interval from the first alternative, r, is calculated by

$$y/(1 + r)^2 + (-w_1) = 0 \qquad (6.1)$$

and that from the second alternative, r', is obtained from

$$y/(1 + r')^3 + (-w) = 0 \qquad (6.2)$$

where y denotes per head output of wage goods. Note that the period of production is still twice as long as the market interval but the period of investment is three times as long as the market interval for the second alternative, since capital is left idle for the first market interval, t_1t'.[2]

By using first order approximation, we can solve (6.1) and (6.2) respectively for r and r' as

$$r = (y/2w_1) - \tfrac{1}{2} \qquad (6.3)$$

and

$$r' = (y/3w) - \tfrac{1}{3} \qquad (6.4)$$

From (6.3) and (6.4), we can see that two alternatives are indifferent if the condition

$$w_1 = 3yw/(w + 2y) \qquad (6.5)$$

is satisfied. Since y should be larger than w, (6.5) implies that $w_1 > w$. Suppose that expectation w is inelastic with respect to current w_1. If w_1 is higher than the level that satisfies (6.5), given w, the capitalist firm will not expend its stock of wage goods to employ labor at t_1 and will choose the second alternative.

Since different capitalists have different expectations, we can say that more and more capitalists will choose the second alternative as the current rate of wage gets higher. The aggregate wages fund actually offered to be exchanged against labor is not predetermined but a decreasing function of the current real wage, given the distribution of expected wage. Since the demand for labor is of unitary elasticity with respect to real wage when the real wage fund to be offered is predetermined, the elasticity of demand for labor is now larger than 1. This is the result of the abandonment of the annual harvest assumption. It cannot be said, therefore, that the annual harvest assumption is not essential for the wages fund doctrine, in spite of the argument of Ekelund to the contrary.

Now two remarks are in order.

We have considered a real model of an economy in which capitalists are supposed to have stocks of wage goods at hand. If we consider a monetary model of an economy, capitalists who demand labor have money and hoard their money if they consider the current money wage is sufficiently higher than the normal level. With reduced money demand for wage goods, some capitalists who supply wage goods decide not to sell them at the current low price but to hold inventory, expecting a normal price in the future. The wages fund actually used to support labor is again not predetermined. Capital remains idle, however, not in the hands of capitalists who demand labor, but in the hands of those who supply wage goods. In this context, the following statement of Mill may be interesting. "If . . . the supply, being in excess of the demand, cannot be all disposed of at the existing price, either a part will be withdrawn to wait for a better market, or a sale will be forced by offering it at . . . a reduction of price" (Mill 1967, p. 636).

Our argument that the wages fund actually offered is not predetermined is a strictly short-run one. It is concerned with the decisions whether to use capital already accumulated immediately or let it be idle for a while, an idleness whose effect is instantaneous. It is different from the longer run argument of the so-called boomerang effect, the negative effect of high wage and low profit on capital accumulation. The boomerang effect will be realized only after a period of production has passed, since it is the effect on the composition of output between wage goods and nonwage goods. Considering an alternative open to capitalists, we concentrated on the comparison of internal rate of return from different uses of already accumulated capital and we neglected to consider the boomerang effect. This is possible, since the expectation of future wage and profit is assumed to be inelastic with respect to current wage and profit,[3] which is again permissible only in the short-run consideration. If, on the other hand, expectation is static on the sense that the expected wage is perfectly elastic with respect to current wage so that they are always identical, we are back again to the world of the wages fund doctrine, even if the annual harvest assumption is discarded.

Zero elasticity of demand for labor

Mill's recantation was originally a review of Thornton's book, *On Labor, Its Wrongful Claims and Rightful Dues, Its Actual Present and Possible Future.* In this book Thornton presented a criticism of suply–demand equilibrium analysis by adducing several cases of indeterminate prices resulting from the presence of completely inelastic schedules and severe discontinuities. From the point of view that the rate of wage is indeterminate in supply–demand equilibrium analysis, Thornton rejected the notion of a predetermined wages fund, which of course makes the rate of wage determinate. Although Mill did not admit the significance of all the cases Thornton adduced, Mill accepted Thornton's criticism of the predetermined wages fund. This implies that Mill had also in mind a case of the wage indeterminacy due to demand for labor inelastic with respect to wage. Supply being given constant, this is the case where schedules of supply and demand are coincidental, at least within certain limits. "When the equation of demand and supply leaves the price in part indeterminate, because there is more than one price which would fulfil the law; neither sellers nor buyers are under the action of any motives, derived from supply and demand, to give way to one another" (Mill 1967, p. 642).

To make the demand for labor completely inelastic, the wage good assumption has to be discarded, since otherwise the elasticity of demand for labor is unitary or may be larger than 1. Taking the existence of fixed capital into consideration, furthermore, Hollander (1968) argued rightly that the fixed technical coefficients in production are required, so that the demand for labor does not change through the substitution effect between fixed capital and labor caused by changes in wage. Without the wage good assumption, however, the boomerang effect is instantaneous, since investment in and disinvestment out of circulating capital can be effected instantaneously. Wages fund may not be changed proportionally to the rate of wage and the demand for labor may be changed through this boomerang effect caused by changes in the rate of wage. For example, higher wage and lower rate of profit makes capitalists consume more and invest less in (or disinvest from) the circulating capital so that wages fund gets smaller relative to the rate of wage. In other words, the abandonment of the wage good assumption is, though necessary, by no means sufficient for the zero elasticity of demand for labor. To avoid this difficulty the fixed intertemporal coefficients in consumption are required, in addition to the fixed technical coefficients in production, to make the elasticity of demand for labor completely inelastic with respect to wage.

Let us construct a simple model of a capitalist, in which the demand for labor is completely inelastic with respect to the rate of wage, keeping all the assumptions made in Ekelund's (1976) short-run model of wages fund, except the wage good assumption. The economy's real output is assumed to be composed solely of machinery (fixed capital) and the consumables that can be consumed by both laborers and capitalists. Following Mill in the recantation, however, we disregard the existence of the fixed capital.

Suppose the capitalist has been in stationary conditions up to t_1. A given stock of the consumables Y is in the hands of the capitalist at t_1, which can be either consumed by himself or advanced to employ laborers; that is,

$$Y = wL + c_1 \tag{6.6}$$

where w, L, and c_1 signify, respectively, the real rate of wage, the current level of employment (i.e., the demand for labor), and the current level of consumption, all at time t_1. Let us denote the average product of labor by a, which is considered as technically given, in view of Hollander's (1968) assumption of the fixed technical coefficients in production. Then after the technologically given period of production $t_1 t_2$, a stock of the consumables aL is available, which can again be either consumed or advanced as wages fund at t_2; that is,

$$aL = wL' + c_2 \tag{6.7}$$

where L' and c_2 denote, respectively, the demand for labor and the level of the capitalist's consumption, all at t_2, and the rate of wage is expected to be still at w in t_2.

The rate of profit r corresponding to w is implicitly defined by

$$a = (1 + r) w \tag{6.8}$$

As the result of the maximization of utility, which is a function of c_1 and c_2, under the conditions (6.6) and (6.7), then, we have the following familiar condition[4]

$$U_1 = (1 + r) U_2 \tag{6.9}$$

where U_1 is the marginal utility of current consumption c_1 at t_1, and U_2 is the marginal utility of the next period's consumption, c_2 at t_2.

As for the demand for labor at t_2, that is, L', let us suppose that the capitalist firm expects the economy to return to the stationary condition in which it has been up to t_1, after a short-run variation in the rate of wage at t_1 and t_2, and plans to employ such a number of laborers at t_2 as is sufficient to rebuild its stock of the consumables Y at t_3. With unchanged productivity of labor, this requires that L' should be Y/a. If L' can be given in this way, we have now four conditions (6.6)–(6.9) to determine

c_1, c_2, r, and L as functions of w. As is easily seen, however, the demand for labor L is, in general, not completely inelastic with respect to the rate of wage w.

We have to impose restrictions on the form of utility function, therefore, to make the demand for labor inelastic with respect to wage. Let us first, however, generalize (6.9) into

$$U_1^{(-)} \geqq (1 + r)\, U_2^{(+)} \tag{6.10}$$

and

$$U_1^{(+)} \leqq (1 + r)\, U_2^{(-)} \tag{6.11}$$

where $U_1^{(-)}$ and $U_2^{(+)}$ are, respectively, the left-hand-side derivative of the utility function with respect to current consumption and the right-hand-side derivative of the utility function with respect to the next period consumption and the like. The condition (6.10) implies that the marginal utility to be lost by the unit reduction of the current consumption is not smaller than the marginal utility to be gained by the increased consumption in the next period made possible by the unit reduction of the current consumption. Similarly, condition (6.11) means that the marginal utility to be gained by the unit increase in the current consumption is not larger than the marginal utility to be lost by the reduction in the next period's consumption which is the inevitable sacrifice due to the unit increase in the current consumption. Obviously these two conditions have to be satisfied if the consumption stream is optimal through time.

If, incidentally, the utility function is differentiable and the right- and left-hand derivatives are identical, (6.10) and (6.11) are combined into the single (6.9). In the case of the fixed intertemporal coefficients in consumption, however, the utility function is, though continuous, not differentiable since the right-hand-side marginal utility of (utility gain of an increase in) the consumption of any period at the optimal consumption stream is zero, while the left-hand-side marginal utility of (utility loss of a decrease in) the consumption of any period at the optimal consumption stream is positive. Indifference curves of this case are shown in Figure 6.2, where the current consumption c_1 is measured horizontally, and the next period consumption c_2 is measured vertically. The ($c_1 = c_2$) line $0A$ indicates the fixed intertemporal coefficients in consumption, and indifference curves are L shaped with a kink on the line $0A$. With any intertemporal price ratio i.e. $(1 + r)$, the optimal consumption is always at the kink, on the line $0A$.

In the case of fixed intertemporal coefficients in consumption, the conditions (6.10) and (6.11) require merely that $c_1 = c_2$, as is seen in Figure 6.2. Since the right-hand-side marginal utilities are zero while the

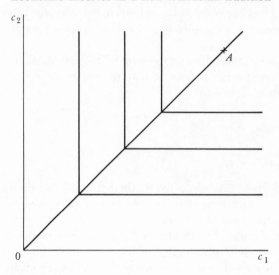

Figure 6.2

left-hand-side marginal utilities are positive, any point on the line $0A$ satisfies conditions (6.10) and (6.11). On the other hand, all other points violate either (6.10) or (6.11), since the marginal utility in both directions of either c_1 or c_2 are positive and that of the other are zero. From (6.6) and (6.7) with $c_1 = c_2$, then, we have

$$(w + a)(Y - aL) = 0 \qquad (6.12)$$

in view of our supposition that $L' = Y/a$. The demand for labor L is Y/a from (6.12), and independent of w.

A rise in wage merely reduces the capitalist's consumption and the wage fund increases proportionally to the rate of wage, so that demand for labor is completely inelastic with respect to wage. This nonexistence of the boomerang effect is a strictly short-run story, however, since the capitalist is assumed to expect that changes in wage rate are merely temporary. In spite of Ekelund's (1976) argument, on the other hand, this can be explained by the endogenous decision process of the capitalist under, of course, certain restrictive conditions.

Thus in his recantation of the wages fund doctrine, Mill not only denied the existence of the predetermined wages fund but also argued that the rate of wage is indeterminate. This is a strong case "in which there is nothing to restrain competition; no hindrance to it either in the nature of the case or in artificial obstacles; yet in which the result is not determined by competition, but by custom or usage; competition ... producing its effect in quite a different manner from that which is ordinarily assumed to be natural to it" (Mill 1965, p. 239). The wage once raised by a well-organized strike remains unchanged even if laborers returned thereafter to competitive suppliers. The wage changed exogenously is supported bv endogenous decisions of competitive demanders and suppliers.

CHAPTER 7

Marx and exploitations in production and in circulation

Ricardo defined the principal problem in political economy as the determination of the laws that regulate distribution (Ricardo 1951, p. 5). It is no wonder, therefore, that the key concept in Marx's *Das Kapital* is also the law of distribution, since "Marx used the Ricardian apparatus: he adopted Ricardo's conceptual layout and his problems presented themselves to him in the forms that Ricardo had given to them" (Schumpeter 1954, p. 390). In volume I of *Das Kapital* Marx analyzed the problem of distribution between the exploiting class in general and the exploited class, laborers, by the use of labor theory of value, while the redistribution among exploiters is considered in volume III of the same book. I examine critically Marx's treatment of the former problem in this chapter, and consider the latter problem and its relation to the former in the next chapter.

The crux of Marxist labor theory of value is to explain how and why surplus value or profit is created and exploited, not in circulation, but in production, even if commodities are exchanged according to their values. It should be criticized, therefore, not so much from the point of view of the theory of relative prices as from the point of view of the theory of profit. This is why Böhm-Bawerk's famous criticism of Marx in his *Karl Marx and the close of his system* was rather pointless while more important is his criticism against exploitation theory of interest in his *Capital and interest.*[1] As Böhm-Bawerk argued, the exploitation theory fails as a persuasive theory of interest because it fails to recognize that the same physical good at different points in time is in effect different goods. If one uses the rate of interest to discount the value of goods in the future (that is, the output available after the period of production), to compare with goods in the present (that is, inputs to be advanced), there exists no exploitation in the production, though the rate of interest is by no means the only possible discount factor. Depending on different ideas of how to compare goods in the future and goods in the present, there can be many different theories on whether exploitation exists and to what degree it exists.

Despite this difficulty with Marx's theory of exploitation in production, a theory of exploitation in circulation may be hidden in Marx's assumptions in *Das Kapital*. Both Marxist and anti-Marxist economists do not necessarily grasp the fact that the time difference between output and input exists not only for the production of goods but also for the reproduction of labor power, and that surplus value and profit may appear in the reproduction of labor power. In Marxist economics, this point is most recognized in the discussion of the problem of the heterogeneity of labor – how skillful labor is produced from unskilled labor.[2] The reproduction of labor power is, however, not the capitalistic process aimed at maximum profit and therefore will not adjust smoothly to the demand for labor. In the face of the industrial reserve army created by capitalists with labor saving technical changes, it is natural that the rate of profit in the reproduction of labor power is much lower than the rate of profit in capitalistic production. Just as monopolistic capital with its higher rate of profit exploits other capitals (Sweezy 1942, p. 272; Steedman 1977, pp. 180–81), capital in general with higher rate of profit exploits labor, and a necessary condition for this exploitation in circulation is the industrial reserve army that Marx regarded as "a condition of existence of the capitalistic mode of production" (Marx 1954, p. 592).

In the next section, I point out how important is the concept of period of production in classical and Marxist theories of capital and I show, by the use of a simple model, that Marxist theory of exploitation in production is based on an implicit assumption that physically identical but differently dated goods are valued equally. Presented subsequently is the fatal criticism Böhm-Bawerk raised against this assumption, a criticism that has not received proper attention from Marxian economists including Hilferding. Different assumptions on how to compare differently dated goods generate different views on whether there exists exploitation in capitalistic production. Three different views on exploitation are compared next: those of Marx, Böhm-Bawerk, and Weizsäcker. Some Marxist arguments on heterogeneity of labor are surveyed which recognize that the reproduction of labor power is a time-consuming process. The final section of this chapter is devoted to arguing that there is a possibility of exploitation in circulation due to the existence of an industrial reserve army, an argument that is independent of the Marxist assumption criticized by Böhm-Bawerk.

Period of production and exploitation

The exploitation theory of interest is based on the fundamental assumption of the capital theory of the classical economics, to which Marx identifies himself as the sole orthodox successor. The assumption is that variable capital (food and necessaries – the wage goods) is advanced by capitalists to laborers, which is quite in contrast to the post-Walrasian neoclassical assumption that wages are paid out of current, not past, output. We may consider, as was pointed out by Eagly (1974, pp. 3–9), that the classical assumption is originally due to time structure of production in the Quesnaysian model. Capital must be advanced because there is a time lag between input of labor and output of commodities and laborers are stripped of any means of subsistence. By making a distinction between productive labor employed by capital advanced and unproductive labor employed by revenue, Adam Smith clearly saw that commandable and embodied labors are identical and there is no surplus in the case of output of unproductive labor, since there is no time delay between labor input and service output. Smith wrote, "The labour of the menial servant does not fix or realize itself in any particular subject or vendible commodity. His services generally perish in the very instant of their performance, and seldom leave any trace or value behind them, for which an equal quantity of service could afterwards be procured" (Smith 1976, p. 330).

In view of the reproduction schema developed in the volume II of *Das Kapital*, it is evident that Marx assumed the advancement of the variable capital by capitalists so as to support the reproduction of labor power in the households of laborers. Unless wages are advanced by capitalists, those who have nothing but labor power to sell cannot live and reproduce labor power. Marx makes a confusing statement, however, to the effect that laborers advance the use-value of labor power to capitalists.

In every country in which the capitalist mode of production reigns, it is the custom not to pay for labour-power before it has been exercised for the period fixed by the contract, as for example, the end of each week. In all cases, therefore, the use-value of labour-power is advanced to the capitalist; the labourer allows the buyer to consume it before he receives payment of the price; he everywhere gives credit to the capitalist. (Marx 1954, p. 170)

It is true, certainly, that weekly wages are paid at the end of the week and that laborers sometimes lose their wage when the capitalist is bankrupt. Even so, it is the capitalists who advance on the average, in the sense that wages must be paid before the realization of the sale of output, though they are often paid after the consumption of the labor power. Otherwise the variable capital cannot claim to be taken into consideration alongside constant capital (materials, depreciation of fixed capital, etc.) in the calculation of the average rate of profit in volume III of *Das Kapital*.

There is also the same kind of statement in Marx's *Theorien über den Mehrwert*, in which he argued the absurdity of speaking of wages as an advance by the capitalist to the laborer.

This also makes it clear how absurd it is to explain the profit of the capitalist from the fact that he advances money to the labourer before he has converted the commodity into money.... The capitalist pays for the labour only after he has consumed it, while other commodities are paid for before they were consumed.... The capitalist has always appropriated to himself the commodity labour before he pays for it. (Marx 1963, p. 305)

The fact that wages are paid after the use of labor power does not, however, deny the advancement by capitalists to laborers in the sense that wages are paid before the realization of value of output – the labor embodied in the output. Following the statement just quoted, Marx continued to argue lengthily that there can be no profit if capitalists advance merely constant capital, which seems to imply that there should be profit if variable capital is advanced.

Marxist rate of exploitation is defined as surplus value over variable capital. It is positive if and only if the value of output is larger than the value of input. To see the essence of the exploitation theory of interest, let us consider a simple Ricardo-like case (Blaug 1978, p. 95) of an economy composed of labor power and wheat. Homogeneous land is assumed to exist infinitely, and the existence of constant capital is ignored, as was done by Marx himself (Marx 1954, pp. 205–206), so as to make the story as simple as possible. The only capital to be advanced is variable capital, to be paid in exchange for labor power to laborers who are stripped of any means of subsistence; this capital takes the form of wheat. Exchanges are carried out according to embodied labor values and therefore the amount of variable capital to be advanced is given by the amount of wheat necessary to reproduce the labor power used up in the production of wheat. The period of production is naturally one year and the harvest of new wheat is one year later than the payment of wheat wage from the capitalists' stock of wheat accumulated from past harvests. Since output and input are physically identical with the same unit value of embodied labor, exploitation exists if and only if the amount of output of new wheat is larger than the amount of wheat advanced as the variable capital, which is possible because of the peculiar property of labor power to be the source of surplus value. Since exchanges are made according to values, this surplus and exploitation originate, not from circulation, but from production. The whole product is a labor product, but only a part of its embodied labor value corresponding to the advanced variable capital is paid, while the rest corresponding to surplus product is unpaid and exploited by the capitalists.

If the new wheat harvested at the end of the production period and the old wheat advanced by capitalists to laborers are identical, not only physically, but also socially and economically, the exploitation theory makes sense and there is no objection to it. Although the input of old wheat and output of new wheat are physically identical, however, how can we compare them, since they are differently dated and there is no assurance that they are identical in their relations to capitalists and laborers? Since wheat markets differently dated are not perfectly related in the sense that goods cannot be transferred from the market dated later to the market dated earlier, differently dated wheats should be considered socially and economically different goods. When the old wheat is advanced, it might be very scarce while new wheat is not yet available until it is redundant. Suppose the Marxist rate of exploitation is 100 percent and all the surplus is reinvested. A bushel of wheat in 1980 grows into 4 bushels in 1982 while a bushel in 1981 grows only to 2 bushels in 1982. To regard 1980 wheat and 1981 wheat as identical means to make 4 bushels of wheat identical to 2 bushels of wheat in 1982.

Unless they are socially and economically identical, there is no guarantee of being able to compare the physical amount of new and old wheat and to talk about the surplus and exploitation. It is of no use in this respect merely to translate physical amount of wheat into expressions in terms of money, abstract human labor, or anything else. Since there can be no labor movement between different time periods, embodied labors cannot be used to compare the value of commodities differently dated. As a matter of fact, embodied labor can be a measure of value even in the same time period if and only if labor can freely move between different sectors of production and the concept of identical abstract human labor can be formed from many different concrete useful labors. Since Marx did not offer any plausible argument that present and future goods physically identical are also identical, socially and economically, the exploitation theory remains incomplete as a theory of interest.

Böhm-Bawerk and Hilferding

Böhm-Bawerk's *Karl Marx and the close of his system* (1975) has been regarded as a criticism of Marx's theory of value so representative that "the arguments advanced by the others are either directly borrowed from Böhm-Bawerk or are variations on the same tune deserving no particular attention" (Boudin 1907, p. 85). As is well known, Böhm-Bawerk is mainly concerned here with two problems: whether the embodied labor or value in use should be a common factor of which the same amount exists in the things exchanged and whether volume I and volume III of *Das Kapital* are contradictory. The former problem is not original to Böhm-Bawerk, since it was already raised by Wicksteed.[3] It is a philosophical problem rather than a scientific one. We can accept, at least as a working hypothesis, that being products of abstract human labor is the common factor existing in commodities exchanged, since most, though certainly not all, of the goods in the markets are labor products. If the share of direct and indirect wage costs in the cost of production is 93 percent (Stigler 1965, pp. 326–42), furthermore, it is quite natural to assume, for the starting hypothesis, that relative prices are proportional to the quantities of labor embodied.

The latter point raised by Böhm-Bawerk, the so-called great contradiction of Marx, is derived from the interpretation of Marx's system to the effect that volume I of *Das Kapital* as such is a complete theory of relative price which is different from another theory of relative price given in volume III. This interpretation is wrong, since Marx was well aware, as was argued by Schumpeter (1954, p. 597), from an early stage of his thought that exchange ratios do not confirm to Ricardo's equilibrium theorem on value; that is, they are proportional to the ratios of labor embodied, which Marx developed in volume I. We cannot blame Böhm-Bawerk, however, since, as was admitted by Schumpeter, he could not see the *Theorien über den Mehrwert*, in which the material indicating this recognition of Marx was published.[4] Volumes I and III should be considered, therefore, jointly and systematically. One should not consider them separately as did Böhm-Bawerk. The labor theory of value in volume I is to be considered as a theoretical hypothesis of the first approximation, which was modified into the theory of prices of production in volume III in view of the equalization of the rate of profit among sectors with different organic compositions of capital.

Neoclassical economists generally expect the theory of value, whether it is the labor theory of value or not, to explain the ratio of exchange or relative prices in the exchange of goods against goods. In spite of the criticism of Marx given by Böhm-Bawerk, it seems that Marx's labor theory of value scores fairly high for this role, if volumes I and III of *Das Kapital* are considered as a single theory of relative price, in which the labor theory of value in volume I is a first step to the final stage developed in volume III. The role of the theory of value in Marxist economics is, however, different from the one expected by neoclassical economists. As rightly argued by Hilferding (1975) in his reply to Böhm-Bawerk's criticism of Marx, the theory of value in volume I aims to show that the surplus value or profit originates from production and not from circulation. It is the confusion of these two roles of the value theory which explains why the critiques of Marx in the past were mostly unproductive.

If the aim of Marx's labor theory of value is to explain how and why surplus value is created and exploited in the process of production, we can find the best argument against it, not in Böhm-Bawerk's *Karl Marx and the close of his system*, nor in his section on Marx in *Capital and interest*, but in his section on Rodbertus. Böhm-Bawerk (1959a, pp. 263–65) attacked the exploitation theory of interest of Rodbertus on the ground that future and present goods are wrongly considered identical and stated that the same argument can be applied to the theory of Marx. Even though surplus value is produced by labor alone, it accrues only after the passage of time. Criticizing Rodbertus, Böhm-Bawerk argues that there is no exploitation if workers receive at present the entire present value of their future output, which is smaller than the future value since the physically same goods located at different time points are not identical in view of the existence of the rate of interest. He considered the following example.

Suppose a single worker spends five years to complete independently a steam engine from the beginning, which commands, when completed, a price of $5,500. There is no objection to giving him the whole steam engine or $5,500 as the wage for five years' continuous labor, but when? Obviously it must be at the expiration of five years. It is impossible for him to have the steam engine before it is in existence. He cannot receive the steam engine valued at $5,500 and created by him alone, before he has created it. His compensation is the whole future value at a future time.

But the worker having no means of subsistence cannot and will not wait until his product has been fully completed. Suppose our worker wishes, after the expiration of the first year, to receive a corresponding partial compensation. The worker should get all that he has labored to produce up to this point, say, a pile of unfinished ore, or of iron, or of steel material, or the full exchange value that this pile of material has now. The question is how large will that value be in relation to the price of the finished engine, $5,500. Can it be $1,100, since the worker has up to this time performed one-fifth of the work?

Böhm-Bawerk said "no." One thousand one hundred dollars is one-fifth of the price of a completed, present steam engine, which is different from what the worker has produced in the first year, one-fifth of an engine that will not be finished for another four years. The former fifth has a value different from that of the latter fifth, in so far as a complete present machine has a value different from the value of an engine that will not be available for another four years. Our worker at the end of a year's work on the steam engine that will be finished in another four years has not yet earned the entire value of one-fifth of a completed engine, but something smaller than that value. Assuming a prevailing interest rate of 5 percent, Böhm-Bawerk concluded that the worker should get the produce of the first year's labor, which is worth about $1,000 at the end of the first year.

By using this example, Böhm-Bawerk criticized Rodbertus and Marx, who claimed, ignoring wrongly the difference between present and future goods, that there is exploitation unless the worker does receive now (not in the future) the entire future (not the present) value of his product though it is available only in the future. Unfortunately, Böhm-Bawerk developed this criticism mainly in his section on Rodbertus in *Capital and Interest*, and did not repeat it sufficiently in his section on Marx, nor in his *Karl Marx and the close of his system*. This might be the reason why there seems to be no rejoinder from Marxist economists to this most important critical comment on the value theory of Marx. It is natural that Hilferding's famous rejoinder to Böhm-Bawerk merely emphasized the significance of value theory as exploitation theory and did not touch the problem of the difference of present and future goods.

In *Karl Marx and the close of his system*, Böhm-Bawerk referred to this problem only when he discussed the theory of value in the precapitalistic conditions. According tto Marx, prices were in accordance with the embodied labor values under simple commodity production in which the worker has his own means of production and subsistence. Böhm-Bawerk raised the criticism that, in exchanges in accordance with value, workers whose products require longer to be completed are unfavorable in comparison with other workers whose products need not much time, and that prices diverge from values as a result of the movement of workers between occupations. Hilferding considered that the crux of this comment lies not so much in the problem of the time required in production as in the problem of simple commodity production. Therefore, he even argued that workers are not free to move between occupations under simple commodity production.[5] Hilferding misunderstood, furthermore, the point of Böhm-Bawerk's comment and argued that the workers whose products require not much time have to await as well, after the completion of their own work, the completion of products of those workers whose output requires longer. This is, of course, not the case with Böhm-Bawerk. Böhm-Bawerk considered the exchange of two products that are completed at the same time but require different lengths of time for completion. It is very unfortunate that by such a funny misunderstanding Hilferding was robbed of the opportunity to make his rejoinder, if any, to Böhm-Bawerk's most important and serious comment (Böhm-Bawerk 1975, pp. 42–45; Hilferding, 1975, pp. 166–168).

Different views on discount and exploitation

To consider whether there exists exploitation in production, we have to compare the value of output and the value of input. In the wheat economy considered earlier in this chapter, output and input are physically identical, but differently dated. The difference in date between output and input is, of course, due to the existence of the period of production, which is recognized in classical as well as Marxist economic theories. To compare differently dated goods, we have to use discount ratio, just as we have to use exchange ratio to compare physically different goods. Böhm-Bawerk used, as just shown, the rate of interest to discount future output so as to make it comparable to input. In the wheat economy, the rate of interest in the sense of *Kapitalzins* (the real rate of interest) or the rate of profit is exactly the Marxist rate of exploitation. If the output of wheat is discounted by the interest rate, therefore, it is equal to the input – wheat advanced as wage – and there is no exploitation. The difference between Marx and Böhm-Bawerk is that the former applies a zero discount rate to goods available in the future to compare them with present goods while the latter applies a positive rate of interest as the discount rate. There seems to be no reason that Marx is right and Böhm-Bawerk is wrong.

Weizsäcker (1973) (see also Samuelson 1972, pp. 312–14) also emphasized the importance of the difference in time. Generalizing the Marxian concept of exploitation, he argued that the original Marxian concept can be meaningful only in a stationary state. Otherwise, "the Marxian socially necessary labor time to produce a certain commodity becomes economically rather meaningless" since "those labor particles which had to be available when there was abundance of labor are added with equal weight together with particles which had to be provided at times of labor scarcity" and "this expression gives little information about the social opportunity costs of the production of this commodity in terms of other commodities" (Weizsäcker 1973, p. 265).

From national accounting relations, we have

$$c + gv = w + rv \tag{7.1}$$

where c, v, w, r, and g are, respectively, real consumption and the value of capital per head, the wage rate, the rate of interest, and the growth rate. In other words, the sum of consumption and investment is equal to the sum of wages and profit, in aggregate, and therefore, per head, including both laborers and capitalists. Similarly, for capitalists only,

$$c' + gv' = w + rv' \tag{7.2}$$

where c' is the capitalists' consumption per head, and v' is the value of capital per capitalist. The rate of wage for capitalist overseeing labor is assumed to be equal to laborers' wage. From (7.1) and (7.2),

$$c' - c = (r - g)(v' - v) \tag{7.3}$$

Weizsäcker considers that capitalists' social duty is to save and accumulate capital. He defines capitalist exploitation of society as $c' > c$, the condition that pertains when capitalists consume profit or consume more than their wage income of overseeing labor. If they save all the profit, $r = g$ and there is no exploitation.

What Weizsäcker proposed is to use the rate of growth to discount the future goods to the present. If $r = g$, therefore, he agrees with Böhm-Bawerk, who discounted future goods with the rate of interest and denied the exploitation by capitalists. Since g falls short of r as capitalists consume a part of profit, Weizsäcker's discount ratio is not larger than Böhm-Bawerk's, and Weizsäcker's position with respect to the possibility of capitalists' exploitation is located between Marx and Böhm-Bawerk. Weizsäcker insists that he can agree with Marx only when $g = 0$, that is, only in a stationary state. If $r \neq 0$ in such a state, as in the case of Marx's simple reproduction, Böhm-Bawerk disagrees both with Marx and Weizsäcker. As was emphasized by Schumpeter (1926), however, the rate of interest can be considered to be zero in a stationary state (Kuenne 1963, pp. 275–79).

Since we are assuming the subsistence wage just sufficient to reproduce labor power, laborers remain laborers and cannot become capitalists.[6] Similarly, let us assume that each capitalist does not dissave (does not consume his capital) and remains capitalist. Stationary state is possible, then, if and only if each capitalist consumes all his profit and keeps his capital unchanged. Since the level of consumption as well as the social milieu around themselves are unchanged in a stationary state, the marginal rate of substitution between consumptions in different periods is equal to 1 for rational capitalists who do not underevaluate the future wants. Such capitalists are indifferent, roughly speaking, if the current consumption is reduced by one small unit (in terms of either value or money) and the consumption is increased by the same amount in a future period.[7] If the rate of interest is positive, however, they can increase their consumption in future more than they reduce their consumption currently. Since capitalists can reproduce themselves by their wage income from overseeing labor, they do begin to save their profit to increase their satisfaction in the long run. A stationary state cannot be maintained as a result of such capital accumulation, unless the rate of interest is zero.

In Figure 7.1, an indifference curve for a capitalist is shown and its slope at a stationary state S ($0S_1 = 0S_2$) is -1. In other words, the indifference curve is tangent to line AB ($0A = 0B$) at the point S. If the rate of interest is positive, the capitalist can move along the line SP, which is steeper than AB, by reducing the present consumption and increasing the future consumption. By so doing the capitalist can achieve higher satisfaction at G than at S. Stationary state S is impossible, therefore, unless the rate of interest is zero and line SP coincides with line SB.

In a stationary state with zero rate of interest, both Böhm-Bawerk and

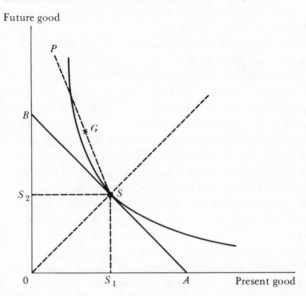

Figure 7.1

Weizsäcker agree with Marx that undiscounted future goods can be compared with present goods. All three would agree, furthermore, that there is no exploitation, since output is at the subsistence level, which is just sufficient to reproduce labor power, and there is no room for the exploitation. Except for such a case, which is uninteresting from the point of view of a theory of distribution, the three views would not agree.[8] Böhm-Bawerk assumed the existence of the positive rate of interest to argue the difference of physically identical goods located at different time points. This might sound, at least to Marxist economists, a circular reasoning, since the exploitation theory of interest is denied by assuming the existence of the positive rate of interest, which the theory aims to prove. Weizsäcker's view on exploitation is very attractive from the point of view of the maximum rate of growth of the economy, but Weizsäcker may not be able to persuade those economists who do not evaluate the value of economic growth so highly. Different views on exploitation, on what discount factor is to be used to compare future and present goods seem, therefore, to suggest that this is a problem of value judgment or ideology. We may conclude that not to discount, to discount with interest rate, and to discount with growth rate represent, respectively, the ideologies of laborers, capitalists, and technocrats.[9]

Period of reproduction of labor power

If future goods are discounted by the rate of interest, there exists no exploitation in the production of goods. Though it is a necessary condition, however, this is not a sufficient condition for the nonexistence of exploitation in an economy. To complete the story, we have to consider the production of labor power along with the production of goods.

Marx described the process of reproduction of labor power as follows.

The owner of labour-power is mortal. If then his appearance in the market is to be continuous, and the continuous conversation of money into capital assumes this, the seller of labour-power must perpetuate himself, "in the way that every living individual perpetuates himself, by procreation." The labour-power withdrawn from the market by wear and tear and death, must be continually replaced by, at the very least, an equal amount of fresh labour-power. Hence the sum of the means of subsistence necessary for the production of labour-power must include the means necessary for the labourer's substitutes, i.e., his children, in order that this race of peculiar commodity owners may perpetuate its appearance in the market. (Marx 1954, p. 168)[10]

This description suggests that the reproduction of labor power is also a time-consuming process in which cost of production must be advanced. As in the case of production of goods, then, do surplus or profit appear in the process of reproduction of labor power?

The fact that reproduction of labor power is a time-consuming and surplus-creating process is most clearly seen in Marxists' explanation of the production of skilled labor from unskilled labor. Following Hilferding (1975), Okishio (1965), and Itoh (1981), we may sketch it as follows.

Suppose there are s different types of labor, and let b_{ik} and h_k denote, respectively, the amount of the kth labor necessary to produce one unit of the ith commodity, and the reduction ratio of the kth labor to simple unskilled labor. The value of the ith commodity is given as

$$t_i = \sum a_{ij} t_j + \sum b_{ik} h_k \qquad (7.4)$$

where a_{ij} and t_j denote, respectively, the amount of the jth commodity necessary to produce one unit of the ith commodity and the value of the jth commodity. Suppose further that H_{ki} amount of the ith commodity and T_{kj} amount of the jth labor are necessary to train a kth type skilled laborer. Then we have

$$L_k h_k = L_k + \sum H_{ki} t_i + \sum T_{kj} h_j, \quad k \neq 1 \qquad (7.5)$$

where L_k is the lifetime labor hours of this laborer and the first type of labor is assumed to be simple unskilled labor, that is, $h_1 = 1$. Itoh justified Hilferding's supposition that "the rate of exploitation might be much lower" for the skilled labor than for the unskilled labor, by arguing that necessary labor (labor hours necessary to reproduce labor power) and surplus labor (the difference between the total labor hours $L_k h_k$ had necessary labor) of a kth type skilled laborer are, respectively,

$$(L_k/2) + \sum H_{ki} t_i + \sum T_{kj} h_j \quad \text{and} \quad L_k/2$$

if the rate of exploitation for the simple unskilled labor is 100 percent and that the rate of exploitation for the kth skilled labor,

$$L_k/(L_k + 2\sum H_{ki} t_i + 2\sum T_{kj} h_j)$$

is clearly less than 100 percent (Hilferding 1975, p. 143; Itoh 1981, p. 246).

Not only the necessary labor but also the surplus labor of the jth type labor used to train the kth type labor are included in the definition of the necessary labor of the kth type labor, the value of the kth labor power. Since the kth labor pays only the necessary labor (the value of the jth labor power), the process of training skilled labor is time consuming and surplus creating. In other words, educating labor is productive, and the educands exploit the educators. This is because parent skilled laborers pay the wage of educators in advance of the sale of the labor power of the children skilled laborers; that is, they pay the advance cost of the education of their children.[11]

Fujimori (1982, pp. 82–84, 157) is critical of what was originally Okishio's formulation, Equation (7.5), on the ground that the dimension of dead labor is to be clearly distinguished from that of living labor. He deletes the second term from the right-hand side of (7.5) and adds equations to determine the value of labor powers, which are in our notation,

$$v_k = \sum H'_{ki} t_i + \sum T_{kj} v_j \tag{7.6}$$

where v_k denotes the value of the kth labor power, H'_{ki} contains, in addition to H_{ki}, the ith commodity consumed by a kth type laborer not for technical training but for his physiologic reproduction, and both H_{ki} and T_{kj} are 0 for $k = 1$. In other words, he considered that educaters' value-creating force of labor is merely transferred to educands and that the surplus labor of the educators is not realized in the training process of skilled labor, but in the production process of goods when the skilled labor power of the educands is exerted. This interpretation might be more loyal to what Hilferding had in mind. "The labor of the technical educator thus transmits, not only value, but in addition its own value-creating power. The formative labors are therefore latent as far as society is concerned, and do not manifest themselves until the skilled labor power begins to work" (Hilferding 1975, pp. 144–145).

In terms of prices and the rate of profit, however, Fujimori (1982, pp. 94–95) considers the following system (in our notation).

$$p_i = (1 + r)(\sum a_{ij}p_j + \sum b_{ik}w_k) \tag{7.7}$$

$$w_k = (1 + r)(\sum H'_{ki}p_i + \sum T_{kj}w_j) \tag{7.8}$$

where p_i and w_k are price of the ith commodity and the wage of the kth type labor, and r is the rate of profit. "In the system of commodity production, where all kinds of good are produced and exchanged as commodities, skills are also subject to the law of commodity production. In the capitalist mode of production, skills are evaluated at their production prices.... $(w_1, \ldots, w_s)$ is the transformed form of the value of labor power, and hence represents wage rates of various types of labour" (Fujimori 1982, pp. 94–95; notation is changed).

From the Marxists' arguments already cited, though we are not particularly interested in the heterogeneity of labor, we may conclude that the reproduction process of labor power is, like the production process of goods, time consuming, requires advancement of costs, and creates surplus or profit. Unlike the case of slave economy, where slave owners pay the costs of reproduction of labor power, laborers in a capitalist economy have to advance the costs by themselves. If we discount future goods and labor powers by the rate of interest, and the rate of profit in both processes is identical and equal to the rate of interest, then there will be no exploitation not only in the production of goods but also in the reproduction of labor power.

An industrial reserve army and exploitation

The rates of profit in different sectors can differ, however, as in the case where the price of the product of a sector is the monopoly price – the price higher than the level of the price of the production. Marx wrote that

the monopoly price of certain commodities would merely transfer a portion of the profit of the other commodity producers to the commodities having the monopoly price. A local disturbance in the distribution of the surplus value among the various spheres of production would indirectly take place, but it would leave the limit of this surplus value itself unaltered.... the monopoly price would be paid by a deduction ... from the profit of the other capitalists. (Marx 1959, p. 861)

In the Marxist system profit is defined as a transformed form of surplus value, a redistribution of the given surplus value exploited from labor. That is the reason why Marx claims that the existence of a monopoly price and higher rate of profit in a sector implies the lower rate of profit common in all the other competitive sectors.

If we start directly from the system of prices and the rate of profit, however, we can also show that a departure of price of the output in a sector from the level of the price of production, in either direction for whatever reason, implies a change in the opposite direction in the rate of profit common to all the other sectors. Suppose there are n sectors, the nth sector being either the sector of monopoly price or that of reproduction of homogeneous labor power. Let A_{ij} denote the amount of the output of the jth sector necessary as input to produce a unit of the output of the ith sector, p_i denote the price of the output of the ith sector, r denote the common rate of profit, and e_i's are parameters initially equal to 1. From the system of the so-called price of production,

$$p_i = (1 + r) e_i \sum_j A_{ij} p_j, \quad i = 1, \ldots, n \tag{7.9}$$

which shows the equality of price and cost (including profit), we can see that r decreases (increases) when any e_i, say, e_n, increases (decreases). This can be easily seen when $n = 2$, by making the first good *numeraire*; that is, $p_1 = 1$. In the first equation in (7.9), r and p_2 must be changed in the opposite direction, since p_1 is constant. In the second equation in (7.9), however, an increase in e_2 is inconsistent with increase in r and decrease in p_2. The departure of monopoly price p_2 from the price of the production, therefore, is caused by an increase in e_2 and lowers the common rate of profit r. In the general case, $(1 + r)$ is the inverse of the Frobenius root of an $n \times n$ positive matrix $[e_i A_{ij}]$, which increases when elements of the matrix increase through an increase in e_n (Morishima 1964, p. 195).

Contrary to the case of the monopolistic sector, wage, that is, the price of the output of the nth sector, assumed to reproduce homogeneous labor power, is more likely lower than the level of the price of production. In (7.9), we have e_n smaller than 1 and therefore r gets larger. This is due to the existence of the relative surplus population or industrial reserve army, which Marx emphasized.

The accumulation of capital, though originally appearing as its quantitative extension only, is effected, as we have seen, under a progressive qualitative change in its composition, under a constant increase of its constant, at the expense of its variable constituent. . . . if a surplus labouring population is a necessary product of accumulation or of development of wealth on a capitalist basis, this surplus population becomes, conversely, the lever of capitalistic accumulation, nay, a condition of existence of capitalist mode of production. . . . there must be the possibility of throwing great masses of men suddenly on decisive points without injury to the scale of production in other spheres. Overpopulation supplies their masses. (Marx 1954, p. 592)[12]

The replacement of variable capital by constant capital may not increase the rate of profit, since it increases some and decreases other elements of

A_{ij} and may not increase r in (7.9). However, excess supply of labor created depresses the wage (or prevents the wage from rising) and increases the rate of profit (or prevents it from falling); that is, e_n is reduced (or prevented from rising) and r is increased (or prevented from falling) in (7.9).

If the nth sector is one of the capitalistic production sectors aiming for maximization of profit, the excess supply of its output would quickly be absorbed by the contraction of output and the reduction of its price would be temporary. As a matter of fact, the system of the price of production, (7.9) with $e_i = 1$, presupposes the equality of demand and supply.[13] The household is, however, not a capitalistic production sector and the reproduction of labor power is only a byproduct of human life. This is why an excess of labor, the industrial reserve army, created by the labor-saving technical progress in the case capitalistic production sectors continues to exist and to depress the wage below the level of the production price of labor power.

Just as the monopolistic capital with a higher rate of profit exploits other competitive capitals with lower common rate of profit, we can say that the nth sector reproducing labor power with the rate of profit $(re_n + e_n - 1)$, which is smaller than r when e_n is smaller than 1, is exploited by other sectors producing goods with the common rate of profit r. Unlike the Marxist concept of exploitation in production, this exploitation is independent of how output in the future is discounted to be comparable to input in the present, since the order of the different sectorial rates of profit remains undisturbed by changes in the common rate of discount. The reason is, of course, that this exploitation arises not in the time-consuming process of production but in the exchange at a point of time between capitalistic production sectors and the noncapitalistic household sector.[14]

Some remarks on the industrial reserve army are in order. Although, first, Marx emphasized the importance of the existence of the industrial reserve army for the capitalist economy, its role in the theory of value is quite ambiguous. In Marxist theory, labor power has to be sold at value (that is, at the cost of reproduction), in order to argue that the surplus and profit arise not in the circulation and exchange but in the production. If commodities are sold at value, however, there has to be no excess demand nor excess supply.

Nothing is easier than to realize the inconsistencies of demand and supply, and the resulting deviation of market-prices from market-values. The real difficulty consists in determining what is meant by the equation of supply and demand. Supply and demand coincide when their mutual proportions are such that the mass of commodities of a definite line of production can be sold at their market-value, neither above nor below it. That is the first thing we hear. The second is this: If commodities are sold at their market-values, supply and demand coincide. (Marx 1959, p. 189)

Certainly if there is no excess supply in labor market, the price of labor power may deviate occasionally upward from the value, and the existence of surplus or profit is not absolutely assured. An industrial reserve army, which prevents the wage from deviating upward from the level corresponding to the value of labor power, is indeed a necessary condition to assure the capitalistic exploitation in production. It results, however, in a downward deviation of the wage from the level of value, which implies that exploitation arises in the circulation or exchange. This result is not avoidable since laborers have nothing to sell but labor power in a Marxist world.

Samuelson criticized neoclassically, moreover, the Marxist concept of an industrial reserve army to the effect that wages continue to fall until the industrial reserve army is eliminated or the wage falls to zero (Samuelson 1966, pp. 365–68). As in the case of Keynesian equilibrium with unemployment, therefore, it has to be explained why the existence of reserve army is compatible with the unchanged level of wage. Following the idea of Harris and Todaro (1970; see also Corden 1974, p. 145), we may consider that what matters to laborers is the expected value of wage, the level of wage multiplied by the employment probability that coincides with the ratio of those employed to the total labor supply when the latter is very large. This presupposes that labor is homogeneous, those who are employed and those who are unemployed are chosen at random, with an equal probability of employment for each identical laborer and with no serial correction in employment; in other words, labor force steadily turns over and jobs are not tenured. Suppose that the number of laborers is much larger than that of employers and that the consideration of laborers' morale prevents employers from introducing wage differentials. Each single laborer cannot, then, expect a large increase in the probability of employment by accepting a wage cut, since it is impossible for him to underbid rivals so that he alone can be employed. Laborers are, therefore, reluctant to accept wage cuts proposed by employers, particularly when the level of wage has already fallen to a fairly low point. In such a case, employers are also reluctant to cut wages, fearing a possible drop in productivity as a result of a wage cut (Negishi 1979a, pp. 87–123).

CHAPTER 8

Marx's dichotomy between exploitation and redistribution of surplus products

Böhm-Bawerk (1975) claimed that a contradiction exists between volume I and volume III of Marx's *Das Kapital*, supporting that claim by interpreting arguments in these two volumes as two different theories of relative prices (see Chapter 7). In view of the reply to Böhm-Bawerk given by Hilferding (1975, pp. 160–61) that in volume I, "Marx's concern is with the value newly created within a period of production, and with the ratio in which this newly created value is distributed between the working class and the capitalist class, thus furnishing the revenues of two great classes," however, it is more appropriate to say that there is a dichotomy between the theory of distribution of income between property owners and wage earners (the theory of value) in volume I and the theory of distribution among property owners (the theory of prices of production and the theory of rent) in volume III.

Like Walras and many other neoclassical economists who started with the simple real models of exchange and of production and later introduced money into consideration, Marx also started with the simple world of value and rate of surplus value (volume I) and later introduced the price of production and the equality of rates of profit, and rent and landownership (volume III). Such a two-step approach, source of the dichotomy, is certainly useful since we can separate a simpler, but more important problem from other, more complex problems and can study the former without being bothered by the latter. The dichotomous procedure has demerits, however, as well as merits. The trouble with the dichotomy of real and monetary theories of Walras and neoclassical economists is that the role of money is minimized by them and they failed consequently to see the problem of effective demand. To recognize the significance of money fully, therefore, the neoclassical dichotomy should be discarded (Chapter 14). Similarly, in my opinion, the Marxist dichotomy cannot work unless value is independent of the pattern of demand from property owners, because the latter is certainly not independent of distribution among property owners. If there exist scarce lands, however, it is impossible to define value that is independent of the pattern of demand. Marx's dichotomy between theory of value and theory of rent fails. The existence of land rent is the Achilles' heel in Marx's labor theory of value considered as a macroeconomic theory of distribution of income between property owners and wage earners.

In view of detailed discussions on the theory of rent in *Das Kapital* and *Theorien über den Mehrwert* (Marx 1959, ch. 37–47; 1968, ch. 8, 9, and 11–14), it is rather strange that most recent attempts to reconstruct Marx's economic model by using modern techniques have paid little attention to the problem of rent and landownership (Samuelson 1966, pp. 341–72; Morishima 1973). Samuelson criticized Ricardo's attempt to deduce price ratio from labor alone, independently of changes in the pattern of landlord demand. He called such a deduction a mathematical impossibility, arguing that "the same criticism holds also for Marx, but he at least had the grace to assume away land rent explicitly thereby avoiding Ricardo's logical error and being guilty only of the misdemeanor of unrealism" (1966, p. 400).

If it can be said that Marx gracefully assumed away land rent, however, it also must be admitted that Walras assumed away money and Marx similarly assumed away the equality of rates of profit. In fact, they did not assume these problems away, but simply postponed consideration of them until later stages of their studies. Marx is guilty, on the other hand, not of the misdemeanor of being unrealistic, but of logical error.

In the following sections I shall define formally what I mean by Marx's dichotomy and shall argue that such a dichotomy does work so far as it is concerned with the distribution between the representative capitalist and wage earners and the distribution among capitalists. In other words, theory of value is independent of theory of price of production. I then present an explanation of the concept of absolute rent, since that concept is unfamiliar to non-Marxist economists in general. As a matter of fact, absolute rent is the only rent that is consistent to Marx's dichotomy. Unfortunately, however, we must argue that absolute rent has a fatal conceptual difficulty. In the final section I shall demonstrate the failure of Marx's dichotomy between distribution between the capitalist, who represents property owners, and wage earners, on one hand, and the distribution between capitalists and landowners in the form of differential rent, on the other.

Value and price of production

The dichotomy can be defined formally as follows. Suppose there are two variables X and Y that are, in general, to be determined by two conditions,

$$F(X, Y) = 0 \tag{8.1}$$

and

$$G(X, Y) = 0 \tag{8.2}$$

If we can find that the condition (8.1) is actually

$$F(X) = 0, \tag{8.3}$$

then there is a dichotomy between the determination X in (8.3) and the determination of Y in (8.2) by the substitution of X, already obtained from (8.3), into (8.2). For the dichotomy to be possible, it is essential that the determination of X be independent of changes in Y, as in the case of (8.3). If the determination of X is influenced by changes in Y, as in the case of (8.1), the dichotomy is impossible and those who consider X without paying attention to Y are guilty of logical error.

Between volume I (i.e., Book I, *The process of production of capital*) and volume III (i.e., Book III, *The process of capitalist production as a whole*) of *Das Kapital*, Marx considered the dichotomy, since in the former he argued as follows.

The capitalist who produces surplus-value, i.e., who extracts unpaid labour directly from the labourers, and fixes it in commodities, is, indeed, the first appropriator, but by no means the ultimate owner, of this surplus-value. He has to share it with capitalists, with landowners, &c., who fulfil other functions in the complex of social production. Surplus-value, therefore, splits up into various parts. Its fragments fall to various categories of persons, and take various forms, independent the one of the other, such as profit, interest, merchants' profit, rent, &c. It is only in Book III that we can take in hand these modified forms of surplus-value.... we treat the capitalist producer as owner of the entire surplus-value, or, better perhaps, as the representative of all the sharers with him in the booty. (Marx 1954, pp. 529–30)

In other words, X is the distribution between laborers and the capitalist who represents property owners, which Marx calls the exploitation of surplus products, and Y is the redistribution among various property owners, like various capitalists and landowners, which Marx calls the redistribution of surplus products.

In the rest of this section, we consider the dichotomy between exploitation of surplus products and the redistribution of surplus products among various capitalists, assuming away the existence of land and landowners. This is the dichotomy between the theory of value and the theory of the price of production. We shall consider in the following sections, on the other hand, the dichotomy between exploitation and redistribution between capitalists and landowners – that is, the dichotomy between the theory of value and the theory of rent.

By assuming away the existence of land, we can safely assume in the rest of this section that input coefficients are technically given constants. For the sake of simplicity, let us consider a two-good (two-sector) economy, assuming away the existence of durable capital and joint production.

The input–output relation is

$$x_1 = a_{11}x_1 + a_{12}x_2 + y_1 \tag{8.4}$$

$$x_2 = a_{21}x_2 + a_{22}x_2 + y_2 \tag{8.5}$$

where x_i, y_i, and a_{ij} denote, respectively, the gross output of the ith good, net output of, or final demand for, the ith good, and the constant input coefficient of the ith good in the production of the jth good. The dual value system to (8.4) and (8.5) is

$$v_1 = a_{11}v_1 + a_{21}v_2 + L_1 \tag{8.6}$$

$$v_2 = a_{12}v_1 + a_{22}v_2 + L_2 \tag{8.7}$$

where v_i and L_i are, respectively, the value of the ith good and the constant labor input coefficient in the production of the ith good.

Total employment of labor is defined as

$$L = L_1 x_1 + L_2 x_2 \tag{8.8}$$

and it is easily seen that

$$L = v_1 y_1 + v_2 y_2 \tag{8.9}$$

which indicates that the value of net output is equal to the input of living labor. Wage is assumed to be equal to the real reproduction cost of labor power,

$$v = c_1 v_1 + c_2 v_2 \tag{8.10}$$

where c_1 and c_2 are physiologically or socially given constants.

The distribution of newly created value between wage earners and the representative capitalist is denoted by the rate of surplus value, or the rate of exploitation, $(L - vL)/vL = (1 - v)/v$, which indicates the ratio of surplus products exploited and wage paid, both given in terms of value. In other words, this is X in Marx's dichotomy. This remains constant, in view of (8.6), (8.7,) and (8.10), provided that input coefficients in production, including the reproduction of labor power, are constant.

Surplus products exploited by the representative capitalist are, then, redistributed among capitalists so that the rate of profit r is equalized between two sectors. This is Y in Marx's dichotomy between the theory of value and the theory of prices of production. This is obtained by transforming values v_i into prices of production p_i, so that

$$p_1 = (1 + r)(L_1 w + a_{11} p_1 + a_{21} p_2) \tag{8.11}$$

$$p_2 = (1 + r)(L_2 w + a_{12} p_1 + a_{22} p_2) \tag{8.12}$$

are satisfied, where

$$w = c_1 p_1 + c_2 p_2 \tag{8.13}$$

The prices of production, which are determined only up to scalar multiplication,[1] and the rate of profit are independent of the level of output and therefore the pattern of capitalists' demand. The distribution ratio between wage earners and capitalists in terms of price, $wL/(p_1 y_1 + p_2 y_2)$, is, however, not independent of the pattern of capitalists' demand, since the pattern of final demand y_i's which can induce the given level of L is not unique, in view of (8.4), (8.5), and (8.8).

The pattern of demand depends, in general, on the pattern of distribution, as Marx clearly pointed out:

the social demand, i.e., the factor which regulates the principle of demand, is essentially subject to the mutual relationship of the different classes and their respective economic position, notably therefore to, firstly, the ratio of total surplus-value to wages, and, secondly, to the relation of the various parts into which surplus-value is split up (profit, interest, ground-rent, taxes, etc.). (Marx 1959, p. 181)

In particular, the pattern of capitalists' demand depends on the distribution among different capitalists – that is, on whether the rate of profit is equalized between different sectors or not. In other words, y_1 and y_2 in (8.4) and (8.5) are not independent of the determination of Y in Marx's dichotomy.

Changes in y_1 and y_2 are, however, absorbed into changes in x_1 and x_2 in (8.4) and (8.5). Values are determined in (8.6) and (8.7) independently of the pattern of the final demand. The determination of the rate of exploitation, $(1 - v)/v$, the X in Marx's dichotomy, is, therefore, independent of the determination of Y in Marx's dichotomy.

We can now conclude with the proposition that Marx's dichotomy does work between a theory of value and a theory of prices of production.[2] The distribution between wage earners and capitalists in value terms is independent of the distribution among capitalists. In other words, value in the Marxist sense is useful as aggregator (weights of goods in aggregation) in the macroeconomic theory of distribution between capitalists and wage earners (Morishima 1973, p. 10).

On the basis of this dichotomy, we can understand what Marxist economists have in mind when they discuss the transformation of value to price.

The distribution of the surplus value is now no longer effected in accordance with the measure of the labor power which the individual producer has in his particular sphere expended for the production of surplus value, but is regulated by the magnitude of the capital it has been necessary to advance in order to set in motion the labor that creates the surplus value. It is obvious that the change in the distribution makes no difference in the total amount of surplus value undergoing distribution, that the social relationship is unaltered, and that the change in the distribution comes to pass solely through a modification in the price of the individual commodities. (Hilferding 1975, p. 160)

Value and absolute rent

Let us now turn to the problem of the distribution of surplus products between capitalists and landowners – the theory of rent. Marx's theory of rent consists of the theory of absolute rent and that of differential rent. While the latter is essentially not different from that of Ricardo and those of other non-Marxist economists, the former is rather peculiar to Marxist economics but not very well known among non-Marxist economists. Absolute rent is rent paid even on marginal land or even by marginal investment on such land. It was discussed by Rodbertus (1851), and Marx (1968, ch. 8) critically followed it.

Because absolute rent is likely to be a foreign term to many non-Marxists, and Marx's own explanation is not easy, the following fresh interpretation is presented first in a simple mathematical model as a prelude to documentation of Marx's arguments on it.

Since the existence of land is admitted, input coefficients in agriculture are no longer constants but are assumed variable and increasing functions of the level of output.

In order to minimize the problem of differential rent, suppose that the land is homogeneous. The existence of landownership requires that the input of capital and labor on such land, and therefore the output of agricultural product, the first good, remain unchanged when the demand for the product changes. Nonagricultural goods are aggregated and called manufactured good, the second good.

Then, price–cost equations (8.11) and (8.12) are changed into

$$p_1 = (1 + r_1)(L_1 w + a_{11} p_1 + a_{21} p_2) \tag{8.14}$$

$$p_2 = (1 + r_2)(L_2 w + a_{12} p_1 + a_{22} p_2) \tag{8.15}$$

where r_1 and r_2 are, respectively, the rate of return (profit and rent) at the margin in agriculture and the rate of return (profit) in manufacture.[3] Input coefficients in manufacture are constant from the assumption of constant returns while those in agriculture are constant from the assumption of constant output. By substituting (8.13) into (8.14) and (8.15), we have the condition for nonzero prices as

$$(1 - R_1 (L_1 c_1 + a_{11}))(1 - R_2 (L_2 c_2 + a_{22}))$$
$$- R_1 R_2 (L_1 c_2 + a_{21})(L_2 c_1 + a_{12}) = 0 \tag{8.16}$$

where $R_i = 1 + r_i$.[4] It can easily be seen that higher R_1 implies lower R_2 and vice versa. The absolute rent is the difference of rates of return in two sectors: $R_1 - R_2 = r_1 - r_2$.

Marx explained as follows why absolute rent exists.

If capital meets an alien force which it can but partially, or not at all, overcome, and which limits its investment in certain spheres, admitting it only under conditions which wholly or partly exclude that general equalization of surplus-value to an average profit, then it is evident that the excess of the value of commodities in such spheres of production over their price of production would give rise to a surplus-profit, which could be converted into rent and as such made independent with respect to profit. Such an alien force and barrier are presented by landed property; when confronting capital in its endeavour to invest in land, such a force is the landlord vis-à-vis the capitalist. (Marx 1959, pp. 761–62)

whether this absolute rent equals the whole excess of value over the price of production, or just a part of it, the agricultural products will always be sold at a monopoly price, not because their price exceeds their value, but because it equals their value, or because their price is lower than their value but higher than their price of production. (p. 762)

It is clear that my interpretation of absolute rent is slightly different from Marx's definition, in that the latter requires that the price of agricultural good exceed its price of production but not exceed its value. This definition is based on Marx's supposition that organic composition of capital is higher in manufacture than in agriculture and therefore the price of production is lower than value in agriculture. My interpretation is rather similar to what Ricardo had in mind when he admitted that

the corn and raw produce of a country may, indeed, for a time, sell at a monopoly price, but they can do so permanently only when no more capital can be profitably employed on the lands, and when, therefore, their produce cannot be increased. At such time, every portion of land in cultivation, and every portion of capital employed on the land, will yield a rent, differing, indeed, in proportion to the difference in the return. (Ricardo 1951, pp. 250–51)

For such a monopoly rent, Marx argued that "monopoly price ... is determined neither by price of production nor by value of commodities, but by the buyers' needs and ability to pay" (Marx 1959, p. 764).

In view of the fact, however, that Marx admitted, "whether the rent equals the entire difference between the value and price of production, or only a greater or lesser part of it, will depend wholly on the relation between supply and demand and on the area of land newly taken under cultivation" (Marx 1959, p. 762), the distinction between absolute rent and monopoly rent is a matter of definition, which is important from the point of view of whether the rent is due to the difference in the organic composition, but is uninteresting from the point of view of whether the rent is due to the relation between demand and supply which is limited by the landownership (Bortkiewicz 1911, p. 423; Ouchi 1958, p. 197). This is the reason for extending Marx's definition of absolute rent so as to include the case where the price exceeds the value.

Let us return to the model of Equations $(8.13)-(8.15)$. Since the output of agricultural product is fixed, the relative price p_1/p_2 has to be determined in a larger general equilibrium model including (8.14) and (8.15) so as to satisfy the equality of demand and supply, and any demand shift results in a change in the relative price p_1/p_2 (and corresponding changes in r_1 and r_2). In view of $(8.13)-(8.15)$, r_1 changes in the same direction as p_1/p_2 and r_2 changes in the opposite direction. Distribution in terms of prices between landowners and capitalists is, therefore, not independent of changes in the demand. Nor is the distribution in terms of prices between wage earners and property owners (capitalists and landowners) independent of demand, since price changes generally do not change wL and $(p_1y_1 + p_2y_2)$ proportionally, when L (total employment of labor) and therefore x_i's and y_i's are given.[5]

Distribution in terms of value between wage earners and property owners is, however, independent of changes in demand, since input co-efficients in agriculture are given by our assumption of given output and values are still obtained from (8.6) and (8.7). The pattern of property owners' demand depends on the distribution between capitalists and landowners – that is, on whether absolute rent is paid by the former to the latter. The rate of exploitation $(1 - v)/v$, nevertheless, remains independent of demand, if it is calculated under the assumption of given agricultural output. In other words, X in Marx's dichotomy is independent of Y, the redistribution of surplus products between capitalists and landowners.

We can now conclude as a proposition that Marx's dichotomy does work between theory of value and theory of absolute rent. The distribution between wage earners and property owners in value terms is independent of the distribution between capitalists and landowners, if the latter takes the form of absolute rent.

Unfortunately, however, absolute rent, which as we just saw makes Marx's dichotomy workable even if land exists, has a conceptual difficulty, which can be seen in the following definition of absolute rent given by Marx. "Just as it is the monopoly of capital alone that enables the capitalist to squeeze surplus-labor out of the worker, so the monopoly of

Returns

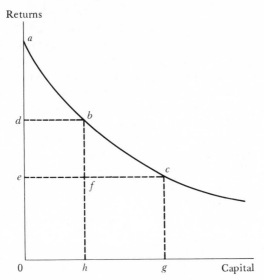

Figure 8.1

landownership enables the landed proprietor to squeeze that part of surplus labor from the capitalist, which would form a constant excess profit" (Marx 1968, p. 94). Note that the word *monopoly* should be interpreted here, not in the modern sense that capitalists or landowners act jointly so as to maximize common gains, but in the classical sense that the supply of capital or land is limited (at least in the short run) so that it is scarce or in the Marxist sense that capital (land) is owned exclusively by capitalists (landowners). The monopoly of capital, therefore, does not exclude competition among capitalists. Otherwise, there would be no equality of the rate of profit. Similarly, the monopoly of landownership does not exclude the possibility that each landowner acts independently. Though Marx made some confusing statements (Bortkiewicz 1911, p. 432), it is clear that he did not have joint action of all the landowners in mind. Then, for a single landowner, there is no reason not to invite additional investment on land when there is absolute rent – that is, when the price of agricultural products exceeds price of production. The joint result of such individual actions is, however, the reduction of absolute rent because of increase in the supply of agricultural products, which continues until absolute rent disappears.

Graphically, we can see this as follows. In Figure 8.1, the amount of capital invested on a given land is measured horizontally, and returns from investment vertically. Investment here consists solely of advancement of wage costs and costs of materials, since durable capital is assumed away. Curve *abc* denotes the diminishing marginal productivity of capital invested on a given land. With first investment $0h$, value of total products is $0abh$, from which $0efh$ is required by the capitalist to assure the average rate of profit. In other words, $0e$ indicate the level of price of production. Rent is represented by *abfe*, where *dbfe* is absolute rent and *abc* is the so-called differential rent II (see notes 3 and 6). By inviting additional investment up to hg, the landowner can make the rent larger, from *abfe* to *ace*. This process ends only when absolute rent disappears – when the last investment yields only the average rate of profit.

Bortkiewicz has already denied Marx's argument for the existence of absolute rent, but he concluded that Marx's failure to prove the absolute rent is not fatal to Marx's theory of value (Bortkiewicz 1911, p. 434). I am not so optimistic, however, and am afraid that Marx's value theory is wrong in the sense that distribution of income between property owners and wage earners is not independent of the distribution among property owners, if rent is explained, not by absolute rent, but by differential rent only.

Value and differential rent

Marx's discussion of differential rent is much more complicated but essentially identical to Ricardo's in the sense that both intensive and extensive margins of cultivation are considered.[6] For our purposes, however, it suffices to consider the former under the assumption that land is homogeneous.

Unlike the case of absolute rent, input coefficients in agriculture, the first sector, have to be assumed explicitly to be increasing functions of the level of output, since the latter is now variable. Input coefficients in manufacture, the second sector, are assumed to be technically given constants.

Price–cost equations (8.11) and (8.12) are changed into

$$p_1 = (1 + r)(L_1(x_1)w + a_{11}(x_1)p_1 + a_{21}(x_1)p_2) \qquad (8.17)$$

$$p_2 = (1 + r)(L_2w + a_{12}p_1 + a_{22}p_2) \qquad (8.18)$$

where L_1, a_{11}, and a_{21} are marginal input coefficients and increasing functions of the level of output in agriculture, x_1 while L_2, a_{12}, and a_{22} are given constants. Differential rent is implicitly defined by (8.17), since (8.17) says that price is equal to the cost, including average profit for the marginal unit, while price exceeds cost including average profit for intra-marginal units. If x_1 is given, p_1/p_2, w/p_2, and r are obtained as functions of x_1 from (8.17), (8.18) and (8.13). The amount of differential rent is, then, calculated more explicitly in terms of the second good as

$$
R = p(x_1)x_1 - \int_0^{x_1} (L_1(x)\bar{w}(x_1) + a_{11}(x)p(x_1) + a_{21}(x))dx
$$
$$(8.19)$$

where p is the relative price p_1/p_2 and $\bar{w}$ is the real wage w/p_2.

Change in the pattern of demand induce, in general, changes in distribution between capitalists and landowner, since r and R are both functions of x_1. Nor can the distribution between wage earners and property owners (capitalists and landowners), in terms of prices, be independent, in general, of the pattern of demand. The problem is, however, whether the distribution between wage earners and property owners, in terms of value, X in Marx's dichotomy, is independent of the distribution among property owners (capitalists and landowners). In other words, it is the question of whether value is independent of changes in demand, since the pattern of demand certainly depends on the distribution among property owners, Marx's Y in the dichotomy.

Unfortunately, values independent of demand are not obtained from (8.6), (8.7), and (8.10), since input coefficients in agriculture are not given constants. The question is, then, how value should be defined for our problem, to calculate the rate of exploitation, when input coefficients are variable. Since this is a problem similar to the one of value under the choice of techniques, it may be natural to use the concept of the minimum required labor cost, which was given in Marx's *Poverty of philosophy* and has recently been emphasized by Morishima, to deal with the case of joint production in general and particularly the case of durable capital (Morishima and Catephores 1978, pp. 22–58, especially p. 36). In the *Poverty of philosophy* Marx states, "It is important to emphasize the point that what determines value is not the time taken to produce a thing but the minimum time it could possibly be produced in" (Marx 1920, pp. 70–71).

The total value newly created and to be distributed between wage earners and property owners is equal to the total employment of labor, L. Incidentally, this is to follow the so-called circulation theory of differential rent, as proposed for example, by Bulgakov (Liubimov 1930, ch. 40; Sakisaka 1977, p. 72). According to this theory, the origin of the differential rent is the surplus value produced in manufacture and circulated into agriculture, since the market value is higher than individual value for agricultural products obtained by intramarginal investments on land, even if they are identical for marginal investment. Rent is purely a distributional phenomenon and total value created remains L, being independent of the differential rent.[7]

To compute the rate of exploitation, then, it is necessary to define the value, the reproduction cost, of labor power corresponding to L. This is obtained, in view of (8.10) and (8.13), by minimizing the labor input to produce c_1L of the first good and c_2L of the second good. This is done by calculating

$$N = M_1(x_1)x_1 + L_2x_2 \tag{8.20}$$

being subject to

$$x_1 = A_{11}(x_1)\,x_1 + a_{12}x_2 + c_1L \tag{8.21}$$

$$x_2 = A_{21}(x_1)\,x_1 + a_{22}x_2 + c_2L \tag{8.22}$$

where M_1, A_{11}, A_{21} are average, not marginal, input coefficients of labor, the first good and the second good in the production of the first good, and all increasing functions of x_1. The rate of exploitation is then calculated as $(L - N)/N$, which is constant if L is given.

Unlike the case of neoclassical full-employment economics, however, the aggregate employment is variable in classical and Marxist economics. In classical full-employment economics, the level of employment is variable on the basis of the Malthusian principle of population. In Marxist economics, the existence of an industrial reserve army assures the variability of the level of employment. Suppose the economy is at a simple reproduction equilibrium where property owners keep the level of consumption of two goods (z_1, z_2) unchanged. The aggregate level of employment L is obtained by calculating

$$L = M_1(x_1)\,x_1 + L_2x_2 \tag{8.23}$$

being subject to

$$x_1 = A_{11}(x_1)\,x_1 + a_{12}x_2 + c_1L + z_1 \tag{8.24}$$

$$x_2 = A_{21}(x_1)\,x_1 + a_{22}x_2 + c_2L + z_2 \tag{8.25}$$

It is clear that L is generally changed as the pattern of demand (z_1, z_2) changes. In view of (8.20)–(8.22), N is not linearly homogeneous with respect to L and does not change proportionally to L.

We have to conclude as the final proposition that Marx's dichotomy between a theory of value and a theory of differential rent fails. The distribution between property owners and wage earners – that is, the rate of exploitation – is not independent of distribution among property owners.[8]

CHAPTER 9

Böhm-Bawerk and the positive rate of interest in a stationary state

It is well known that Böhm-Bawerk adduced three causes for the existence of interest, *Kapitalzins*, defined as a premium (*agio*) attached to the present consumers' goods in the exchange against the future consumers' goods. They are (1) better provision for wants expected in the future than in the present, (2) undervaluation of future wants, and (3) the superiority of more roundabout or more protracted methods of production (Böhm-Bawerk 1959b, pp. 259–89, especially p. 283; see also Schumpeter 1954, pp. 927–30). The first cause implies that the marginal utility of future consumption is lower than that of present consumption, since one is given more goods in the future than in the present. If everybody is in such a situation, a positive rate of interest is necessary, because otherwise everybody wishes to borrow to consume more in the present and nobody will lend to consume more in the future. Under Böhm-Bawerk's second cause, on the other hand, the marginal utility of future consumption is lower than that of present consumption, even if one is provided equally as well in the future as in the present. In other words, the rate of interest is positive because people are myopic and consume more in the present unless the rate of interest is positive. While the first two causes are concerned with the supply of capital, the third cause implies that capital is demanded even if the rate of interest is positive, since a more roundabout and more capital intensive method of production is technically superior to a less roundabout and less capital intensive one.

The mutual relation among these three causes has not been clearly recognized in recent literature, which, in my opinion, is the reason why the present state of capital theory is confused with respect to whether the rate of interest can be positive in a stationary state. As Orosel (1981) rightly pointed out, the distinguishing characteristic of the Austrian school of economics is that the time structure of primary inputs plays a central role in the theory of production. The standard interpretation seems to be, furthermore, that Böhm-Bawerk himself tried to show that the third cause is by itself capable of producing interest even if operating in the absence of the first two causes (Schumpeter 1954, p. 930).[1] Wicksell (1977), following Böhm-Bawerk, developed a stationary state model in which positive rate of interest is explained by the marginal productivity of the period of production.[2] In such a one-sided productivity model, however, one equation is missing.[3] This problem was solved by Hirshleifer (1967) by introducing time-preference relation, Böhm-Bawerk's second cause. This solution may not be unanimously acknowledged (see Pasinetti 1979 and Sandelin 1980), but Bernholz (1971) and Faber (1979) also seem to show the positive rate of interest in a stationary state on the basis of the second and third causes of Böhm-Bawerk.[4] What has become of the first cause?

Böhm-Bawerk (1959b, c) admitted that the third cause generates and works through the first cause. The fact that the first cause can explain the supply of capital independently of the second cause implies that the third cause and the first cause (which is generated by the third cause), without the help of the second cause, can cause a positive rate of interest in a stationary economy, despite the arguments of Hirshleifer (1967) and many other recent writers. As was already pointed out by Arvidsson (1956), however, the consideration of the first cause in a stationary state requires a life-cycle model in which people live for finite periods, have rising incomes, and consume their life incomes.[5] In Negishi (1982c), therefore, I tried to justify such an explanation of a positive rate of interest on the basis of the first and third causes by constructing a stationary two-period life-cycle model in which younger savers can have larger consumption when they are old.

In the present chapter, on the other hand, I emphasize the fact that a general life-cycles model can generate, as special cases, two explanations of the positive rate of interest in a stationary state, one based on the first and third causes and the other based on the second and third causes. If the period of production is shorter relative to the life span of individual persons, a positive rate of interest can be explained by the third cause and the first cause (which is generated by the third cause). If the period of production is longer relative to the life span of individual persons, however, we have to rely on the second cause, which has to be introduced independently of the third cause to explain positive rate of interest.

The next section, "Wicksell's missing equation," explains why an equation is missing in Wicksell's model and how it was supplied by Hirshleifer by using the second cause of interest. The third section, "Böhm-Bawerk's three causes of interest," is devoted to documenting the first cause and its relation to the second and third causes in the writings of Böhm-Bawerk. A two-period life-cycle model is then constructed, in the section, titled "The life-cycle and the first cause," and the positive rate of interest is demonstrated in a stationary state without using the second cause in the case where the period of production is relatively shorter. Finally, to deal with the case where the period of production is relatively longer, a model with the inheritance is offered and the positive rate of interest is shown in a stationary state by the use of the second cause in the sense that people undervalue the wants of future generations.

Wicksell's missing equation

Let us first see how an equation is missing in Wicksell's model, where only the third cause of Böhm-Bawerk, superiority of a roundabout method of production, is considered and how the problem is solved in Hirshleifer (1967) by introducing the second cause of Böhm-Bawerk – time preference. For the sake of convenience in considering a life-cycle model later, let us develop a descrete, period analysis version (Lutz 1956, pp. 25–36, 186–187, Böhm-Bawerk 1959b, pp. 351–65, Wicksell 1977, pp. 172–184, Hirshleifer 1967).

A point input–point output production function of the representative firm is

$$Y = f(t)I \tag{9.1}$$

where Y is the volume of output of a consumers' good, L is labor input, t is the period of production (nonnegative integer), and $f(t)$ is an increasing concave function of t, indicating the superiority of a more roundabout method of production.[6] Rate of return or rate of interest r is implicitly defined by

$$pY = (1 + r)^t wL \tag{9.2}$$

where p is the price of consumers' good and w is the rate of wage, both assumed stationary. Given p and w, we can solve for r as a function of t. The maximization of r with respect to t, such that $r(t - 1) \leqslant r(t)$, and $r(t) \geqslant r(t + 1)$, requires that

$$f(t)/f(t - 1) \geqq 1 + r \geqq f(t + 1)/f(t) \tag{9.3}$$

Finally, the assumption of full employment gives

$$aL = \bar{L} \tag{9.4}$$

where $\bar{L}$ denoted the total available labor, a given constant, and a is the given scale ratio of the representative firm and the total economy. We can make consumers' good *numeraire* ($p = 1$). To determine Y, t, L, w, and r, one equation is still missing, unless we assume that the value of capital

$$K = \sum_{s=0}^{s=t-1} awL(1 + r)^s \tag{9.5}$$

is given, as Wicksell actually did. It is clear, however, that to give K exogenously is quite unsatisfactory, capital here being not homogeneous but heterogeneous so that its composition should be determined endogenously.[7] In other words, the value of capital cannot be given exogenously because it is not independent of endogenous variables r and w.

To supply a missing equation, Sandelin (1980) extended production function (9.1) into a more generalized one,

$$Y = F(L, t) \tag{9.6}$$

where F is increasing and concave with respect to both L and t, not linear with respect to L. From (9.2) and (9.6), then, r is a function not only of t but also of L. The maximization of r with respect to L requires

$$\partial F/\partial L = F/L \tag{9.7}$$

Sandelin claimed that this is the equation missing from Wicksell's model, since Y, L, t, w, and r can now be determined by (9.2), (9.3), (9.4), (9.6) and (9.7). It may seem that positive interest as well as capital to be maintained, from (9.5) are determined by a one-sided productivity model, since (9.3) implies that r is positive. The third cause alone may seem to generate positive interest in a stationary state, even if there exist no first and second causes. What will happen, however, if capitalists do not agree to maintain such an amount of capital at such a rate of interest? Our solution of this overdeterminacy problem is as follows. If the production function (9.6) is not linear with respect to L – that is, if the marginal productivity is diminishing – there must be an implicit factor of production besides labor, say, land. In the long run, then, the market for it is created and rent is established. Production function is now

$$Y = F(L, T, t) \tag{9.8}$$

where T is land input, and F is linear homogeneous with respect to L and T. In addition to (9.4), the clearance of the newly created market for land requires

$$aT = \bar{T} \tag{9.9}$$

where $\bar{T}$ denotes the given total amount of land available, and a is the scale ratio of firm and economy. If we denote land rent by v, wL in (9.2) and (9.5) should be replaced by $wL + vT$. Because of new variables T and v, an equation is still missing, even if (9.9) is added and $\bar{T}$ is given.[8]

To keep the amount of capital stationary, capitalists have to keep the level of consumption unchanged, neither saving nor to dissaving. Hirshleifer (1967) introduced a utility function of the representative household of capitalists,

$$U = U(c_1, c_2) \tag{9.10}$$

where c_1 and c_2 are the level of consumption in any two consecutive periods. From the maximization of (9.10) being subject to the budget constraint, the condition for the stationary consumption ($c_1 = c_2 = aY/b$) is

$$U_1(aY/b, aY/b)/U_2(aY/b, aY/b) = 1 + r \tag{9.11}$$

where U_1 and U_2 are partial derivatives of U with respect to c_1 and c_2, aY is the aggregate supply of consumers' good, and b is the given scale ratio of the representative household and the whole economy. Equation (9.11) is the missing equation found by Hirshleifer, since we can determine Y, L, t, w, and r from (9.1)–(9.4) and (9.11).

The fact that r is positive, from (9.3), implies that a positive rate of interest is demonstrated in a stationary economy. From the point of view of Böhm-Bawerk's three causes of interest, the second and third causes are utilized in this demonstration, because (9.11) implies the undervaluation of future wants, while the superiority of a more roundabout method of production is represented by the assumption that $f(t)$ is an increasing function in (9.1). What has become of the first cause, the better provision for wants in the future than in the present, which (in my opinion) Böhm-Bawerk considered more important than the second cause, in its relation to the third cause? Since the first cause has not been much discussed in the recent literature, let us see how it is explained by Böhm-Bawerk himself.

Böhm-Bawerk's three causes of interest

Böhm-Bawerk's explanation runs as follows for his first cause of the interest:

A first principal cause capable of producing a difference in value between present and future goods is inherent in the difference between the relation of supply to demand as it exists at one point in time and that relation as it exists at another point in time.... If a person suffers in the present from appreciable lack of certain goods, or of goods in general, but has reason to hope to be more generously provided for at a future time, then that person will always place a higher value on a given quantity of immediately available goods than on the same quantity of future goods. This situation occurs with very great frequency in our economic life.... [Of course,] it must be admitted that the counterpart is no rarity in economic life. There are people who at the moment are relatively well provided for and for whom there will presumably be less provision in the future.... [However,] most goods are durable, especially money, which with its aspect of non-particularization is capable of representing all classes of goods, hence they can be reserved for the service of the future. (Böhm-Bawerk 1959b, pp. 265–68)

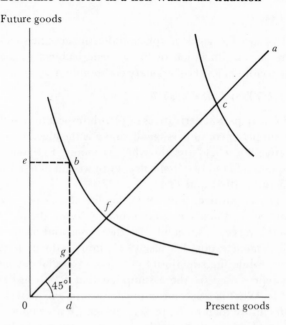

Figure 9.1

On the average, therefore, people expect to be able to provide better for their wants in the future than in the present.

The situation is shown in Figure 9.1. Present goods are measured horizontally, and future goods, vertically. Line $0a$ has slope 1 and indicates the equal provision for wants in the present as well as in the future. If a person is provided with $0d$ amount of present goods and expects to be provided with $0e$ amount of future goods, the indifference curve passing point b which has slope -1 at f (no underevaluation of future goods) has slope less than -1 at b (the curve is steeper at b than at f) indicating the positive rate of interest, since marginal utility of future goods is less than that of present goods.

The situation where the second cause of Böhm-Bawerk (1959b, pp. 268–73) exists can be seen at the point c in the Figure 9.1. Since future wants are systematically undervalued, the slope of the indifference curve at point c is less than -1. The rate of interest is positive even if there exists no "difference between the relation of supply to demand as it exists at one point in time and that relation as it exists at another point in time." The second cause is independent of the first cause and can explain by itself a positive rate of interest. It is also clear that the first cause is independent of the second cause and can explain by itself a positive rate of interest. Furthermore, "it can be easily demonstrated that this phenomenon [the second cause] necessarily contributes to enhance the effectiveness of our first principal cause of the lesser valuation of future goods," since the slope of the indifference curve at b is all the steeper if its slope at f is steeper in Figure 9.1. The first and second causes "work cumulatively" (Böhm-Bawerk 1959b, p. 283).

It is clear that the third cause, technical superiority of present goods, is independent of the second one, Equation (9.11) being a condition independent from the specification of $f(t)$ in (9.1). The relation to the first cause is subtler, however. The third cause is independent of the first one only when the first cause is created by other factors than the third cause. Moreover, the third cause, without the help of such other factors, can create the first one.

Indeed, Böhm-Bawerk argued for the latter fact as follows.

As for the difference in provision for wants in different periods of time, elimination of that factor would give the situation an appearance lacking every semblance of verisimilitude. It would, in fact, be a thorough contradiction of itself. For if the value of a unit of product were the same in all periods of time ..., if such a situation ever occurred at any time at all, it would inevitably nullify itself immediately. For if every utilization for future periods were not only technically but also economically more remunerative than utilization for the present ... then people would naturally withdraw the bulk of their goods from the service of the present in order to devote them to the more lucrative service of the future. But that would immediately cause an ebb tide in provision for the present, and a flood tide in provision for the future.... As a result, the difference in the situation as to provision for wants which had momentarily been set aside, would automatically be restored. (Böhm-Bawerk 1959b, pp. 279–80)

... third cause of the higher value of present goods is completely independent of the other two previously discussed. It is far removed from any necessity of borrowing strength and effectiveness from any difference arising out of other sources in the situation relating to provision for wants. So far removed is it, in fact, that this cause itself is capable of creating such a difference, should that become necessary. (p. 280)

Furthermore, Böhm-Bawerk argued for the independence of the third cause from the first one in the controversy raised by Fisher and Bort-kiewicz whether the third cause constitutes an independent reason besides the first one, or whether it merely constitutes a partial reason within the first one. He tried, though unsuccessfully in my opinion, to show the independence by demonstrating that the technical superiority of present goods can bring forth a value advantage, that is, interest, also if the final state of demand and supply in present and future is constant, when there is another counteracting factor in the sense of negative first cause (Böhm-

Bawerk 1959c, pp. 181–82). In Figure 9.1, the example of Böhm-Bawerk corresponds to the case where a debt, *bg*, falls due. This, of course, does not deny the fact that the third cause itself works to provide future wants better than the present one.

Finally, however, Böhm-Bawerk admitted,

I could have maintained that I am correct at least formerly in my own arrangement because my third reason indubitably differs from my first reason insofar as I defined the latter as supply divergencies resulting from other sources. (Böhm-Bawerk 1959c, pp. 192–93)

Indeed it is a trifle whether the third reason outwardly is independent or must be grouped under the main heading first reason. (p. 193)

The arrangement of reasons can be changed in such a way that the first and third reasons stand combined. (p. 192)

The life cycle and the first cause

In view of Böhm-Bawerk's arguments we have just seen, it seems more natural, from the point of view of economic theory as well as that of the history of economic thought, to demonstrate positive interest in a stationary state by the combination of the third cause and the first cause, which necessarily follows from the third cause, rather than by the combination of the second and the third causes, whose coexistence is accidental. As was pointed out by Arvidsson, we have to consider a life-cycle model of individual members of the economy, to apply the first cause in a stationary state where the economy as a whole is equally provided in the future as well as in the present. A life-cycle model is not alien to Böhm-Bawerk, since he considered the case of "all the indigent beginners in every calling, especially the budding artist or jurist, the first year medical student, the civil servant or business man just breaking in," as examples of those who expect future wants to be better provided for than present ones and value future goods less, and admitted also the counterpart, "a clerk in an office, for instance, who is fifty years old and is earning sixty dollars a week must face the prospect that in ten or fifteen years he will have nothing of his own but a few hundred dollars a year from an annuity, perhaps, that he purchased from an insurance company" (Böhm-Bawerk 1959b, p. 266).

Let us consider an economy of stationary population, where each individual lives for two periods (twice as long as the period of production), so that the size of the young, working population and that of the old, retired population are equal in each period. In the first period, each individual works for given hours but consumes less than he or she earns and lends the

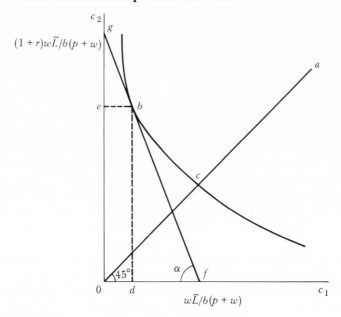

Figure 9.2

saved capital to firms, while, in the second period, the individual not only consumes the yield from his or her capital but also dissaves all of that capital. The second cause, time preference, is assumed away, so that

$$U_1(c_1, c_2)/U_2(c_1, c_2) = 1 + r, \quad c_1 = c_2 \tag{9.12}$$

which corresponds to Equation (9.11) is satisfied only when r is zero. If people consume only the produced, consumers' good, the younger population cannot consume and has to save all the income in the first period, since what the older population dissaved must be saved by younger population, which is equal to the wage payments advanced. To avoid this difficulty, we assume that people always consume a unit of labor service in conjunction with their consumption of a unit of consumers' goods.[9] Of course, this is a simplifying assumption to make a graphic exposition (Figure 9.2) possible and we can make, in general, the ratio of consumers' goods and labor service variable.

The lifetime budget equation for the representative individual is

$$(p + w)c_1 + (p + w)c_2/(1 + r) = w\bar{L}/b \tag{9.13}$$

where c_1 and c_2 denote, respectively, the amount of consumption of consumers' goods (and also of labor service) in the first and second periods, and p, w, r, $\bar{L}$, b, are, as before, the price of consumers' goods, wage, rate of interest, given total labor supply and the scale ratio of representative individual and the whole economy. If the lifetime utility $U(c_1, c_2)$ is maximized being subject to (9.13),

$$U_1(c_1, c_2)/U_2(c_1, c_2) = 1 + r \tag{9.14}$$

should be satisfied, where U_i denotes the partial derivative of U with respect to c_i. Since time preference is assumed away, the left-hand side of (9.14) is 1, if $c_1 = c_2$. When r is positive, therefore, c_2 should be larger than c_1 from the usual assumption of quasi-concavity of U, which implies that the future want is better provided than the present one (the first cause). In Figure 9.2, c_1 is measured horizontally, and c_2, vertically. Budget equation (9.13) is represented by the line fg whose slope is such that $\tan \alpha = (1 + r)$. The condition (9.14) is satisfied at b, where an indifference curve whose slope is -1 at c (when $c_1 = c_2$) is tangent to the budget line fg. As b in Figure 9.1, b in this Figure 9.2 also indicates that the future want is better provided for than the present one.

The possibility for the better provision of future want is, as we shall see, to be assured by the third cause, the assumption that $f(t)$ is increasing in the production function of the representative firm given as Equation (9.1):

$$Y = f(t)L$$

though we have to restrict the form of $f(t)$, so that we can exclude the solutions with $t \geqq 2$ safely.[10] If $t \geqq 2$, the existing capital (defined in Equation (9.5)) will exceed, as we shall see later, what the old population saved, which is impossible in a model where the problem of the inheritance is assumed away. The rate of return or the rate of interest r is defined, as before, by Equation (9.2), which is

$$pY = (1 + r)^t wL$$

and the period of production t maximizes r for given p and w and must satisfy Equation (9.3), which is

$$f(t)/f(t - 1) \geqq 1 + r \geqq f(t + 1)/f(t)$$

whenever the equation is applicable.

In each period, the labor market must be cleared; instead of Equation (9.4),

$$aL + b(c_1 + c_2) = \bar{L} \tag{9.15}$$

is required, because bc_1 and bc_2 denote, respectively, and demand not only for consumers' goods but also for labor service, from young and old

populations. On the other hand, the clearance of the market for consumers' goods requires

$$b(c_1 + c_2) = aY. \tag{9.16}$$

Now, these seven conditions, (9.1)–(9.3) and (9.13)–(9.16), can deter-
mine seven unknowns: w, r, c_1, c_2, L, Y, and t, while $p = 1$ by the choice of
consumers' good as *numeraire*. Suppose $t = 0$. From the right-hand side of
(9.3), r is positive, since $f(1) > f(0)$; that is, roundabout production is
superior to hand-to-mouth production. From (9.2), (9.15), and (9.16),
however, we have

$$p(c_1 + c_2) + w(c_1 + c_2) = w\bar{L}/b \tag{9.17}$$

which is in contradiction to (9.13) when r is positive. Therefore, the case of
$t = 0$ is not possible. When $t \geqq 1$, on the other hand, $r > 0$ is assured again
from the right-hand side of (9.3); that is, more roundabout production is
superior to less roundabout. We can restrict our consideration, therefore,
to the case of $t \geqq 1$.

Incidentally, if $t = 1$, we have $pc_1 = wc_2$ from (9.2), (9.13), (9.15), and
(9.16). The value of the consumers' goods consumed by the younger
population is equal to the value of the labor service consumed by the older
population. If people consume only consumers' goods and no labor
service, the younger population cannot consume at all. It can be seen
furthermore that the value of capital, given by Equation (9.5):

$$K = \sum_{s=0}^{s=t-1} awL(1 + r)^s$$

In this case, awL is equal to the value of saving, $w\bar{L} - b(p + w)c_1$, in view
of (9.13), (9.15), and $pc_1 = wc_2$. This justifies our assumption that $t = 1$,
since otherwise K exceeds the value of saving, which is impossible in a
model with no inheritance.

Of course, solving Equations (9.1)–(9.3) and (9.13)–(9.16) does not, in
general, yield the case of $t = 1$, unless some restrictions are imposed on the
utility function $U(c_1, c_2)$ and the production function $f(t)$. For example,
suppose $U(c_1, c_2) = \log c_1 + \log c_2$ so that there is no undervaluation of
future wants (the second cause) and $f(1) = 1$. We can see that the case of
$t = 1$ is possible, since any r that satisfies (9.3) with $t = 1$ (that is,
$1/f(0) \geqq 1 + r \geqq f(2)$), also satisfies other conditions, in view of $c_1 = wc_2$,
as was just derived, $U_1/U_2 = c_2/c_1 = (1 + r)$, from (9.13) and (9.14), and
$f(1) = 1 = w(1 + r)$, from (9.1) and (9.2). In other words, r is indeterminate if we solve (9.1), (9.2), and (9.13)–(9.16) by assuming that $t = 1$.
Another example is the case where $U(c_1, c_2) = c_1^{(1/2)} + c_2^{(1/2)}$ and $f(1)^2 \geqq$

$f(0), 1 \geqq f(2)$. In this case, we get $(1 + r) = 1/f(1)$ by assuming $t = 1$ and solving (9.1), (9.2), and (9.13)–(9.16), in view of $U_1/U_2 = (c_2/c_1)^{(1/2)} = (1 + r), c_1, = wc_2$, and $f(1) = w(1 + r)$. Because of restrictions on $f(t)$, we can see that this solution satisfies also condition (9.3) for $t = 1$.

More generally, we have a set A of r, the domain of r that satisfies (9.3) for $t = 1$. In view of $c_1 = wc_2, f(1) = w(1 + r)$, we have $c_2/c_1 = (1 + r)/f(1)$. If utility is homothetic (that is, the slope of indifference curve is a function of c_2/c_1 only), we can associate for any r in A, the slope of the indifference curve, U_1/U_2, which is to be equated with $(1 + r)$. In this way, a new set B of r corresponds to the set A of r. To justify the assumption that $t = 1$ and the life span of individuals is twice as long as the period of production, we have to restrict the shape of $U(c_1, c_2)$ as well as that of $f(t)$ so that there is at least a value of r that belongs both to A and B. In the first of the preceding examples, two sets A and B are identical and any r that satisfies (9.3) for $t = 1$ can be an equilibrium rate of interest. In the second example, on the other hand, $r = (1 - f(1))/f(1)$ belongs to both A and B and is the equilibrium rate of interest.

Inheritance and the second cause

A positive rate of interest in a stationary state is demonstrated by using Böhm-Bawerk's first and third cause, but without using the second cause. One might be dissatisfied, however, with the model given in the previous section on the ground that the length of the period of the production is arbitrarily assumed not to exceed that of individual life minus 1. To get rid of this assumption, we have to introduce the inheritance of capital into the model so that the value of existing capital can be larger than the value of the saving. In a stationary state the representative individual cannot dissave all his capital at the end of his life but must leave the capital to the next generation, the value of which is equal to that of what he inherited at the beginning of his life. Because of the inherited capital, one can consume more when he is young than when he is old, if he wishes to do so. The first cause of the rate of interest is, therefore, not applicable to explain the positive rate of interest. As one's lifetime consumption is related to the capital inherited at the beginning of his life, so is the lifetime consumption of the next generation related to the capital he is going to leave at the end of his life. A positive rate of interest is, therefore, impossible in a stationary state, unless the representative individual undervaluates the consumption of the next generation in comparison with his own consumption. This seems to introduce Böhm-Bawerk's second cause by the backdoor, however.[11]

To make sure the period of production is not shorter than the life span of the individual person, let us consider the latter as a unit of time of length such that the former is not shorter than the latter unless production is instantaneous, hand-to-mouth. If the period of production is not shorter than his life span, an individual cannot enjoy the fruit of his saving himself and has to leave it to his next generation. The budget constraint of the sth generation of the representative individual is

$$(pK_{s+1}/(1 + r)) + pc_s = (w\bar{L}/b) + pK_s \tag{9.18}$$

where K_s denotes the heritage from the $(s - 1)$-th generation to the sth generation, c_s is the consumption of the consumers' good by the sth generation, and p, r, w, $\bar{L}$, and b are as defined in the preceding section. For the sth generation, K_s is already given, while he can choose c_s and K_{s+1} freely. For this decision he has to take into consideration not only his own utility but also the utility of the next generation, i.e., $(s + 1)$-th generation, since the latter is influenced by K_{s+1}. Since the latter is also a function of K_{s+2} from the budget constraint of the $(s + 1)$-th generation, the sth generation has also to take the utility of the $(s + 2)$-th generation into consideration, and so on.

To decide on c_s and K_{s+1}, the sth generation has, therefore, to take the utility of all the future generations into consideration. It is natural for him, however, to discount the significance of the utility of future generations in comparison with that of his own utility and to discount more for the more remote generations. The sth generation of the representative individual maximizes, therefore,

$$\sum_{x=s}^{x=\infty} d^{(x-s)} U(c_x) \tag{9.19}$$

where $d(<1)$ is a given constant discount ratio and $U(c_x)$ is the utility of the xth generation, being subject to the budget constraint

$$\sum_{x=s}^{x=\infty} (pc_x/(1 + r)^{(x-s)}) = \sum_{x=s}^{x=\infty} (wL/b(1 + r)^{(x-s)}) + pK_s \tag{9.20}$$

which is obtained by combining the budget equations like (9.18) for all the xth generations such that $x \geqq s$. This constrained maximization requires that

$$d^y(\partial U/\partial c_y)/d^z(\partial U/\partial c_z) = (1 + r)^z/(1 + r)^y \tag{9.21}$$

for all y, $z \geqq s$. This condition is, however, reduced to

$$d = 1/(1 + r) \tag{9.22}$$

since all c_z's are identical, i.e., $c_x = c$ for all x in a stationary state.

The condition (9.22) corresponds to Hirshleifer's condition, (9.11). Together with the other four conditions given earlier, repeated here for convenience:

$$Y = f(t)L \tag{9.1}$$

$$pY = (1 + r)^t wL \tag{9.2}$$

$$f(t)/f(t - 1) \geqq 1 + r \geqq f(t + 1)/f(t) \tag{9.3}$$

and

$$aL = \bar{L} \tag{9.4}$$

Equation (9.22) can determine five unknowns Y, L, t, w, and r. By assuming that $1/d < f(1)/f(0)$, we can make the case of $t = 0$ impossible, in view of (9.22) and the right-hand side of (9.3). Since $Y = bc$, it can be easily checked that

$$pK_s = w\bar{L} \sum_{s=1}^{s=t} (1 + r)^s/b \tag{9.23}$$

from (9.20) and (9.2), so that

$$pK_s = (1 + r)K/b = (1 + r) \sum_{s=0}^{s=t-1} awL(1 + r)^s/b \tag{9.24}$$

in view of (9.4) and (9.5). In other words, the value of the heritage the representative individual receives is the value of the economy's capital stock per head and interest on it.

Böhm-Bawerk (1959b, pp. 270–71) raised three contributory or partial causes for the lesser valuation of future utility – that is, erroneous valuation by reason of fragmentary imagery of future wants, lack of will power, and consideration of the brevity and uncertainty of human life. In view of this last partial cause, we may conclude that we have to rely on the second cause of the positive rate of interest in the sense that people undervalue the wants of future generations, if the life span of individuals is shorter relative to the period of production.

PART III

International trade and investment

CHAPTER 10

The role of exporters and importers
in classical and Keynesian theories

Unlike the neoclassical theory of international trade, the classical theory of international trade emphasized the role of exporters and importers. This can be seen in Ricardo's chapter on foreign trade (1951, pp. 128–49) as well as in the following arguments of Adam Smith on the different employment of capitals.

The capital of the wholesale merchant replaces, together with their profits, the capitals of the farmers and manufacturers of whom he purchases the rude and manufactured produces which he deals in, and thereby enables them to continue their respective trades. It is by this service chiefly that he contributes indirectly to support the productive labour of the society, and to increase the value of its annual produce. His capital employs too the sailors and carriers who transport his goods from one place to another, and it augments the price of those goods by the value, not only of his profits, but of their wages. (Smith 1976, pp. 362–63)

The capital employed in purchasing foreign goods for home-consumption, when this purchase is made with the produce of domestic industry, replaces too, by every such operation, two distinct capitals; but one of them only is employed in supporting domestic industry. The capital which sends British goods to Portugal, and brings back Portuguese goods to Great Britain, replaces by every such operation only one British capital. The other is a Portuguese one. Though the returns, therefore, of the foreign trade of consumption should be as quick as those of the home-trade, the capital employed in it will give but one-half the encouragement to the industry or productive labour of the country. (p. 368)

Let us first note that a role exists for exporters and importers even if the cost of transport is ignored. This role is to replace the capital of the producers. The role is clearly related to the time structure of the classical theory of production; that is, production requires time and the wage cost must be advanced by capitalists until the product is sold to consumers. There is, therefore, no room for this role of exporters and importers in the neoclassical theory of international trade, which is based on either a theory of timeless or instantaneous production or the assumption that there is no need to advance wage cost (Eagly 1974, pp. 3–9).

In the neoclassical theory of international trade, it is assumed that domestic consumers can buy directly from foreign producers in the foreign market. This assumption may not be so unrealistic in international trade

117

among countries, like European ones, located close to one another and socially and culturally very similar. In international trade between countries far away and dissimilar, say the United States and Japan, however, the role of consumers is very limited and international trade is carried out almost exclusively in the hands of exporters and importers. Domestic consumers buy the importables in domestic markets from foreign exporters or domestic importers, because consumers have neither enough information nor suitable credit to buy directly from foreign producers, cannot finance transportation cost individually, and are not well accustomed to do foreign exchange business.

This is the reason why some neoclassical interpretations fail to grasp the essential points of the classical theory of international trade. On the other hand, we can expect a new perspective to current economic problems, which neoclassical theory cannot offer, by taking the role of exporters and importers explicitly into consideration. In this chapter are presented two examples of the former, the classic price-specie-flow mechanism and Ricardo's theory of terms of trade, as well as one example of the latter, foreign exchange gains in a Keynesian situation.

Classical economists' refutation of the mercantilist principle favoring a chronic export surplus is derived from the Cantillon–Hume price-specie-flow mechanism. By this mechanism an inflow of bullion raises domestic prices and selling dear and buying cheap tends to turn the balance of trade against the country. The neoclassical theory of international transfer has made it clear, however, that the resulting changes in prices can be in either direction, depending on international differences in demand patterns, and are not necessarily in the direction suggested by the classical price-specie-flow theory, which states that prices rise in the surplus country and fall in the deficit country (Kemp 1964, pp. 79–81). Dornbusch, Fisher, and Samuelson (1976) constructed a model in which there is no price effect associated with a redistribution of the world money supply and therefore no effects on real variables in the adjustment process for monetary disequilibrium, contrary to the classical price-specie-flow mechanism, unless there exist nontraded goods. The reason is that their model is a neoclassical one with exporters and importers assumed away. It can be shown that the classical price-specie-flow mechanism is rescued by incorporation of importers and exporters into their model, even if nontraded goods are assumed away.

The standard interpretation in neoclassical theory of international trade as well as in the history of economic thought is that Ricardo's comparative cost principle can only determine the possible range of terms of trade and the equilibrium terms of trade cannot be determined unless Mill's reciprocal demand is taken into consideration. It is argued that this

fact signifies the failure of labor theory of value or cost theory of value
(Schumpeter 1954, pp. 612–13). There are some arguments, however,
like those of Kojima (1952, p. 77) and Morita (1977), which claim that
Ricardo's theory can uniquely determine terms of trade by the conditions
in production without having recourse to demand factors, by combining
the comparative cost principle and his theory of international distribution of gold. In Negishi (1982b), I demonstrated that Ricardo's theory of
trade can determine the terms of trade by explicitly taking into consideration the role played by exporters and importers, though the theory of
international distribution of gold cannot help us in this respect. The
essence of the labor theory of value lies not so much in the proportionality
of relative values and quantities of labor embodied as in the explanation of
the profit created not in the process of circulation but in the process of
production (see the section titled "Böhm-Bawerk and Hilferding," in
Chapter 7). In other words, what is important is the fact that relative
prices and the rate of profit are determined by the conditions of production independently of the demand conditions (Chapter 8). In this sense we
can say that Ricardo's labor theory of value does not fail in the theory of
international trade.

It is interesting to consider the incorporation of exporters and importers
into the Keynesian theory of international trade. Keynesian economics
considers that prices are sticky in general, except that the price of the
importables to be charged to domestic consumers is flexible when the rate
of foreign exchange is changed. This exceptional flexibility of price is
clearly based on the supposition that domestic consumers can buy directly
from the foreign producers. In Negishi (1979b), I demonstrated that the
domestic prices of importables as well as those of exportables are sticky in
the face of a changing rate of foreign exchange, if domestic consumers
have to buy the importables exclusively from domestic importers or
foreign exporters. This demonstration is, I believe, worthwhile, in view of
recent experience showing that, at least in the short run, the domestic
prices of importables are sticky and that foreign exchange gains (losses)
mainly accrue not to domestic consumers but to exporters and importers.

Classical price-specie-flow mechanism

The classical economists did not doubt that the arguments of their predecessors, the mercantilists, in favor of a chronic export surplus were
based on an intellectual confusion. Even Thomas Mun, who realized that
an inflow of bullion raises domestic prices and turns the balance of trade
against the country did not hesitate to advocate the indefinite accumula-

tion of hard money (McCulloch 1954, pp. 115–209). This is the so-called mercantilist dilemma. The classical refutation of the mercantilist principle is derived from Cantillon–Hume price-specie-flow mechanism. Purely automatic forces tend to establish a natural distribution of specie between the trading countries of the world and such levels of domestic prices that each country's value of exports equals that of imports.

The crux of the classical price-specie-flow mechanism is thus the changes in prices caused by redistribution of specie due to the trade imbalance. Hume posed the problem thus:

> suppose four-fifths of all the money in Great Britain to be annihilated in one night and the nation reduced to the same condition, with regard to specie, as in the reigns of the Harrys and Edwards, what would be the consequence? Must not the price of all labour and commodities sink in proportion, and everything be sold as cheap as they were in those ages? What nation could then dispute with us in any foreign market, or pretend to navigate or to sell manufactures at the same price, which to us would afford sufficient profit? In how little time, therefore, must this bring back the money which we had lost, and raise us to the level of all the neighbouring nations? . . . [And] suppose that all the money of Great Britain were multiplied fivefold in a night, must not the contrary effect follow? Must not all labour and commodities rise to such an exorbitant height, that no neighbouring nations could afford to buy from us, while their commodities, on the other hand, became comparatively so cheap, that, in spite of all the laws which could be formed, they would be run in upon us, and our money flow out, till we fall to a level with foreigners, and lose that great superiority of riches, which had laid us under such disadvantages? (Hume 1955, pp. 62–63)

The other side of the specie flow is, however, the international transfer of real resources. The modern literature on international transfer has made it clear that the resultant changes in prices can be in either direction, depending on international difference in demand patterns, and are not necessarily in the direction suggested by the classical price-specie-flow theory; that is, prices rise in the surplus country and prices fall in the deficit country (Kemp 1964, pp. 79–81). If, for example, two countries are identical in taste, which can be expressed by a homothetic social indifference map (so that Engel curves are straight lines through the origin), the equilibrium prices are independent of the distribution of income between the two countries, including the distribution of specie. In this case, as is pointed out by Dornbusch, Fisher, and Samuelson (1976), there is no price effect associated with a redistribution of the world money supply and therefore no effects on real variables in the adjustment process for monetary disequilibrium, contrary to the classical price-specie-flow mechanism.

Let me outline a simplified version of Dornbusch, Fisher, and Samuelson (1976). For the sake of simplicity, we consider the case of two-good, two-country model, in which each country competely specializes in the production of the exportables.[1] The production is of constant returns to scale with respect to the sole factor of production, called labor.[2] As for the demand side, let us assume that the level of aggregate expenditure of each country is proportional to the supply of money in the country[3] and that the ratio of expenditure on each good to the aggregate expenditure is a given constant.[4] The sum of supplies of money in two countries is assumed to be constant.

The condition for the equilibrium of demand and supply of labor in the home country is then

$$wL = aV(M/G) G + a^*V^* (1 - (M/G))G \qquad (10.1)$$

where L is the given supply of labor, w is the money rate of wage, a is the ratio of expenditure on the exportables of the home country, V is the constant velocity of the circulation, M is the domestic money supply, G is the world money supply, variables with(out) asterisk are those of foreign (home) country, and rate of foreign exchange is assumed to be 1. Similarly, for the labor in the foreign country, we have

$$w^*L^* = (1 - a) V(M/G) G + (1 - a^*) V^*(1 - (M/G))G \qquad (10.2)$$

If the distribution of specie, M, is given, we can solve (10.1) and (10.2) for w and w^*. If two countries have identical taste, such that $a = a^*$ and $V = V^*$, furthermore, it is easily seen that equilibrium w and w^* are independent of the distribution of specie.

The specie-flow mechanism is given as

$$dM/dt = wL - VM \qquad (10.3)$$

where t denotes time; the supply of money is increased as a result of a trade surplus that is equal to the difference of income and absorption. Since w remains unchanged when M changes, if the two countries are identical in taste, it can be easily seen that the solution of (10.3) is stable and a trade balance is eventually established. Since the price of each good is completely determined by wage cost in our model, there is no price effect of specie flow in this special case. Something must be done to explain the changes in prices in the direction suggested by the classical price-specie-flow theory.

Dornbusch, Fisher, and Samuelson showed that even in this special case the introduction of nontraded goods revitalizes the classical conclusion that in the adjustment process prices decline along with the money stock in the deficit country while both rise in the surplus country. Let us therefore introduce the nontraded goods in our model and assume that the ratio of expenditure on nontraded goods in each country is constant; that is, $(1 - k)$. Nontraded goods and the exportables are produced in each country but there is still no import competing production. In view of identical taste, then, (10.1) and (10.2) are, respectively, modified into

$$wL = aVG + (1 - k)(M/G)VG \tag{10.4}$$

and

$$w^*L^* = (k - a)VG + (1 - (M/G))(1 - k)VG \tag{10.5}$$

from which equilibrium w and w^* are obtained if M is given.[5] Now equilibrium wages are no longer independent of the distribution of specie. An increase in M increases w and reduces w^*. The prices of goods produced in a country change in the same direction as the supply of money in the country. Since we have from (10.4)

$$dw/dM = (1 - k)V/L \tag{10.6}$$

the right-hand side of (10.3) is decreasing with respect to M and therefore the price-specie-flow mechanism is stable.

In view of the importance of nontraded goods, if not in the classical and neoclassical models of international trade, then in the actual world of international trade, there is no doubt that the preceding result is important and interesting. There is, however, an important difference between the classical model of international trade and the neoclassical model of international trade on which are based Dornbusch, Fisher, and Samuelson's discussion as well as the modern discussions of the transfer problem. This is the role of exporters and importers in international trade, which is a leading role in classical theory but one completely neglected in neoclassical theory. As will be shown, prices change in the direction suggested by the classical price-specie-flow theory even in the case of identical and homothetic demands and no nontraded goods, if the role of exporters and importers is taken into consideration.

Our model, which is supposed to be that of classical economics, remains that of neoclassical economics unless the role of exporters and importers is explicitly incorporated. In view of the fact that the role of exporters and importers in the classical economics is derived from the time structure of the classical theory of production, to replace the capital of producers advanced, we have to consider that conditions (10.1) and (10.2) or (10.4) and (10.5) are, in classical economics, not so much the conditions for equilibrium of demand and supply of labor service in the neoclassical sense as the conditions for equilibrium of demand and supply of funds, or resources in general, to support labor in the period of production. In other words, w and w^* represent the prices of the resources in general, which include wages as well as profits.

If we assume away the nontraded goods but take the role of exporters and importers into consideration, conditions (10.1) and (10.2) are modified, in the case of identical taste, into

$$wL = aMV + aM^*Vr + (1 - a)MV(1 - s) \qquad (10.7)$$

and

$$w^*L^* = (1 - a)M^*V + (1 - a)MVs + aM^*V(1 - r) \qquad (10.8)$$

where $M + M^* = G$ and r and s are positive constants less than 1. Let us assume that domestic importers replace $100(1 - s)$ percent of the capital of foreign producers and foreign importers replace $100(1 - r)$ percent of the capital of domestic producers. The equilibrium values of w and w^* are obtained from (10.7) and (10.8) if M and M^* are given. An increase in M coupled with a decrease in M^* so as to keep G unchanged clearly increases w and decreases w^*. The specie-flow changes prices in the direction suggested by classical theory even in the case of identical taste, if the role of exporters and importers is properly taken into consideration. The stability of (10.3) is also easy to show.

Ricardo's theory of terms of trade

The labor theory of value fails as a theory of international trade if one regards it simply as stating that the relative prices are proportional to the quantities of labor embodied. Thus even Ricardo admitted that "the same rule which regulates the relative value of commodities in one country does not regulate the relative value of the commodities exchanged between two or more countries" (Ricardo 1951, p. 133). According to Schumpeter, this is very serious for Ricardo's theory of value.

We may look upon the comparative cost principle as an exception from the labor quantity law, for it describes a case where commodities no longer exchange according to this law. This exception is the more serious because it covers not only international values but also, in all cases of less than perfect mobility of labor, domestic values. In fact, together with all the other exceptions and qualifications that Ricardo was forced to make, it really rips up the entire fabric of Ricardo's theory of value. (Schumpeter 1954, p. 612)

In the standard theory of international trade, therefore, the theory of international value is that of reciprocal demand developed by Mill (1965, p. 596), who claims that we have to fall back upon an antecedent law, that of supply and demand, when the law of cost of production is not applicable. As shown in the Chapter 7 section on Böhm-Bawerk and Hilferding, however, the essence of the labor theory of value lies not so much in the proportionality of relative values and quantities of labor embodied as in the explanation of the profit created not in the process of circulation but in the process of production. In other words, what is important is the fact that relative prices and the rate of profit are determined by the conditions of production independently of the demand situation. From such a point of view, it is interesting that Kojima (1952, p. 77) and Morita (1977) consider the terms of trade to be determined in Ricardo's theory without taking reciprocal demand into consideration. Morita argues as follows.

Since the day of J.S. Mill the standard interpretation of Ricardo has been that there is no theory in Ricardo to determine the terms of trade and therefore demand factors must be introduced so as to supplement Ricardo in this respect. This interpretation is clearly wrong. By combining the comparative cost principle and the theory of international distribution of gold, Ricardo presented a mechanism which can uniquely determine terms of trade (international prices) by the conditions in production without having recourse to demand factors.

Ricardo's numerical example of the comparative cost principle is as follows. Suppose one unit of cloth made in England is being exchanged against one unit of wine made in Portugal.[6]

England may be so circumstanced that to produce the cloth may require the labour of 100 men for one year, and if she attempted to make wine, it might require the labour of 120 men for the same time. England would therefore find it her interest to import wine, and to purchase it by the exportation of cloth. To produce the wine in Portugal might require only the labour of 80 men for one year, and to produce the cloth in the same country might require the labour of 90 men for the same time. It would therefore be advantageous for her to export wine in exchange for cloth. . . . Thus England would give the produce of the labour of 100 men, for the produce of the labour of 80. (Ricardo 1951, p. 135)

Ricardo assumed that one unit of cloth is exchanged internationally against one unit of wine. From the point of view of the theory of reciprocal demands, the commodity terms of trade can be anything, depending on the conditions of demand, between two domestic price ratios (120/100 and 80/90), and there is no reason why the ratio should be 1 irrespective of demand conditions. Kojima and Morita argue, however, the terms of trade can be uniquely determined if this comparative cost principle of a trade of pure barter is combined with the theory of international distribution of gold.

Ricardo's argument concerning the international distribution of gold may be interpreted as the theory of the redistribution of a given amount of gold through the trade balance – the theory of a specie-flow mechanism. Ricardo states that "gold and silver having been chosen for the general medium of circulation, they are, by the competition of commerce, distributed in such proportions amongst the different countries of the world as to accommodate themselves to the natural traffic which would take place if no such metals existed, and the trade between countries were purely a trade of barter," (1951, p. 137), so that the balance of trade is established. In other words, the system is completely dichotomized so that real variables are unchanged by the introduction of monetary factors (see Chapter 14). If the terms of trade are not determined independently of demand in the case of pure barter trade by the comparative cost principle, therefore, they cannot be so determined merely by the introduction of gold as the general medium of circulation, in spite of arguments of Kojima and Morita.[7]

The model of classical price-specie-flow mechanism given in Equations (10.7), (10.8), and (10.3), is reproduced here for convenience.

$$wL = aMV + aM^*Vr + (1 - a)MV(1 - s) \tag{10.7}$$

$$w^*L^* = (1 - a)M^*V + (1 - a)MVs + aM^*V(1 - r) \tag{10.8}$$

$$dM/dt = wL - VM \tag{10.3}$$

Suppose the home country is England, specialized in the production of cloth, and the foreign country is Portugal, specialized in the production of wine. Since w and w^* represent wages and profits on capital advanced to support labor, the price of a unit of cloth is $100w$ and that of wine, $80w^*$. The equilibrium terms of trade $(80w^*/100w)$ can be obtained by solving (10.7) and (10.8) under the condition that trade balances, so that $wL = VM$ and $w^*L^* = VM^*$, in view of (10.3). It is not independent of a sole demand factor in the model: a.

If w and w^* are different, however, r and s may no longer be assumed to be constant. Suppose w is lower than w^*. Given the consumers' preference in the choice of foreign exporters and domestic importers, it is profitable for British exporters and importers to expand their business and for Portuguese exporters and importers to reduce their business, so that s is decreased and r is increased in (10.7) and (10.8). Although w increases and w^* decreases from (10.7) and (10.8), this process of shift of capital from British producers to British exporters and importers and from Portuguese exporters and importers to Portuguese producers will be terminated before w and w^* are equalized. This is because shift of British capital from domestic production to export and import business requires a risk premium, as Ricardo recognized.

Experience, however, shows that the fancied or real insecurity of capital, when not under the immediate control of its owner, together with the natural disinclination which every man has to quit the country of his birth and connections, and intrust himself, with all his habits fixed, to a strange government and new laws, check the emigration of capital. These feelings, which I should be sorry to see weakened, induce most men of property to be satisfied with a low rate of profits in their own country, rather than seek a more advantageous employment for their wealth in foreign nations. (Ricardo 1951, pp. 136–37)

Because domestic importers buy foreign goods in foreign markets and sell them in domestic markets and domestic exporters buy domestic goods in domestic markets and sell them in foreign markets, they naturally require a risk premium and do not expand their businesses unless their rate of profit is much higher than the general rate of profit in their country. Suppose in our example, therefore, that British exporters and importers do not expand their business unless w is lower than dw^*, where $d(< 1)$ is a constant discount factor corresponding to risk premium. Since we now have $w = dw^*$ at equilibrium, equilibrium terms of trade can be determined as $(80w^*/100w) = 80/100d$, independently of demand factor a. If the discount factor d is 0.8, we have the case Ricardo assumed: one unit of cloth is exchanged with one unit of wine.

This conclusion is independent of our model of a specie-flow mechanism, which is the theory of international distribution of gold. Therefore, we have to say that Ricardo's theory can determine equilibrium terms of trade, not because, as Kojima and Morita supposed, the theory of international distribution of gold combines with the principle of comparative cost, but because the role of exporters and importers is properly recognized in classical economic theory.

Foreign exchange gains in a Keynesian situation

In the neoclassical theory of international trade, where perfect information is assumed, it is not unreasonable to suppose that domestic consumers can buy directly from foreign producers without the help of exporters or importers. In a Keynesian situation, however, we cannot assume perfect information. As a matter of fact, as I have argued elsewhere, the principle of effective demand can be explained only by imperfect information without being inconsistent with observed behavior of money and real wages (Negishi 1979a, ch. 3). If information is not perfect, we have to consider that the role of consumers is very limited in international trade and export and import are carried out almost exclusively by specialized firms of exporters and importers. Domestic consumers buy the importable in the domestic market from foreign exporters or domestic importers, because domestic consumers do not have enough information on the foreign market and, on the other hand, foreign producers do not have enough information on the domestic market.

Suppose in the domestic market foreign exporters or domestic importers as well as domestic producers have Sweezy-type kinked demand curves, even though they are perfectly competitive. Unlike the case of oligopoly, however, the kink is explained by the asymmetric behavior of customers due to imperfect information (see the Chapter 2 section titled "Demand deficiency and increasing returns"). A firm cannot expect a large increase in demand by reducing its price, since customers currently buying from other firms are not perfectly informed. It has to expect, on the other hand, a large reduction of demand when it raises the price, since customers currently buying from it are fully informed of the price rise and will quickly shift to other firms charging unchanged price. If short-term expectation is realized, the profit is being maximized at the current level of the sale where the demand curve is kinked. At this level the marginal revenue is discontinuous and the marginal cost curve passes between two separate parts of the marginal revenue curve. As was explained by Sweezy (1939), then, it is very likely that the price remains unchanged if the level of effective demand is changed or if the marginal cost curve is shifted.

The effect of the introduction of exporters and importers into the Keynesian model of international trade is the possible rigidity of domestic price of the importables in the face of floating foreign exchange rates, since shifts of marginal cost curves of domestic importers and foreign exporters are very likely to keep the price of the importables to be charged to the domestic consumers unchanged. Only flexible price, a floating rate of foreign exchange, can affect the economy merely through the income effects that are due to foreign exchange gains (losses) accrued to exporters and importers. These gains and losses arise from the fact that domestic exporters buy at the price given in terms of home currency and sell at the price given in terms of foreign currency, and domestic importers buy at the price given in terms of foreign currency and sell at the price given in terms of home currency. Such an absence of changes in consumers' price is, of course, a short-run phenomenon. In the long run, foreign exchange gains induce entry of new firms into profitable sectors. New entering firms have to undersell old existing firms so that prices charged to consumers are reduced in such sectors. In the short run, however, income effects are dominant. The stability of foreign exchange depends, then, not on the price elasticities of import demands, which are essential for the stability in the traditional Keynesian model without exporters and importers (Kemp 1964, p. 286), but on propensities to consume and to import and on whether foreign exchange gains (losses) accrue to the exporting or importing country.[8]

The level of output of the home country X and that of the foreign country X^* are determined in the Keynesian model by the level of effective demand; that is,

$$X = D(x) + M^*(x^*) \tag{10.9}$$

and

$$X^* = D^*(x^*) + M(x) \tag{10.10}$$

where x and x^* are, respectively, the level of national income of the home country and that of the foreign country, D and D^* are, respectively, the domestic demand for domestic goods of home and foreign countries, and M and M^* are, respectively, home and foreign demand for import.[9]

Suppose first that international trade is exclusively carried out by importers, so that foreign exchange gains or losses, if any, accrue entirely to importers of the importing country. Then we have

$$x = X + (1 - R) M(x) \tag{10.11}$$

and

$$x^* = X^* + (1 - (1/R)) M^*(x^*) \tag{10.12}$$

where R is the rate of exchange defined as the price of foreign currency in terms of home currency, which is equal to 1 initially. In other words, the national income of the home country in terms of home currency is defined as the sum of the output, which includes services of importers, and the foreign exchange gains (negative in case of losses), and similarly for the foreign country. Note that the price home importers pay for M is given in terms of foreign currency, while the price foreign importers pay for M^* is given in terms of home currency. By substituting (10.11) and (10.12) into (10.9) and (10.10), we have at $R = 1$,

$$dx/dR = (-M(1 - D^{*\prime}) + M^* M^{*\prime})/A \tag{10.13}$$

and

$$dx^*/dR = ((1 - D') M^* - M M')/A \tag{10.14}$$

where D' is the derivative of D with respect to x and the like, and

$$A = (1 - D')(1 - D^{*\prime}) - M' M^{*\prime} \tag{10.15}$$

which is positive if we assume that the marginal propensities to consume are less than 1; that is, $D' + M' < 1$ and $D^{*\prime} + M^{*\prime} < 1$. The numerator of (10.13) is negative if trade between two countries balances – that is, if $B = M^*/R - M = 0$.[10] The appreciation of home currency, or reduction of R, increases x in this case. The numerator of (10.14) is positive if the home country is not in deficit – that is, if $B \geqq 0$. The appreciation of home currency then reduces x^*.

The stability of the foreign exchange market is considered as follows. The change in the balance of payments due to a change in foreign exchange rate is

$$dB/dR = M^{*\prime}(dx^*/dR) - M'(dx/dR) - M^* = C/A \qquad (10.16)$$

where, in view of (10.13) and (10.14),

$$C = (1 - D^{*\prime} - M^{*\prime})(MM' - M^*) - M^*M^{*\prime}D' \qquad (10.17)$$

If, for example, the home country is in surplus ($B = M^*/R - M > 0$) and its currency is appreciated (R is reduced), then B is increased; that is, the surplus is increased, since A is positive and C is negative in (10.16), in view of (10.15) and (10.17).[11]

If international trade between two countries is exclusively carried out by exporters so that foreign exchange gains or losses, if any, accrue entirely to exporters in the exporting country, equations (10.11) and (10.12) are changed into

$$x = X - M^*(x^*) + RM^*(x^*) \qquad (10.18)$$

and

$$x^* = X^* - M(x) + (M(x)/R) \qquad (10.19)$$

where the price home exporters receive from M^* is given in terms of foreign currency and the price foreign exporters receive from M is given in terms of home currency. By substituting (10.18) and (10.19) into (10.9) and (10.10) and differentiating with respect to R, we have at $R = 1$,

$$dx/dR = (M^*(1 - D^{*\prime}) - MM^{*\prime})/A \qquad (10.20)$$

and

$$dx^*/dR = (-(1 - D')M + M'M^*)/A \qquad (10.21)$$

where A is defined as in (10.15). The numerator of (10.20) is positive if the home country is not in deficit, $B = M^* - (M/R) \geqq 0$.[12] The appreciation of home currency reduces x. The numerator of (10.21) is negative if trade balances (if $B = 0$). The appreciation of home currency increases x^*.

The stability of the foreign exchange market is considered as follows. The change in the balance of payment due to a change in foreign exchange rate is

$$dB/dR = M^{*\prime}(dx^*/dR) - M'(dx/dR) + M = C'/A \qquad (10.22)$$

where, in view of (10.20) and (10.21),

$$C' = (1 - D^{*\prime} - M^{*\prime})(M - M^*M' - MD') \qquad (10.23)$$

If, for example, the home country is in deficit ($B = M^* - (M/R) < 0$), and its currency is depreciated (R is increased), then B is increased; that is, the deficit is decreased, since A is positive and C' is positive in (10.22) in view of (10.15) and (10.23).[13]

Finally, let us consider the case where international trade between two countries is exclusively carried out by exporters and importers of a country, say, the home country so that both foreign exchange gains and losses accrue entirely to the home country. The relation between x and y is

$$x = X + (R - 1)M^*(x^*) + (1 - R)M(x) \tag{10.24}$$

while we no longer need to make a distinction between x^* and X^*. Note that both the price importers pay for M and the price exporters receive for M^* are given in terms of foreign currency. By substituting (10.24) and $x^* = X^*$ into (10.9) and (10.10) and differentiating by R, we have at $R = 1$,

$$dx/dR = (M - M^*)(1 - D^{*\prime})/A' \tag{10.25}$$

and

$$dx^*/dR = (M - M^*)M'/A' \tag{10.26}$$

where

$$A' = (1 - D^{*\prime})(D' - 1) + M'M^{*\prime} \tag{10.27}$$

which is negative. There will be no changes in x and x^* induced by a change in R, if trade balances (if $B = M^* - M = 0$).[14] If the home country is in surplus ($B > 0$), both of (10.25) and (10.26) are positive, while if it is in deficit ($B < 0$), both of (10.25) and (10.26) are negative.

The change in the balance of payments due to a change in foreign exchange rate is

$$\begin{aligned} dB/dR &= M^{*\prime}(dx/dR) - M'(dx/dR) \\ &= ((M - M^*)M'(D^{*\prime} + M^{*\prime} - 1)/A' \end{aligned} \tag{10.28}$$

If $B = 0$, $dB/dR = 0$. If the home country is in surplus ($B > 0$), it is negative in view of (10.27), and the appreciation of the home currency increases trade surplus, which implies the instability of the foreign exchange market. If the home country is in deficit ($B < 0$), dB/dR is positive and the depreciation of the home currency decreases the trade deficit, which implies stability.

To summarize: The foreign exchange market is unstable in the short run if trade balances and foreign exchange gains (losses) accrue to importing countries. The market is stable, on the other hand, if trade balances and foreign exchange gains (losses) accrue to exporting countries. Finally, the market is only one-sidedly stable if both foreign exchange gains and losses of exporters and importers accrue to a country. The trade

surplus and appreciation of the currency of a country actively partici-
pating in international trade (like Japan?) in the sense of foreign exchange
risk bearing tends to destabilize the foreign exchange market because the
stabilizing effect of foreign exchange gains of importers to increase imports
is overtaken by the destabilizing effect of foreign exchange losses of
exporters to decrease imports.

CHAPTER 11

Ricardo, the natural wage, and international unequal exchange

The neoclassical theory of international trade presupposes given supplies of factors of production, including labor, and their international immobility. The price of a factor of production is then determined by its value productivity, which in turn depends on physical productivity and the price of the product. This can be clearly seen, for example, in arguments leading to the Stolper–Samuelson theorem that the price of a factor of production that is used relatively more intensively in the production of importables is increased by the imposition of an import tariff. In other words, the price of a factor of production as a quasi-rent is determined exclusively by the demand for it, since the supply is given by assumption.

The neoclassical interpretation of the Ricardian theory of international trade is, naturally, that it is a special case of the more general neoclassical theory, where the labor is the sole factor of production and the specialization is complete rather than incomplete.

In the simplest version of the Ricardian model commodities are exchanged for each other within a country according to the amounts of labor required to produce them. Labor is treated as the only factor of production requiring remuneration and it is assumed to be homogeneous in quality, so that wage rates in all occupations within the country are similar. Labor requirements per unit of output in the prevailing technology are assumed to be invariant with the scale of production. (Caves and Jones 1973, p. 120)

Wage rates are linked both to commodity prices and to physical productivities. Therefore a comparison between home and foreign wage rates must as well involve a comparison in labor productivities in the two countries and the commodity terms of trade. (p. 131)[1]

The wage rate in the neoclassical interpretation of Ricardian theory is the quasi-rent imputed to the given supply of labor, which is determined exclusively by the demand for labor, hence by the productivity of labor. This is quite un-Ricardian, unfortunately, as will be shown in the next section. In the long run, Ricardo as well as other classical economists considered the natural wage, which is independent of demand for labor and determined solely by the reproduction cost of labor power. The supply of labor, on the other hand, is considered to be variable and to adjust to the demand for labor by the Malthusian principle of population. The neoclassical interpretation cannot explain the implications of Ricardo's numerical example in which labor productivity in the cloth industry is lower in England, which seems to be the more advanced country, than in Portugal, which seems to be the less-developed country, since it is strange to consider that the wage is lower in the former than in the latter. It is, however, not the wage but the rate of profit which should be considered to be lower in England, while the natural wage may not be lower in England.

In his neo-Marxist theory of international unequal exchange, Emmanuel (1972) is very critical of the traditional theory of comparative costs and emphasizes the importance of international difference of the natural wage between developed and underdeveloped countries and the importance of capital movements between such countries. Ricardo did not, however, deny the international difference in the natural wage, and capital movements are implicity considered by him, as shown in Chapter 10, through consideration of exporters and importers. Emmanuel's criticism does not apply, therefore, to Ricardo's theory of comparative costs. We have to admit, on the other hand, Emmanuel's emphasis on capital mobility and wage differentials does fit present-day reality much more than does neoclassical theory – to wit, the so-called Heckscher–Ohlin model with international factor price equalization, which excludes the necessity of capital movements. Unfortunately, Emmanuel's demonstration of unequal exchange is given in terms of numerical examples and based on a clumsy process of Marxist transformation of values into prices. Later in this chapter I shall reformulate it in terms of simple price–cost relations so that it can be seriously considered even by non-Marxist economists, who do not accept the labor theory of value.

Emmanuel defined the unequal exchange by the reduction of the terms of trade of the lower wage country in comparison with the situation of no wage differentials and does not deny the gains from international trade and investment as such. Saigal (1973), a follower of Emmanuel, however, went further and defined the unequal exchange in terms of comparison of the autarky with the situation with international trade and investment. In other words, Saigal is not only, like Emmanuel, criticizing basic assumptions of the neoclassical theory of international trade but also, unlike Emmanuel, denying the gains from international trade and investment. Saigal's theory is, fortunately, illogical and cannot be supported, since in his model capitalists are not really trying to maximize profit. We can, however, resolve present inconsistencies in Saigal's model by introducing preference in location and risk premium in international investment, which Ricardo and Emmanuel emphasized. By so doing, ironically, we can show, as done later in this chapter, that both of two countries with different wages but identical technology can gain from international trade and investment, in terms of Saigal's criteria, a result stronger than neoclassical one. In a neoclassical model where wage is endogenously determined by marginal productivity of labor, the rate of profit falls in a capital-importing country. In Saigal's model as well as Ricardo's, however, natural wages are given exogenously by socioeconomic or bioeconomic factors, and the rate of profit rises even in a capital-importing country as a result of international trade and investment between countries with identical technology.

Ricardo's theory of comparative costs

Ricardo has two concepts of wage: the short-run market wage and the long-run natural wage.

The natural price of labour is that price which is necessary to enable the labourers, one with another, to subsist and to prepetuate their race, without either increase or diminution. The power of the labourer to support himself and the family which may be necessary to keep up the number of labourers, does not depend on the quantity of money which he may receive for wages, but on the quantity of food, necessaries, and conveniences become essential to him from habit which that money will purchase. The natural price of labour, therefore, depends on the price of the food, necessaries, and conveniences required for the support of the labourer and his family.... The market price of labourer is the price which is really paid for it, from the natural operation of the proportion of the supply to the demand; labour is dear when it is scarce and cheap when it is plentiful. However much the market price of labour may deviate from its natural price, it has, like commodities, a tendency to conform to it. (Ricardo 1951, pp. 93–94)

As we pointed out in the preceding section, the wage rate in the modern interpretation of the Ricardian theory of international trade is the quasi-rent imputed to the given supply of labor, – in other words, short-run wage established before the supply of labor is adjusted to the demand for labor. This is, however, quite un-Ricardian.

Viner wrote: "It is more or less obvious that Ricardo based his analysis on the following assumptions: ample time for long-run adjustments; free competition; only two countries and only two commodities; constant labor costs as output is varied; and proportionality of both aggregate real costs and supply prices within each country to labor-time costs within that country" (Viner 1937, p. 444). It is, therefore, the natural wage that we should consider in the theory of comparative costs.

Ricardo's numerical example of the comparative-cost principle is as follows. Suppose one unit of cloth made in England is being exchanged against one unit of wine made in Portugal.

England may be so circumstanced that to produce the cloth may require the labour of 100 men for one year, and if she attempted to make wine, it might require the labour of 120 men for the same time. England would therefore find it her interest to import wine, and to purchase it by the exportation of cloth. To produce the wine in Portugal might require only the labour of 80 men for one year, and to produce the cloth in the same country might require the labour of 90 men for the same time. It would therefore be advantageous for her to export wine in exchange for cloth. (Ricardo 1951, p. 135)

This exchange takes place notwithstanding that the commodity imported by Portugal could be produced there with less labor than in England and that England gives the produce of her labor of 100 men for the produce of the labor of 80. The reason given by Ricardo for this unequal exchange of labor is the difficulty with which not the labor but the capital moves from one country to another.

Experience, however, shows that the fancied or real insecurity of capital, when not under the immediate control of its owner, together with the natural disinclination which every man has to quit the country of his birth and connection, and intrust himself, with all his habits fixed, to a strange government and new laws, check the emigration of capital. These feelings, which I should be sorry to see weakened, induce most men of property to be satisfied with a low rate of profits in their own country, rather than seek a more advantageous employment for their wealth in foreign nations. (Ricardo 1951, pp. 136–137)

It is, therefore, not the case that "labor is treated as the only factor of production requiring remuneration." Although Ricardo admitted that the natural wage may differ in different countries, furthermore, it is not the wage differentials but the difference in the rate of profit which explains unequal exchange of labor, since it is strange to consider that the natural wage is lower in England, an advanced country, than in Portugal, a less-developed country.

Lower rate of profit in England is in turn explained by lower productivity of labor in England.[2]

If the profits of capital employed in Yorkshire should exceed those of capital employed in London, capital would speedily move from London to Yorkshire, and an equality of profits would be effected; but if in consequence of the diminished rate of production in the lands of England from the increase of capital and population wages should rise and profits fall, it would not follow that capital and population would necessarily move from England to Holland, or Spain, or Russia, where profits might be higher. (Ricardo 1951, p. 134)

Labor productivity in England is lower both in cloth and in wine than in

Portugal, because English lands are more densely populated and more heavily invested than Portuguese lands. In spite of Samuelson (1977b, pp. 657–59) and Amin (1976, p. 134), it is not the case that Portugal is rich and England is poor. One may perhaps consider that in the Ricardian macroeconomic production function, the marginal rate of substitution between cloth and wine is constant and the marginal productivity of labor is diminishing because of the existence of land as a fixed factor of production; that is,

$$C + sV = F(N), \quad F'(N) > 0, \quad F''(N) < 0 \tag{11.1}$$

where C, V, and N are, respectively, the output of cloth, that of wine, and labor input, and s is a constant. Of course s is different for different countries, the comparative advantage. To employ N labor, furthermore, wN amount of capital has to be advanced, where w signifies the natural wage. "Capital consists entirely of the wage-bill; in other words, it is only circulating capital which takes one year to be re-integrated," observed Pasinetti (1974, p. 7).

In the Ricardian numerical example, in which cloth and wine require respectively 100 and 120 units of labor in England, the rate of profit and prices in England before trade (in autarky) are determined by

$$p_1 = (1 + r)\,100w = (1 + r)100(c_1 p_1 + c_2 p_2) \tag{11.2}$$

and

$$p_2 = (1 + r)120w = (1 + r)120(c_1 p_1 + c_2 p_2) \tag{11.3}$$

where r is the rate of profit, p_1 is the price of cloth, p_2 is the price of wine, and the natural wage w purchases just the given specified amount of each commodity: c_1 and c_2. This implies that at the margin where there is no land rent, the price of a product must be equal to the sum of the wage bill advanced and the profit earned on it. By multiplying (10.2) and (10.3) by c_1 and c_2, respectively, and adding them, we have

$$R = 1/(1 + r) = 100c_1 + 120c_2 \tag{11.4}$$

since $(c_1 p_1 + c_2 p_2)$, assumed to be nonzero, can be canceled out.

Similarly, we have for Portugal

$$p_1 = (1 + r')90(c_1' p_1 + c_2' p_2) \tag{11.5}$$

and

$$p_2 = (1 + r')80(c_1' p_1 + c_2' p_2) \tag{11.6}$$

from which we conclude that

$$R' = 1/(1 + r') = 90c_1' + 80c_2' \tag{11.7}$$

where r' is the rate of profit in Portugal and c_1' and c_2' correspond to c_1 and c_2. As is seen in (11.4) and (11.7), the rate of profit is higher in Portugal than in England before trade, if $c_1 \geqslant c_1'$ and $c_2 \geqslant c_2'$.

Finally, when England is specialized in cloth and Portugal in wine, we have

$$p_1 = (1 + r)100(c_1 p_1 + c_2 p_2) \tag{11.8}$$

and

$$p_2 = (1 + r')80(c_1 p_1 + c_2 p_2) \tag{11.9}$$

where for the sake of simplicity it is assumed that $c_1 = c_1'$ and $c_2 = c_2'$, which means the natural wage is identical in the two countries, and r is the rate of profit in England and r' is that in Portugal, both after the trade.[3] From (11.8) and (11.9) we must have

$$RR' - 100c_1 R' - 80c_2 R = 0 \tag{11.10}$$

where $R = 1/(1 + r)$ and $R' = 1/(1 + r')$.

The relation between r and r' depends on the possibility of capital movement between countries. As was argued in the Chapter 10 section on Ricardo's theory of terms of trade, capital can move between countries through the activities of exporters and importers to replace the capital of producers. International trade enables capital to move from England, where the rate of profit was lower before trade, to Portugal, where the rate of profit was higher. It is impossible, however, that r and r', and therefore R and R', are completely equalized, in view of factors that, Ricardo emphasized, induce most men of property to be satisfied with a low rate of profits in their own country rather than to seek a higher rate in foreign nations. In Ricardo's numerical example, where $p_1 = p_2$, so that one unit of cloth is exchanged against one unit of wine, we must have

$$R' = 0.8R, \quad R = 100(c_1 + c_2) \tag{11.11}$$

in view of (11.8) and (11.9). Comparison of (11.4), (11.7) and (11.11), shows that trade increases the rate of profit in both countries.[4]

Emmanuel's theory of unequal exchange

Emmanuel (1972) considered two cases of international unequal exchange: a primary form of nonequivalence (no wage differential or equal rate of surplus value with unequal organic compositions of capital) and nonequivalence in the strict sense (wage differential or unequal rates of surplus value).

Let us begin with the first case (Emmanuel 1972, pp. 52–60). The natural wage and the ratio of profit to the capital in the form of advancement of wage cost are assumed to be equal in both countries, before international trade and investment take place. The rate of profit is, however, different between two countries, since two countries are assumed to have different organic compositions of capital, the different ratios between other forms of capital (fixed capital, advancement of cost of materials and so on) and the advancement of wage costs.[5] When international trade and investment take place, the rate of profit is equalized. This is made possible by unequal exchange from the point of view of the embodied labor theory of value. Exchange ratio is unfavourable for commodities that have lower organic composition, relative to the amount of labor embodied in them.

Although this is a classic case in Marxist economics (Sweezy 1942, pp. 290–91) and the one Samuelson discussed in his criticism against Emmanuel (Samuelson 1977b, pp. 649–60), Emmanuel himself does not regard this type of unequal exchange as truly important. The reason is that this case is the one with the same natural wage (the same rate of surplus value) in two countries, which is considered by Emmanuel to be the result of a bioeconomic law common to the two countries. In Ricardo's system, according to Emmanuel, wages are incapable either of exceeding the physiological minimum or of being reduced below the level, through the working of a kind of biological law, the same for every country, while in Marx's system the social and historical factors can bring about considerable difference in wage levels and make impossible the equalization of wages on a world scale (Emmanuel 1972, pp. xxxiii–xxxiv). In the world of today the notion of the subsistence minimum is sufficiently elastic for no tendency to automatic equalization to be possible. Emmanuel emphasized, therefore, that the second case of unequal exchange is truly important.

Emmanuel showed by numerical examples that the terms of trade of the lower wage country are unfavorable in comparison with the case of no wage differential. This reduction of the terms of trade is the definition of unequal exchange in the second case where the natural wage differs among countries (Emmanuel 1972, pp. 59, 61, 62). It should be emphasized that Emmanuel does not compare autarky and trade situations and therefore does not deny the gains from international trade as such. His criticism is of the neoclassical assumption that wage is endogenous and capital is immobile internationally, which, in the case of the Heckscher–Ohlin theory, leads to international factor price equalization. Emmanuel assumed, on the other hand, that internationally different wages are exogenously given and capital is freely mobile between countries.

In spite of Emmanuel's argument, Ricardo also admitted the possible difference in natural wage among countries: "It is not to be understood that the natural price of labour, estimated even in food and necessaries, is absolutely fixed and constant. It varies at different times in the same country, and very materially differs in different countries. It essentially depends on the habits and customs of the people" (Ricardo 1951, pp. 96–97). Emmanuel's criticism of theory of comparative costs does not, therefore, apply to Ricardo's theory, and his theory of international unequal exchange is quite Ricardian, which enables us to formulate his arguments in Sraffa-like equations of price–cost relations.

Unlike Emmanuel who started with Marxian values and then transformed them into prices, let us consider, from the beginning, price–cost relations,

$$Rp = ap + b \qquad (11.12)$$

and

$$R = cp + d \qquad (11.13)$$

where $R = 1/(1 + r)$ and r is the internationally equalized rate of profit, p is the price of the first good in terms of the second good (the *numeraire*), a and c (b and d) are, respectively, technically given input coefficients of the first (second) good in the production of the first and second goods.[6]

Any change in input coefficients induces changes in R and p. If a and b are unchanged, such changes in R and p must be in the opposite directions from (11.12). If either c or d only is increased, it is impossible, from (11.13), for p to increase and for R to decrease. Therefore, R must increase and p must decrease, for such a change in c or d. Suppose the lower wage country is specialized in the first good, and the higher wage country, in the second good. Let us assume, first, that the first good is the wage good. To compare with the situation of no wage differential, we have to increase c in (11.13) from the level in the no wage differential situation, since the second good has a higher wage cost. This makes p decrease. Let us assume, second, that the second good is the wage good. We have, then, to increase d in (11.13) from the level in the no wage differential situation, which again results in a decrease in p. Terms of trade of the lower wage country p must always have deteriorated, therefore, in comparison with the no wage differential situation, irrespective of whether the country is specialized in wage goods or not.

Saigal's refutation of gains from trade

Although Emmanuel does not deny the gains from trade as such, some of his followers seem to do so, by employing a different definition of unequal

Table 11.1

	Country A			Country B		
	Equipment	Labor hour	Product	Equipment	Labor hour	Product
Good I	10e	40h	30e	10e	40h	30e
Good II	10e	80h	60c	1e	8h	6c

exchange. For example, to Saigal (1973), unequal exchange means that terms of trade are unfavorable to lower wage country in comparison with its domestic price ratio in autarky and that the rate or profit is decreased (increased) in the lower (higher) wage country when international trade (with complete specialization) and investment (with rate of profit equalized) take place. This is a direct refutation of both the classical and neoclassical theories of gains from trade.

Let us examine a case proposed by Saigal (his exercises 1 and 2) where two countries, A, a central economy, and B, a dependent or peripheral economy, and two sectors or two goods, I, equipment or materials, and II, consumption goods, are considered. Input–output data are given in Table 11.1, where identical technology for two countries is assumed and e, c, and h signify equipment, consumption goods, and labor hours. Let us suppose that ratio of wage rates in A and in B is 4:1 and that $W^A = (1/2)c$ and $W^B = (1/8)c$, where W^A and W^B signify wage rates for one labor hour in each country.

In autarky, then, from price–cost equations,[7]

$$10P_e^A (1 + R^A) + 40W^A = 30P_e^A \tag{11.14}$$

$$10P_e^A (1 + R^A) + 80W^A = 60c \tag{11.15}$$

$$10P_e^B (1 + R^B) + 40W^B = 30P_e^B \tag{11.16}$$

$$P_e^B (1 + R^B) + 8W^B = 6c \tag{11.17}$$

We can solve for

$$1 + R^A = 1.5$$
$$1 + R^B = 2.73$$
$$P_e^A = (4/3)c = 1.33c$$
$$P_e^B = (11/6)c = 1.83c$$

where R^A and R^B are rates of profit in two countries, P_e^A and P_e^B are price of the good I (equipment) in terms of the good II (consumption goods) in two countries.[8]

Table 11.2

	Equipment	Labor hour	Product
Country A, Good I	$10e$	$40h$	$30e$
Country B, Good II	$4e$	$32h$	$24e$

When international trade and investment are free and country A (B) is specialized in good I (II), input–output data are given in Table 11.2, and from price–cost equations, taking into consideration that $W^A = (1/2)c$ and $W^B = (1/8)c$,

$$10P_e (1 + R) + 20c = 30P_e \qquad (11.18)$$

$$4P_e (1 + R) + 4c = 24c, \qquad (11.19)$$

we can solve for

$$1 + R = 15/7 = 2.14$$
$$P_e = 7c/3 = 2.33c$$

where R and P_e are rate of profit equalized and the price of the good I in terms of good II.

Saigal observed from this analysis that the conditions for the unequal exchange, $P_e > P_e^B > P_e^A$ and $R^B > R > R^A$ are realized, which implies that (1) country B has to export 2.33 units of consumption goods to import 1 unit of equipment, while it could obtain 1 unit of the latter by sacrificing only 1.83 units of the former in the autarky, and (2) the maximum rate of accumulation falls from 1.73 to 1.14 in B.[9]

Fortunately, we cannot accept this conclusion of Saigal's. In the free capitalistic world, given technology and wage differences as in Saigal's example, Evans (1981a, p. 129; 1981b, p. 125) has pointed out that capital moved from country A to B can profitably be invested in the sector I in B, since price–cost relation is

$$10P_e (1 + R) + 40W^B < 30P_e \qquad (11.20)$$

when $P_e = 2.33c$, $R = 1.14$ and $W^B = (1/8)c$, i.e., $40W^B = 5c$. In other words, the higher wage country, A, cannot compete with the lower wage country, B, in any good, when technology is identical and rate of profit equalized.[10] The result is that all the capital moves from A to B.[11]

Of course, such an extreme solution is highly unrealistic. What we should do to save Saigal's model with wage differential and mobile capital is to admit that the rate of profit is not equalized even though capital is freely mobile between countries. Recall that, according to Ricardo, "insecurity of capital ... together with the natural disinclination ... to quit the country of his birth ... induce most men of property to be satisfied with a low rate of profits in their own country, rather than seek a more advantageous employment for their wealth in foreign nations" (Ricardo 1951, pp. 136–37). And even Emmanuel himself admitted that "if the risk premium in Brazil is + 1/2, compared with the United States, and general rate of profit in the latter country is 10 percent, then parity occurs when the rate of profit in Brazil reaches 15 percent. At 16 percent capital should move from the United States to Brazil, and at 14 percent from Brazil to the United States" (Emmanuel 1972, p. 71).

Let us, then, reconstruct Saigal's model properly, giving the conditions for the complete specialization fully and admitting that mobility of capital does not equate rate of profit completely. The result will be completely contrary to the one claimed by Saigal, that the lower wage country can gain both in the comparison of domestic price ratio and the terms of trade as well as in terms of the rate of profit by international trade and investment.

When country A (B) is specialized in good I (II), not only the price–cost equations

$$P_e = (1 + R)\, aP_e + bW^A \tag{11.21}$$

$$1 = (1 + Rq)cP_e + dW^B \tag{11.22}$$

but also the price–cost relations

$$P_e < (1 + Rq)\, aP_e + bW^B \tag{11.23}$$

$$1 < (1 + R)\, cP_e + dW^A \tag{11.24}$$

have to be satisfied, where a, b and c, d are input coefficients of good I and labor in the production of two goods, respectively, and $q > 1$ implies that capital emigration from A to B is checked by factors mentioned in quotations from Ricardo and Emmanuel cited previously.

In autarky, on the other hand, price–cost equations in country B are

$$P_e^B = (1 + R^B)\, aP_e^B + b\, W^B \tag{11.25}$$

$$1 = (1 + R^B)\, cP_e^B + dW^B \tag{11.26}$$

From (11.22) and (11.26), we have

$$(1 + Rq)\, cP_e = (1 + R^B)\, cP_e^B \tag{11.27}$$

while from (11.23) and (11.25) we have

$$P_e\,(1 - (1 + Rq)\, a) < P_e^B\,(1 - (1 + R^B)\, a) \tag{11.28}$$

Now we are ready to show that, contrary to Saigal's result, (11.21)–(11.24) imply gains from trade and investment; that is, $P_e < P_e^B$ and

$(1 + Rq) > (1 + R^B)$. Suppose that $P_e > P_e^B$. Then, from (11.27) we have $Rq < R^B$. This is a contradiction, however, since we have $P_e < P_e^B$ from (11.28). Therefore, it has to be $P_e < P_e^B$. Then, from (11.27) we have $(1 + Rq) > (1 + R^B)$.

Similarly, in autarky, price–cost equations in A are

$$P_e^A = (1 + R^A) aP_e^A + bW^A \tag{11.29}$$

$$1 = (1 + R^A) cP_e^A + dW^A \tag{11.30}$$

and we have

$$P_e^A (1 - (1 + R^A) a) = P_e (1 - (1 + R) a) \tag{11.31}$$

$$(1 + R) cP_e > (1 + R^A) cP_e^A \tag{11.32}$$

from (11.21), (11.24), (11.29) and (11.30). If we suppose that $P_e < P_e^A$, then we have a contradiction, namely $P_e > P_e^A$ from (11.31) and (11.32). Therefore, we have $P_e > P_e^A$, which implies $R > R^A$ from (11.31).

Both of Saigal's conditions for unequal exchange are not realized, since we have $P_e^B > P_e > P_e^A$ and $Rq > R^B$, $R > R^A$. While the former is common sense from the point of view of classical and neoclassical theories of trade, it may be interesting to see the latter, which is due to the assumption of given wage rates.[12] A rise in the rate of profit in a capital importing country is an unexpected result from a neoclassical model where wage is endogenously determined by marginal productivity of labor.[13]

Saigal (1973, p. 133) argued that international equal exchange is possible between developed and less-developed countries in a socialist world economy while international trade is unequal exchange between such countries in a capitalist world economy. It is quite ironic that unequal exchange in the sense of Saigal is impossible in a free capitalist world, as shown here, while it may be possible in a socialist world when an advanced country imposes a wrong pattern of specialization on other countries.

Markets and money

CHAPTER 12

Jevons, Edgeworth, and the competitive equilibrium of exchange

Walras's regard for Jevons's contribution to the equilibrium theory of competitive exchange was not high since, as he pointed out in his letter to Jevons, the latter had failed to derive "the equation of effective demand as a function of price, which ... is so indispensable for the solution of the problem of the determination of equilibrium price" (Walras 1965, p. 397).[1] This is no wonder. Demand as a function of price implies that traders are price takers. Walras presupposed the existence of market prices accepted by competitive traders as data, in his theory of general equilibrium of competitive exchange. Jevons and Edgeworth tried to justify this Walrasian supposition by explaining such prices established in a competitive market as ratios of exchange eventually resulting from a process of free bargaining and arbitrage, without assuming price-taking behavior of competitive traders.

In a sense, Schumpeter recognized this difference between Walras and Jevons.

The Competitive Hypothesis. This notion had been made explicit by Cournot ... after having started with the case of straight monopoly ... he first introduced another seller and then additional ones until, by letting their number increase indefinitely, he finally arrived at the case of "illimited" (unlimited) competition, where the quantity produced by any one producer is too small to affect price perceptibly or to admit of price strategy. Jevons added his Law of Indifference, which defines the concept of the perfect market in which there cannot exist, at any moment, more than one price for each homogeneous commodity. These two features – excluded price strategy and law of indifference – express, so far as I can see, what Walras meant by *libre concurrence*. (Schumpeter 1954, p. 973)

Both Cournot and Jevons tried to explain what Walras simply assumed.

The basic notions in Jevons's theory of exchange are those of a trading body, piecemeal or divisible trade, and the law of indifference. Edgeworth adopted Jevons's concept of the trading body and showed that in an economy with an infinite number of traders, Jevons's law of indifference and equations of exchange obtain. This result is now familiar as the Debreu–Scarf theorem, which states that as the economy grows in number of participants, the core of exchange game shrinks to the set of competitive equilibria. Whereas Walras did Jevons less than justice, Edgeworth, in a sense, did him more than justice, in so far as Jevons's concept of a trading body was generously interpreted by Edgeworth so as to exclude the case of indeterminate equilibrium of bilateral monopoly and that of competition among the few. In my opinion, however, even Edgeworth did Jevons less than justice, since the implication of Jevons's process of divisible trade, which leads to the law of indifference, was not fully exploited. If indivisible lump-sum transactions are ruled out and competition is assured so that Jevons's law of indifference is established by arbitrage behavior of traders, it is easily seen that the solution of Jevons's equations of exchange is the only stable outcome, even in markets with a small number of traders.

Jevons's approach thus suggests that an infinitely large number of traders is, though sufficient, not necessary for the outcome that traders seem to behave as if they were price takers, a point that has been overlooked in recent studies of the large economy in the tradition of Edgeworth.[2]

This chapter depends largely on Negishi (1982e), though some changes have been made upon further consideration. The next section is devoted to documenting the basic concepts of Jevons's theory of exchange. Edgeworth's limit theorem based on Jevons's concept of trading body is explained in the section after that, where it should be noted that the divisibility of trade is not necessarily assumed and the law of indifference is obtained merely as a by-product of Jevons's equations of exchange. I then argue that arbitrage behavior leading to the law of indifference, together with the divisibility of trade, generates the solution of Jevons's equations of exchange even when the number of traders is small. It is to be noted that the law of indifference is not assumed from the beginning but explained by arbitrage behavior. In the case of Walras, however, the law of indifference is assumed and not explained, as will be shown in the final section.

Jevons's theory of exchange

Let me sketch Jevons's theory of exchange. Before giving his famous equation of exchange, Jevons discussed three concepts – the trading body, divisible trade, and the law of indifference – all of which are very important if we are to understand the true implications of Jevons's theory of exchange.

Jevons considered exchange of goods between trading bodies.

The trading body may be a single individual in one case; it may be the whole inhabitants of a continent in another; it may be the individuals of a trade diffused through a country in a third. England and North America will be trading bodies if we are considering the corn we receive from America in exchange for iron and other goods. The continent of Europe is a trading body as purchasing coal from England. The farmers of England are a trading body when they sell corn to the millers, and the millers both when they buy corn from the farmers and sell flour to the bakers. (Jevons 1888, pp. 88–89)

Though some historians of economic thought are critical of Jevons's use of the trading body (see Blaug 1978, pp. 327–28, and Howey 1960, p. 52), similar concepts have been used very often in various fields of economic theory. For example, countries are regarded, as Jevons himself suggested, as trading bodies and the utility function, or indifference map, of a country is considered in the theory of international trade.[3] Another example concerns the models used in theories of the microeconomic foundations of macroeconomics, in which the representative or aggregate household and representative or aggregate firm exchange labor services and consumers' goods (e.g., see Benassy 1978 and Malinvaud 1977).

The reason why Jevons uses such an artificial invention to explain exchange is that the behavior of the aggregate or average person is much more stable than that of an individual person.

A single individual does not vary his consumption of sugar, butter, or eggs from week to week by infinitesimal amounts, according to each small change in the price. He probably continues his ordinary consumption until accident directs his attention to a rise in price, and he then, perhaps, discontinues the use of the articles altogether for a time. But the aggregate, or what is the same, the average consumption, of a large community will be found to vary continuously or nearly so. (Jevons 1888, p. 89; see also p. 15)

Differential calculus can be used, therefore, only for the case of the aggregate or average person.

Jevons then proceeds to the discussion of the law of indifference and the divisibility of trade.

If, in selling a quantity of perfectly equal and uniform barrels of flour, a merchant arbitrarily fixed different prices on them, a purchaser would of course select the cheaper ones. . . . Hence follows what is undoubtedly true, with proper explanation, that in the same open market, at any one moment, there cannot be two prices for the same kind of article. (Jevons 1888, p. 91)

It follows that the last increments in an act of exchange must be exchanged in the same ratio as the whole quantities exchanged. Suppose that two commodities are bartered in the ratio of x for y; then every m-th part of x is given for the m-th part of y, and it does not matter for which of the m-th parts . . . even an infinitely small part of x must be exchanged for an infinitely small part of y, in the same ratio as the whole quantities. This result we may express by stating that the increments concerned in the process of exchange must obey the equation $dy/dx = y/x$. (pp. 94–95)

Behind this "statical view of the question" there must be a dynamic process of trading. What Jevons had in mind is a piecemeal or divisible exchange process, since "dynamically we could not treat the ratio of exchange otherwise than as the ratio of dy and dx, infinitesimal quantities of commodity" (Jevons 1888, p. 94; see also pp. 92–93).

Now we finally come across the proposition that contains "the keystone of the whole theory of exchange, and of the principal problems of economics":

The ratio of exchange of any two commodities will be the reciprocal of the ratio of the final degrees of utility of the quantities of commodity available for consumption after the exchange is completed. (Jevons 1888, p. 95 [italics in the original])

Let us now suppose that the first body, A, originally possessed the quantity a of corn, and that second body, B, possessed the quantity b of beef. As the exchange consists in giving x of corn for y of beef, ... the quantities exchanged satisfy two equations, ... $[F_1(a - x)/G_1(y) = y/x = F_2(x)/G_2(b - y)]$. (pp. 99–100)

Here the cumbersome notations used by Jevons have been replaced by ordinary ones and F_1 and G_1, and F_2 and G_2, respectively, denote A's final degree of utility (i.e., marginal utilities) of corn and beef, and B's final degrees of utility of corn and beef.

Edgeworth's limit theorem

Jevons's famous law of indifference and equations of exchange to determine the quantities exchanged, which are given in the previous section, are satisfied at point E in Figure 12.1. This figure is the Edgeworth box diagram, where the quantity of corn is measured horizontally, that of beef vertically, the quantities of commodity available to A are measured with the origin at A, those available to B, with the origin at B, curve DEF is the contract curve, which is a locus of points where indifference curves of two bodies are tangent, and profit C denotes the initial allocation of commodities. If each trading body consists of only a single individual, which is the case of isolated exchange or bilateral monopoly, the equilibrium is indeterminate in the sense that any point on the contract curve between D and F is a stable outcome of exchange. There is no reason why only E can be an equilibrium and Jevons's law of indifference and equations of exchange cannot be applied in this case.

Since Jevons said that "the trading body may be a single individual in one case," and considered the indeterminateness of equilibrium only in

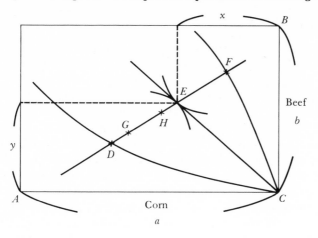

Figure 12.1

the case where a commodity is indivisible (Jevons 1888, pp. 88, 122–125; see also Edgeworth 1881, p. 30), we have to admit that Jevons did not recognize the indeterminateness of bilateral monopoly, let alone that of the competition among the few in general, which Edgeworth claimed.[4] Edgeworth was, however, quite generous in interpreting Jevons when he wrote,

the Jevonian law of indifference has place only where there is competition, and, indeed perfect competition. Why, indeed, should an isolated couple exchange every portion of their respective commodities at the same rate of exchange? Or what meaning can be attached to such a law in their case? ... This consideration has not been brought so prominently forward in Professor Jevons's theory of exchange, but it does not seem to be lost sight of. His couple of dealers are, I take it, a sort of typical couple, clothed with the property of indifference, whose origin in an open market is so lucidly described; not naked abstractions like the isolated couples imagined by a De Quincey or Courcelle-Seneuil in some solitary region. Each is in Berkleian phrase a representative particular; an indivdual dealer only is presented, but there is presupposed a class of competitors in the background. (Edgeworth 1881, pp. 31, 109)

In view of Jevons's reason for using the trading body – namely, the fact that the behavior of an average person is more stable than that of a single individual – Edgeworth's interpretation of Jevons is much more reasonable and productive than those of hairsplitting historians of economic thought (see Black et al. 1973, pp. 120–21).

Edgeworth thus presupposed perfect competition, where the number of traders is infinite (1881, p. 18), to justify Jevons's law of indifference and equations of exchange. Suppose each trading body consists of two persons identical in taste and initial holding, say A_1, A_2, and B_1, B_2. Edgeworth considers a cooperative game of exchange in which coalitions of individual persons are freely formed. It is evident that equal quantities of commodities should be allocated to identical persons in the same trading body. Allocation D in Figure 12.1 can be blocked with gains by a coalition of A_1, A_2 and either of B_1 and B_2. Thus, A_1, A_2 and, say, B_1 can recontract such that both A_1 and B_1 remain at D and A_2 returns to C (by canceling trade with B_2 so that both A_1 and A_2 are better off after paying some side payments to B_1, since the midpoint between D and C which is available to both A_1 and A_2 is located above the indifference curve passing D and C. Any allocation on the contract curve and close to D, say, G, can be similarly blocked by the same coalition. Similarly, allocation F or those on the contract curve and close to F can be blocked by a coalition of both B_1 and B_2 and any one of A_1 and A_2. An allocation like H, which is cose to E, however, cannot be blocked in this case and belongs, therefore, to the core, which is the set of stable allocations that cannot be blocked by coalitions. To block an allocation like H, Edgeworth considered the limiting case, wherein each trading body consists of infinitely many identical persons. However, close H is to E, then, it can be successfully blocked by a coalition of all persons belonging to A and some suitable number of persons belonging to B, since an identical allocation available to each person in A can be sufficiently close to H, on the line CH, so that it is above the indifference curve passing through H. The only allocation to remain in the core is E, since line EC is tangent to the indifference curve passing E.[5]

We have to admit, first, that traders in Edgeworth exchange game are not perfectly rational and are rather myopic, since we are ruling out the possibility of collusive agreements not to engage in blocking activity that eventually leads to a less favorable allocation. With regard to Figure 12.1, there would be an incentive for B traders to enter into a collusive agreement not to engage in any activity that would undermine H and eventually result in the attainment of E. Traders are assumed to engage in any activity, if and only if it instantaneously improves their positions, without considering its eventual effects.[6]

We have to note, second, that the allocation E does not imply the price-taking behavior of traders in the Edgeworth exchange game, though it is also a Walrasian equilibrium in which traders are assumed to be price takers. In the Edgeworth cooperative game of exchange, therefore, there is no possibility of price-making behavior of some traders to take advantage of price-taking behavior of other traders, a problem that, following the suggestion of Hurwicz (1972), Roberts and Postlewait (1976) considered in the case of a decentralized noncooperative game of exchange. The Edgeworth theorem justifies Walrasian theory, however, because it is not the assumptions but the outcome that matters for a theory. Even though traders are actually not price takers, we may make the assumption that they are price takers, provided that we have the same outcome: the allocation E.

It is no use, finally, for a trading body to misrepresent its preference and to shift the contract curve and allocation E. Even if it obtains by such behavior an allocation E' which is preferred to E and satisfies the equations of exchange for the misrepresented preference, such an allocation is blocked by a coalition pursuing allocation more favorable in terms of true preference. If the allocation E is once realized, on the other hand, it cannot be blocked by such misrepresentation, since the trading body first has to return to the allocation C, or to move to an allocation less favorable than E. Since traders are myopic in the Edgeworth game, they will not engage in such activity, even though it might eventually improve their positions. This is true even for the case of the small numbers.

Divisible trade and the law of indifference

In interpreting Jevons's equations of exchange, Edgeworth understood rightly the implication of Jevons's use of the trading body, but he did not perhaps fully understand the implication of Jevons's process of divisible trade, which leads to his law of indifference. In my opinion, Jevons's theory of exchange is so powerful that equations of exchange and the law of indifference hold even if the number of participants in exchange is finite.

Let us consider the case of four-person, two-good exchange, where each trading body consists of two identical persons, A_1, A_2 and B_1, B_2. Figure 12.2 is a reproduction of Figure 12.1 and allocation H on the contract curve DEF cannot, as in Figure 12.1, be blocked by the coalition of A_1, A_2 and B_1 considered by Edgeworth. We can show, however, that H is not a stable outcome of exchange, if the nature of trading process in Jevons's theory of exchange is properly taken into consideration.

First, let us rule out the possibility of an indivisible lump-sum transaction and assume that each single transaction is divisible, so that every portion of a homogeneous commodity is treated indifferently – that is, exchanged against the other commodity at the same rate of exchange. There being no Walrasian auctioneer, either of the two parties may suggest a rate of exchange, in a two-person exchange, and both parties decide what they would like to trade at that exchange rate. The resulting

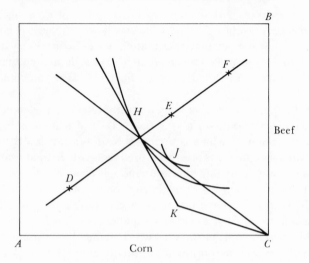

Figure 12.2

provisional contract, determined by the smaller of the two desired trades, is called a single transaction. In other words, the dynamic exchange process of Jevons is a piecemeal one, as I argued previously, and a finite, not infinitesimal, transaction is permissible only when it is divisible.

There must be, then, at least two successive transactions and the ratio of exchange should vary in the course of exchange between C and H, if allocation H can ever be reached by exchange starting from C. Otherwise, if there is only a single transaction and the exchange ratio remains unchanged throughout the exchange process, it must be equal to the slope of line CH and exchange must proceed on line CH, starting from C and moving toward H. Such an exchange process has to be terminated at J, however, since the transaction is divisible and it is unfavorable for A to go beyond J. Further, we can see that the variable ratio of exchange between C and H must be identical to the slope of the tangent to the indifference curve passing through H, for the last infinitesimal or finite transaction arriving at H.

Suppose, therefore, that exchange proceeds like CKH. This means the first transaction is to be done with an exchange ratio favorable to B and unfavorable to A, like CK, and the second transaction is to be done with an exchange ratio favorable to A and unfavorable to B, like KH, though the average ratio is CH. If we suppose that this is the case, not only with exchange between A_1 and B_1 but also with exchange between A_2 and B_2, allocation H can be blocked by the following arbitrage of different exchange ratios.[7]

Suppose B_1 and A_2 form a new trade coalition and B_1 proposes some new transaction to A_2, without canceling his transaction with A_1. B_1 offers A_2 an exchange ratio strictly between CK and KH, and A_2 accepts this proposal of B_1 by canceling a part of his transaction with B_2 at the exchange ratio CK, since "provided that A gets the right commodity in the proper quantity, he does not care whence it comes, so that we need not ... distinguish the source or destination" (Jevons 1888, pp. 117–18). Both B_1 and A_2 can be strictly better off as a result of forming this coalition, if the behavior of B_2 remains unchanged. Because B_2 is not the sole supplier of beef and A_2 canceled only a part of his transactions with B_2, A_2 can safely expect that B_2 would not retaliate by canceling the rest of his transactions with A_2 and throwing away the remaining gains from trade with A_2. Even in the worst case, the case in which A_2's expectation is not realized, B_1 and A_2 can remain at H by canceling all of B_1's transactions with A_1 and by trading exclusively between themselves. We may, therefore, reasonably expect that coalition of A_2 and B_1 is formed and allocation H is blocked.

Not only A_2 and B_1 but also A_1 and B_2 may form coalitions competitively to exploit different exchange ratios. This kind of arbitrage activity is the basis of Jevons's law of indifference. Allocation E, which is the solution to Jevons's equations of exchange, is the only allocation that is not blocked by arbitrage leading to the law of indifference. Taking the divisibility of trade into consideration, furthermore, does not increase the possibility of blocking the allocation E by the misrepresentation of preferences. Once allocation E with the law of indifference is realized, any shift from it by canceling a part of transaction CE necessarily makes traders worse off, since indifference curves are tangent to CE at E.

The preceding argument for the specialized case can be generalized in several directions. First, if the exchange ratio varies, not once, but several times, we can consider that each person tries to replace to part of his transaction with an exchange ratio less favorable than the average (CH) by some transaction with an exchange ratio more favorable than the average. Second, the path of exchange with a varying exchange ratio may be different for different persons in the same trading body, though initial and end points are identical. Still, arbitrage is possible, because for each person some exchange transactions are made with an exchange ratio more favorable than CH and some other transactions are made with an exchange ratio less favorable.[8]

Why can the allocation H, which cannot be blocked by Edgeworth's coalition, be blocked by Jevons's arbitrage in four-person, two-good exchange? This is partly because the coalition considered by Edgeworth, and in modern game theory, is defined too stringently to be used in the theory of exchange. It is a sort of closed group of participants, in the sense that the group's members exchange only among themselves, being completely separated from other participants who do not belong to the coalition. In the actual world, such a pure coalition is rather rare. For example, the Second World War was fought between Axis powers (Germany, Italy, Japan, et al.) and Allied powers (France, the United Kingdom, the United States, the U.S.S.R., et al.), but these two coalitions were not closed and pure, since until the last moment diplomatic relations were kept open between Japan and the U.S.S.R. Coalition as considered in Jevons's arbitrage process is, however, of an impure and open kind, since A_2 cancels only a part of the transaction with B_2 and keeps the rest of transaction with B_2 unchanged, when A_2 forms a coalition with B_1. Since this concept of coalition is not considered by Edgeworth, and lump-sum transactions are not excluded, it is no wonder that H is not blocked. Being dependent on expectations of the behavior of nonmembers, an open coalition is certainly less stable than a closed one, though the stability of the realized coalition itself is not required to block an allocation in Edgeworth's exchange game. There is no reason, however, to exclude the possibility of open coalition, since "any individual is free to contract (at the same time) with an indefinite number" (Edgeworth 1881, p. 18).

Cournot–Walras arbitrage

Jevons's theory of exchange is, of course, not a complete theory. Zawadzki (1914, pp. 110–11) pointed out that Jevons's equations of exchange cannot be considered an attempt at complete solution of the problem of exchange, though they indicate the possibility of it, and that the multiple commodity case is not considered by Jevons.

In the case of three or more commodities, as Walras argued, "we do not have perfect or general market equilibrium unless the price of one of any two commodities in terms of the other is equal to the ratio of the prices of these two commodities in terms of any third commodity" (1954, p. 157). According to Morishima (1977, pp. 18–19), Walras had in mind two models of general market equilibrium, the *tâtonnement* model with auctioneer and *numeraire*, and the arbitrage model without auctioneer. The latter, which is similar to the one considered by Jevons, used the theory of arbitrage that had been developed by Cournot. Morishima admits, however, that "in the two-commodity case the arbitrage theory is trivial, because there is, of course, no arbitrage via a third commodity" (1977, p. 20). This implies that Walras considered only arbitrage among three or more commodities and did not consider arbitrage in the exchange of two commodities, which is the very problem of Jevons. In other words, Walras simply assumed the law of indifference, without considering how it is established through arbitrage, even in his arbitrage model.

This is also the case with Morishima and Majumdar (1978), in an ingenious article arguing that the only possible outcome in a free exchange process is the allocation E in Figure 12.2, even in a finite economy, if Cournot–Walras arbitrage behavior is assumed. Jevons's law of indifference is simply assumed there, with the result that the only possible outcome is the allocation E, even in an isolated exchange of two goods between two persons, the case in which each trading body consists of a single person. If the law of indifference itself is to be explained by arbitrage behavior, however, the allocation E is not the only outcome in an isolated exchange. For example, allocation H in Figure 12.2 cannot be blocked, since person A cannot cancel any part of transaction CK without expecting the worst case that person B retaliates by canceling all the transactions and A has to return to the allocation C. There must be at least four persons, as was argued in the preceding section, so that there is competition in each of two trading bodies and those who tried to block H can at least return to H even in the worst case.

We have to conclude, therefore, that what Jevons suggested to us has not yet been fully developed by Edgeworth and his followers, let alone by Walras and his followers.

CHAPTER 13

Menger's *Absatzfähigkeit*, a non-Walrasian theory of markets and money

In the history of economic science, Menger is usually recognized, with Jevons and Walras, in connection with the marginal revolution, the nearly simultaneous but completely independent discovery in the early 1870s of the principle of diminishing marginal utility as the fundamental building block of static microeconomics. There are, however, more dissimilarities than similarities between, say, Walras and Menger. What Menger was aiming at was rather what may be called disequilibrium process analysis than a theory of static equilibrium, which Walras gave us beautifully (Blaug 1978, pp. 309–24, and Hayek 1973). Indeed, it is Menger who is the first and the greatest non-Walrasian economist (Negishi 1985).

The role of *Unsicherheit* (uncertainty) has been emphasized sufficiently in the modern exposition of Menger's theory of money. For example, Streissler (1973a) pointed out that prices for the same physical commodities are not numbers but stochastic variables in Menger's vision. He argued that Menger suggested a liquidity theory of money, more general than the Keynesian one, on the basis of this stochastic price variation, a variation that is of little economic significance for commodities of everyday regular demand and supply but becomes important only in decisions with regard to the accumulation of wealth.[1] Although I would be the last to undervaluate the importance of the role of uncertainty in the theory of money as an asset suggested by Menger, I would rather consider as important Menger's theory of imperfect markets for commodities of everyday regular demand and supply markets and that of money as a medium of exchange, from the point of view of recent non-Walrasian models of quantity constraints.

The plan of this chapter is as follows.[2] I first sketch Menger's theories of price, the commodity, and money, as far as they are interesting from the viewpoint of recent non-Walrasian economics. I then consider Menger's *Absatzfähigkeit der Waaren*, marketability of commodities, in terms of the so-called non-*tâtonnement* process and short-side principle of non-Walrasian economics. Finally, the role of money in non-*tâtonnement* processes is considered from the viewpoint of Menger's theory of money based on marketability of commodities, and in relation to the Keynesian argument on the essential property of money given in Keynes's *General theory*.

Menger's theory of market

In contrast to Walrasian theory of price, Menger's theory of price is characterized by the fact that he considered isolated exchange and bilateral monopoly as the basic type of economic intercourse. Menger does not begin with the competitive market. He begins with the individual bargain, like Böhm-Bawerk's horse-trading, and then works round, via monopoly, to competition as a limiting case of monopolies (Streissler 1973a, b; Weber and Streissler 1973). The result is that Menger has no notion of the existence of a deterministic market price.

Thus commodities that can be exchanged against each other in certain definite quantities (a sum of money and a quantity of some other economic good, for instance), that can be exchanged for each other at will by a sale or purchase, in short, commodities that are equivalents in the objective sense of the term, do not exist – even on given markets and at a given point in time. (Menger 1950, p. 193)

We must note, above all, that Menger distinguishes the commodity from the good and has a separate chapter on the theory of commodity in his *Grundsätze*. The commodity is defined by him as follows.

Products that the producers or middlemen hold in readiness for sale are called commodities. In ordinary usage the term is limited in its application to movable tangible goods (with the exception of money).... But in scientific discourse a need was felt for a term designating all economic goods held ready for sale without regard to their tangibility, mobility, or character as products of labor, and without regard to the persons offering them for sale. A large number of economists, ... defined commodities as (economic) goods of any kind that are intended for sale. (Menger 1950, pp. 238–39)

Menger explains further the relation between goods and commodities.

From the definition just given of a commodity in the scientific sense of the term, it appears that commodity-character is nothing inherent in a good, no property of it, but merely a specific relationship of a good to the person who has command of it. With the disappearance of this relationship the commodity-character of the good comes to an end. A good ceases to be a commodity, therefore, if the economizing individual possessing it gives up his intention of disposing of it, or if it comes into the hands of a persons who do not intend to exchange it further but to consume it.... Commodity-character is therefore not only no property of goods but usually only a transitory relationship between goods and economizing individuals. Certain goods are intended by their owners to be exchanged for the goods of other economizing individuals. During their passage, sometimes through several hands, from the possession of the first into the possession of the last owner, we call them "commodities," but as soon as they have reached their economic destination (that is, as soon as they are in the hands of the ultimate consumer) they obviously cease to be commodities and become "consumption goods" in the narrow sense in which this term is opposed to the concept of "commodity." But where this does not happen, as in the case very frequently, for example, with gold, silver, etc., especially in the form of coins, they naturally continue to be "commodity" as long as they continue in the relationship responsible for their commodity-character. (Menger 1950, pp. 240–41)

But why do some goods cease to be commodities quickly while coins never cease to be commodities? In other words, why is it that little metal disks apparently useless as such can be commodities and exchanged against useful things that can become consumption goods? This is because of the different degrees of *Absatzfähigkeit der Waaren* – salability or marketability of commodities. Money is the most marketable of all commodities: "*The theory of money necessarily presupposes a theory of the saleableness of goods*" [italics in the original].[3] Degree of *Absatzfähigkeit* is defined by Menger as "the greater or less facility with which they [commodities] can be disposed of at a market at any convenient time at current purchasing prices, or with less or more diminution of the same" (Menger 1892, pp. 243–44).

Behind this definition is Menger's observation that the smaller the difference between the higher buying price and lower selling prices, the more marketable the commodity usually is.

The most cursory observation of market-phenomena teaches us that it does not lie within our power, when we have bought an article for a certain price, to sell it again forthwith at that same price.... The price at which any one can at pleasure buy a commodity at given market and a given point of time, and the price at which he can dispose of the same at pleasure, are two essentially different magnitudes. (Menger 1892, p. 243)

Prices vary between different places, between different times, and between different people. But, as far as the difference between the buying and selling prices is concerned, it is to the determinate direction and by no means stochastic, in spite of Streissler's (1973a) emphasis on the stochastic price variation in Menger's theory of price.

Although Menger detailedly described circumstances upon which the degree of *Absatzfähigkeit* of commodities depends, what is interesting from our point of view is the fact that it depends on whether the relevant market is well organized or poorly organized.

If the competition for one commodity is poorly organized and there is danger therefore that the owners will be unable to sell their holdings of the commodity at economic prices, at a time when this danger does not exist at all, or not in the same degree, for the owners of other commodities, it is clear that this circumstance will be responsible for a very important difference between the marketability of that commodity and all others. . . . Commodities for which an organized market exists can be sold without difficulty by their owners at prices corresponding to the general economic situation. But commodities for which there are poorly organized markets change hands at inconsistent prices, and sometimes cannot be disposed of at all. (Menger 1950, pp. 248–49)

Walras assumed that the market is well organized. Menger's theory of commodity for which the market is poorly organized and for which marketability is not high suggests that Menger's is a non-Walrasian theory of market. Menger's criticism on pre-Mengerian economics, that "investigation into the phenomena of price has been directed almost exclusively to the quantities of the commodities exchanged, and not as well to the greater or less facility with which wares may be disposed of at normal prices" (Menger 1892, 1950, p. 242), can also be applied to Walrasian or neoclassical economics. In other words, Menger's theory of marketability of commodities is a first attempt at non-Walrasian economics.

Absatzfähigkeit and the short-side principle

Recent study of non-Walrasian economics was pioneered, in a sense, by the studies of non-*tâtonnement* processes in the early 1960s. This is a generalization of Walrasian *tâtonnement* process which is, in a simple case of exchange economy, described by

$$dp_j/dt = \sum_i x_{ij}(p_1, \ldots, p_m) - \sum_i \bar{x}_{ij}, \quad j = 1, \ldots, m \tag{13.1}$$

where p_j, t, x_{ij} and $\bar{x}_{ij}$ denote, respectively, the price of jth good, time, gross demand for the jth good by the ith individual, and the initial holding of the jth good by the ith individual. In other words, the rate of price change of a good is proportional to the excess demand in the market of that good. Gross demands are obtained by maximizing utility being subject to budget constraints,

$$\sum_j p_j x_{ij} = \sum_j p_j \bar{x}_{ij} \tag{13.2}$$

and can be expressed as functions of prices only, since in *tâtonnement* exchange transactions are ruled out at disequilibria where prices are changing, and therefore $\bar{x}_{ij}$'s remain constant. If we permit disequilibrium transactions, $\bar{x}_{ij}$'s are no longer constants and x_{ij}'s are functions not only of prices but also of $\bar{x}_{ij}$'s. A non-*tâtonnement* process, then, may be described by

$$dp_j/dt = \sum_i x_{ij}(p, \bar{x}_i) - \sum_i \bar{x}_{ij}, \quad j = 1, \ldots, m \tag{13.3}$$

and

$$d\bar{x}_{ij}/dt = F_{ij}(p, \bar{x}), \quad i = 1, \ldots, n, j = 1, \ldots, m \tag{13.4}$$

where $\bar{x}_i$ is an m-vector of $\bar{x}_{i1}, \ldots, \bar{x}_{im}$ and $\bar{x}$ is an $n \times m$ matrix of $\bar{x}_{ij}$'s. In other words, stock of a good held by an individual changes as a result of disequilibrium exchange transactions that depend on prices and the distribution of goods among individuals.

In the study of non-*tâtonnement* processes, many transaction rules are proposed so as to specify F_{ij} functions in (13.4). A rule called Hahn's rule is to impose the following conditions on F_{ij}'s.

$$\text{sign}(x_{ij} - \bar{x}_{ij}) = \text{sign}(\sum_i x_{ij} - \sum_i \bar{x}_{ij}), \quad \text{if } x_{ij} - \bar{x}_{ij} \neq 0 \tag{13.5}$$

The implication of the rule is this. When there exists aggregate excess supply of the jth good, all individuals demanding the jth good will be able to satisfy their demand, while some supplying individuals will be left with unsold goods. Therefore, after exchange, there remain only negative individual excess (net) demands or positive excess (net) supplies. Similarly, when there exists aggregate excess demand for the jth good, then all supplying individuals will find they can supply all they had planned, while some demanding individuals will have their demand unsatisfied, with the result that individual excess demands are all nonnegative (Hahn and Negishi 1962; Negishi 1962).

This rule reappears in fixprice models or quantity constraint models of recent studies of non-Walrasian economics as the short-side principle that transaction equals the minimum of supply and demand. Following Benassy (1978), consider the situation where quantities are supposed to react infinitely faster than prices so that we have to study equilibria at fixed prices. Since trades are allowed to occur at non-Walrasian (nonequilibrium) prices, there will be in general excess demands or supplies on the different market, and some traders will have to be constrained. When

$$Z_h = \sum_i z_{ih} \neq 0 \tag{13.6}$$

where z_{ih} denotes the ith individual's excess demand in the hth market, a rationing scheme is necessary to obtain actual transaction $\bar{z}_{ih}$. Since actual transactions must sum up to zero, it is assumed that

$$\bar{z}_{ih} = F_{ih}(z_{lh}, \ldots, z_{nh}), \quad \sum_i F_{ih}(z_{lh}, \ldots, z_{nh}) = 0 \tag{13.7}$$

A number of hypotheses are made on F_{ih} functions, among which we have the short-side principle that traders on the short side (suppliers if there is excess demand, demanders if there is excess supply) can realize their demands,

$$\bar{z}_{ih} = z_{ih} \quad \text{if } Z_h z_{ih} \leqq 0 \tag{13.8}$$

It is clear that this is nothing but Hahn's rule in the study of non-*tâtonnement* process (Negishi 1982a).

From the point of view of Menger's *Absatzfähigkeit*, the short-side principle can be seen that commodities are highly marketable when its suppliers are on the short side of the relevant market and not so marketable when they are on the long side of the market. Unlike those recently working in non-Walrasian economics, however, Menger was not so much interested in the fixprice situation of the perfectly competitive market as in the flexprice case of the imperfectly competitive market (Streissler 1973a, b; Weber and Streissler 1973). In the latter type of the market, we can consider that suppliers are likely to be on the long side of the market in general, in the sense that they wish to sell more at the current price if there is enough demand.

This point was well recognized by a pioneer of modern theory of imperfect competition, Piero Sraffa (Hirase 1967, pp. 89–90; Negishi 1979a, p. 35).

It is not easy, in times of normal activity, to find an undertaking which systematically restricts its own production to an amount less than that which it could sell at the current price, and which at the same time is prevented by competition from exceeding that price. Businessmen, who regard themselves as being subject to competitive conditions, would consider absurd the assertion that the limit to their production is to be found in the internal conditions of production in their firm, which do not permit the production of a greater quantity without an increase in cost. The chief obstacle against which they have to contend when they want gradually to increase their production does not lie in the cost of production but in the difficulty of selling the larger quantity of goods without reducing the price, or without having to face increased marketing expenses. (Sraffa 1926, p. 543)

In Figure 13.1, we consider the case of a firm under imperfect competition and measure the level of output x horizontally, and price p and cost vertically. A downword sloping demand curve DD is perceived by this firm, not particularly because it is a monopolist, nor because its product is differentiated, but more fundamentally because the market in which the commodity is sold is poorly organized, so that the larger amount of the commodity can be disposed of in the market only with the less favorable price. The equilibrium of the firm is shown to be at A, or $(\bar{p}, \bar{x})$, with the marginal revenue MR equalized with marginal cost MC at $\bar{x}$. At the current price $\bar{p}$, the firm wishes to sell as much as x', but is quantitatively constrained at $\bar{x}$, since there is not enough demand. There exists

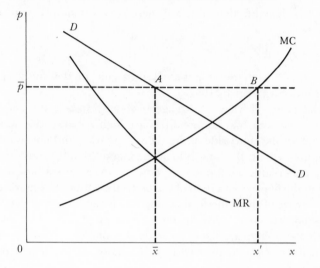

Figure 13.1

an implicit excess supply AB or $x' - \bar{x}$, and the marketability of the commodity is not high. The only exception is the case where the firm is at the full capacity and MC curve is perpendicular at $\bar{x}$ so that A and B coincide. In the poorly organized market, therefore, the commodity is not highly marketable when firms are operating at less than full capacity.[4]

There are two kinds of demand and supply: regular, stable demand and supply, and irregular, casual demand and supply. For example, the demand curve in Figure 13.1 is concerned with regular demand as perceived by a regular supplier. When A and B do not coincide and there exists an excess supply of regular supplier, casual demand will be easily satisfied by regular suppliers with current price $\bar{p}$. Casual supply has to compete with regular excess supply to catch casual demand and will not be easily satisfied, unless price is reduced.[5] The marketability of the relevant commodity is low and the resale price of those casual suppliers who want to get rid of the commodity they just bought will be much lower than the price at which they bought as regular demanders. When, on the other hand, A and B coincide with supply inelasticity of regular suppliers, casual suppliers do not have to compete with regular suppliers to catch demand and their supplies will be easily satisfied. The marketability of the commodity is high and there is no gap between resale price of those casual suppliers who wanted to get rid of the commodity they just bought and the price at which they bought.

Table 13.1

	Good (price)		
	Cow (3)	Bread (1)	Bean (1)
Excess demand			
Jack	−1	3	0
Witch	2	1	−7
Market	1	4	−7

A theory of money

Besides the short-side principle, another plausible rule for a disequilibrium transaction is that of voluntary exchange. By this rule, no one can oblige any agent to exchange more than he wants, or in the other direction. Following Benassy (1978), this rule requires that

$$|\tilde{z}_{ih}| \leqq |z_{ih}| \quad \text{and} \quad \tilde{z}_{ih}\, z_{ih} \geqq 0 \tag{13.9}$$

This rule conflicts with the short-side principle, however, unless there exists a medium of exchange. Consider the example given in Table 13.1.[6] The short-side principle requires that a transaction should be made so as to make the sign of individual excess demands identical to that of market excess demand. Jack's supply of a cow should, therefore, be satisfied. This must be paid by the Witch either with bread or beans. In the former case, the Witch has involuntarily to supply bread, which she would rather demand. In the latter case, Jack has to accept beans, which he does not wish to have. At this stage it is possible that the utility of a trader has been decreased by the transaction.[7] Price, of course, changes. Since the price of beans is to be decreased relative to the price of bread, it will eventually be possible for the Witch to regain bread by supplying some beans to Jack, or that Jack can part with beans to accept bread from the Witch. In other words, either bread or beans plays the role of medium of exchange: money.

Arrow and Hahn (1971, pp. 326–46) introduced money explicitly into the non-*tâtonnement* process using Hahn's rule (Equation (13.5) here), they ruled out direct exchange of nonmonetary goods, and they required the voluntary exchange rule only for nonmonetary goods.[8] What they call "target excess demand," $x_{ij} - \bar{x}_{ij}$, is obtained by maximizing utility $U_i(x_{i1}, \ldots, x_{im}, m_i)$ being subject to

$$\sum_j p_j x_{ij} + m_i = \sum_j p_j \bar{x}_{ij} + \bar{m}_i \tag{13.10}$$

where m_i and $\bar{m}_i$ denote the demand and current stock of money of the ith individual, respectively. Active excess demand is, on the other hand, obtained by taking the constraint

$$\sum_j p_j (x_{ij} - \bar{x}_{ij})^+ \leqq \bar{m}_i \tag{13.11}$$

into consideration, where the superscript plus sign implies that negative $(x_{ij} - \bar{x}_{ij})$ is replaced by 0. This constraint implies ruling out of direct exchange between nonmonetary goods and requires that one cannot purchase goods without having cash on hand. Active excess demands A_{ij}'s are identical to target excess demands $(x_{ij} - \bar{x}_{ij})$'s if they are negative or unless the condition (13.11) is binding. If it is binding, it is assumed that

$$A_{ij} = (x_{ij} - \bar{x}_{ij})\bar{m}_i / \sum_j p_j (x_{ij} - \bar{x}_{ij})^+ \tag{13.12}$$

In other words, positive target excess demands are reduced proportionally to active demands. Now the right-hand side of (13.3) is replaced by $\sum_i A_{ij}$ and Hahn's rule is given as

$$A_{ij} \sum_i A_{ij} > 0, \quad \text{if } A_{ij} \neq 0 \tag{13.13}$$

But why is a good chosen as the money? Recent neoclassical explanations in the tradition of Walras assume the existence of a transaction cost for each good as the exogenously given data and consider money as the best good chosen by people in terms of these costs (Niehans 1971; Karni 1973; Niehans 1978, p. 113). It is unsatisfactory that these costs, being given exogenously, are concerned with the physical characteristics of goods and not with the conditions of the markets where goods are exchanged as commodities. As Nagatani (1978, pp. 118–30) argued, then, it is more appropriate to use Menger's degrees of marketability of commodities and explain the money as the most marketable commodity.

For this purpose we have to reformulate our exposition in the previous section of Menger's marketability of commodities in terms of the short-side principle that supplying firms are in general on the long side of the market. The reason is that the income account of firms already presupposes the existence of money, which, however, is to be explained (Niehans 1978, p. 125). Let us, therefore, consider an exchange economy where an individual is regularly supplying a certain good in exchange for whatever other goods he is in need of. Suppose the elasticity of supply is not zero in the sense that the amount of supply, denoted by x, can be increased at disutility, say, by working harder. Since the markets are poorly organized, the exchange ratio between the good(s) the individual needs and the good he supplies is (are) assumed to be a diminishing function (functions) of x. His utility to be maximized is denoted by

$$U(G(x)x, x) \qquad (13.14)$$

where U is increasing with respect to the first argument, the amount of other good(s) the individual can obtain in exchange, decreasing with respect to the second argument, the amount of the good he supplies, and $G(x)$ is the exchange ratio and diminishing with respect to x.

The maximization of (13.14) with respect to x gives

$$G(x) (1 + xG'(x)/G(x)) = -U_2(G(x)x, x)/U_1(G(x)x, x) \qquad (13.15)$$

where G' denotes the derivative of G, and U_i denotes the partial derivative of U with respect to the ith argument. Condition (13.15) can also be described by Figure 13.1, if p is replaced by G, and curve DD, MR and MC are considered to describe $G(x)$, the right-hand side and the left-hand side of (13.15), respectively. The equilibrium of the individual under consideration is at A and he is on the long side of the market in the sense that he wishes to, but cannot, supply more than $\bar{x}$ at the current exchange ratio.

Since the relevant good has thus limited marketability as a commodity, it cannot be received by other individuals as a medium of exchange. If an individual accepts this good once, he cannot dispose of it easily at the same exchange ratio, since he is a casual supplier and has no market share while regular supplier(s) can supply more at the same exchange ratio. The possible exception is the case where no suppliers can increase supplies – that is, the supply elasticity is zero – and the MC curve in Figure 13.1 is perpendicular at $\bar{x}$. Only commodities that have such a supply condition can enjoy high marketability and be accepted as a medium of exchange by individuals who have no intention of consuming the commodity themselves but plan to dispose of it subsequently in exchange for other commodities they wish to consume.

This requirement for money to be of zero supply elasticity is well recognized by Keynes in the chapter titled "The essential properties of interest and money" in the *General theory*, where supply elasticity is divided into elasticity of production and elasticity of substitution.[9]

Money has, both in the long and in the short period, a zero, or at any rate a very small, elasticity of production, so far as the power of private enterprise is concerned, as distinct from the monetary authority; ... elasticity of production meaning, in this context, the response of the quantity of labor applied to producing it to a rise in the quantity of labor which a unit of it will command. Money, that is to say, cannot be readily produced; ... labor cannot be turned on at will by entrepreneurs to produce money in increasing quantities as its price rises in terms of the wage-unit. In the case of an inconvertible managed currency this condition is strictly satisfied. But in the case of gold-standard currency it is also approximately so, in the sense that the maximum proportional addition to the quantity of labor which can be thus employed is very small, except indeed in a country of which gold-mining is the major industry. (Keynes 1936, p. 230)

Obviously, however, the above condition is satisfied, not only by money, but by all pure rent-factors, the production of which is completely inelastic. A second condition, therefore, is required to distinguish money from other rent elements. The second *differentia* of money is that it has an elasticity of substitution equal, or nearly equal, to zero; which means that as the exchange value of money rises there is no tendency to substitute some other factor for it; ... except, perhaps, to some trifling extent, where the money-commodity is also used in manufacture or the arts. This follows from the peculiarity of money that its utility is solely derived from its exchange-value, so that the two rise and fall *pari passu*, with the result that as the exchange value of money rises there is no motive or tendency, as in the case of rent-factors, to substitute some other factor for it. (p. 231)

It must be emphasized, however, that the importance of the zero supply elasticity as an essential property of money lies not so much in the fact that the supply cannot be increased when the price is bid up as in the fact that there is no potential excess supply at the current price, the potential excess supply meaning that the supply can be increased even if price is kept unchanged at the current level.

In a well-organized market considered in Walrasian economics, *DD* in Figure 13.1 is horizontal and identical to MR so that *A* and *B* coincide. Every commodity has high marketability and, in this sense, can be accepted as a medium of exchange, even if MC is not perpendicular. If a special commodity called money is introduced, therefore, its role is limited in Walrasian economics.

CHAPTER 14

The Marshallian foundation of macroeconomic theories

The aim of macroeconomics is, particularly after Keynes's *General theory*, to explain changes in the aggregate output or employment as well as those in price level. Currently, we have two competing theories of macroeconomics: the monetarists' equilibrium theory and Keynesian disequilibrium theory. The former revives the traditional quantity theory of money and emphasizes the importance of changes in absolute price level, but extends the quantity theory so as to explain changes in aggregate output and employment, induced by changes in prices, while the latter claims the existence of involuntary unemployment and argues that changes in the effective demand induce changes in aggregate output and employment. The aim of this chapter is to consider how microeconomically such changes in aggregate output and employment can be explained in monetarist as well as in Keynesian theories.

Microeconomics, or price theory, is currently dominated by Walrasian theory, in which the real theory and monetary theory can be dichotomized and money can be neutral. Such a possibility of dichotomy and neutrality is, as we shall see, a necessary consequence of Walrasian procedure, in which an abstract nonmonetary real economic system is first considered before money is introduced into consideration. No one can deny the fact that in this way we can see better, in a sense, the working of the real economic forces hidden behind the monetary curtain of contemporary economy. We have nevertheless to pay the cost, because the role of money is extremely limited in the Walrasian system. After the real economic system is solved without using money by *tâtonnement*, the smooth functioning of relative prices, no role is left to money when it is introduced but the determination of absolute prices. In other words, any changes in the supply of money are absorbed in changes in the price level, with the level of output and employment unchanged, even in the short run.[1] Another by-product of aggregate relative price *tâtonnement* economy is that its demands and supplies are completely symmetric, so that there can be no Keynesian equilibrium with demand and supply unequalized.

It is clear that the Walrasian theory cannot be a microeconomic foundation of macroeconomics, irrespective of whether macroeconomics is monetarist or Keynesian. The natural question is, then, whether the Marshallian theory of microeconomics cannot be a microeconomic foundation of macroeconomics. As we shall see, unlike Walras, Marshall did not dichotomize his system into an abstract moneyless system and a monetary system. In Marshall's system, money does exist from the beginning, though its purchasing power is assumed to be constant when relative prices are considered. We can start from Marshall's microeconomic theory of a non-*tâtonnement* market to construct a microeconomic foundation to Keynesian macroeconomics. When Marshall considered trade cycles, on the other hand, he emphasized the importance of the changes in absolute price level with accompanying changes in relative prices, which have influences in industrial production and employment. We can also say, therefore, that Marshall paved the way to the microeconomic foundation of monetarist macroeconomics.

In the next section I explain in detail why Walrasian economics cannot be a microeconomic foundation of macroeconomics, which aims to explain changes in aggregate output and employment. Marshall's theory of trade cycle is then documented, its relation to what Keynes called monetary economics is discussed, and its similarity to recent monetarism is pointed out. Finally, I explain Marshall's non-*tâtonnement* theory of the market and argue that it suggests a theory of the firm facing a kinked demand curve, which can be a microeconomic foundation to Keynesian macroeconomics.

The classical dichotomy and the neutrality of money

Walras (1954) developed the dichotomized system of neoclassical economics most systematically.[2] Complicated phenomena can be studied scientifically, Walras said, only if the rule of proceeding from the simple to the complex is always observed. Walras first decomposes a complicated real economy into several fundamental elements like individuals, firms, consumer goods, factors of production, newly produced capital goods, and money. He then composes a simple model of an economy by picking up a very limited number of such elements, namely individuals and consumer goods, disregarding the existence of other elements. This is the model of pure exchange, where goods to be exchanged among individuals are simply assumed to be available to them and not considered as produced at cost. A journey from the simple to the complex proceeds from this simple, though closed and self-compact, model by introducing new elements one by one. First, firms and factors of production are introduced, in the model of production, where service of capital is available, but investment or the production of new capital goods simply does not exist. Then newly produced capital goods and credit are introduced, in the model of credit and capital formation, where a kind of bond is introduced but still there is no money. Finally, money and inventories are introduced, in the model of circulation and money. It should be noted that in the Walrasian world, in the theory of exchange, the theory of production, and the theory of credit and capital formation, there exists no money at all, until it is finally introduced in the theory of circulation and money. Real theories and monetary theory are completely dichotomized.

The reason or justification for such dichotomy is that the fundamental significance of such elements as exchanges among individuals, firms, production, investment, and the rate of interest, can be considered without taking money into consideration. In some sense this is certainly true. A by-product of this procedure of considering real economy first without introducing money is, however, the ingenious device of *tâtonnement*, on which Walras had to rely to solve the general equilibrium problems of nonmonetary economics. This device, although successful for solving problems of general equilibrium without using money and by so doing to make clear the significance of real economic factors, is responsible for the limited role of money when introduced later in the Walrasian system and for the resulting negligence of monetary influence on the allocation of real economic resources.

In Walrasian nonmonetary models, – those of exchange, of production, and of credit and capital formation – there are many individuals and many firms as well as many goods (including bond) and many factors of production. A general equilibrium is a state in which not only each individual (firm) achieves the maximum obtainable satisfaction (profit) under given conditions but also demand and supply are equalized in all markets. How can we make such a situation possible without introducing money? It seems in general almost impossible to satisfy all individuals by barter exchange, unless mutual coincidence of wants accidentally prevails everywhere. The solution suggested by Walras is *tâtonnement*, in which we can find the essence of Walrasian economics.

Suppose all the individuals and the representatives of firms meet in a big hall. Since all of them are assumed to be competitive price takers, it is convenient to assume the existence of an auctioneer whose sole role is to determine relative prices. At first, the auctioneer announces all relative prices (including the rate of interest) at random. Individuals and firms make decisions on the supply and demand of all goods, factors and bond, assuming that prices called by auctioneer are unchanged and whatever amount they wish can actually be supplied and demanded at these prices. If the total demand equaled the total supply for each good (including factors and bond), the exchange would take place (or the contract is made) at these prices and the problem would be solved. If not, on the other hand, there should not be any exchange taking place even for goods for which total demand is equal to total supply and every contract, if any, should be canceled among those who have already found the other party of the exchange. The auctioneer cancels relative prices that fail to establish a general equilibrium and announces new relative prices by following the law of supply and demand, thus raising the price of goods for which the demand is larger than the supply and lowering the price of goods for which demand is smaller. The same procedure is repeated until a general equilibrium is established. Actual exchanges take place and enforceable contracts are made only when all parties can realize their respective plans of demand and supply.

Preliminary adjustments of prices in *tâtonnement* can be very short if the auctioneer is smart enough. We can, then, ignore this process and safely consider that economic activities like exchange, production, and consumption are carried out continuously under the condition of market equilibrium. In other words, nonmonetary *tâtonnement* is a logically extreme, ideal model of a non-*tâtonnement* economic process in which relative prices are rapidly and smoothly adjusted so that we can safely disregard the effect of economic activities in market disequilibrium. The point is not the institutionally unrealistic assumption of an auctioneer but the basic supposition that resources are to be fully employed as a result of price adjustment.

Since money is not utilized in Walrasian nonmonetary models, demand and supply of a good are completely symmetric. Goods can be bought by goods and there is no problem that "the merchant finds it generally more easy to buy goods with money than to buy money with goods" (Smith 1976, p. 438). According to Walras: "The effective demand for or offer of one commodity in exchange for another is equal respectively to the effective offer of or demand for the second commodity multiplied by its price in them of the first. . . . No one ever makes an offer simply for the sake of offering. The only reason one offers anything is that one cannot demand anything without making an offer. Offer is only a consequence of demand" (Walras 1954, p. 23).

After working out the *tâtonnement* of nonmonetary models, Walras introduced money into his system in the model of circulation and money, but he still retained *tâtonnement* in his monetary model, with the result that the role of money is limited only to the determination of absolute prices, that is, prices in terms of itself. In other words, changes in output and employment cannot be explained by monetary factors, since they have no influence on allocations of real resources. Since exchanges are carried out only under the condition of market equilibrium, where every individual can buy or sell whatever amount he wishes at an unchanging price, there is no need to take changes in price into consideration and no problem of marketing difficulty in a *tâtonnement* economy. Almost any good, unless physically inconvenient, can serve as a medium of exchange. Money, which is the measure of value, can be the sole medium of exchange only in the case of non-*tâtonnement*, disequilibrium exchanges. In view of the marketing difficulty in such exchanges, the use of money is considered by people to be more advantageous than other goods, the changing prices of which make them not generally acceptable as means of payment. It is only in such a case, that "the merchant finds it generally more easy to buy goods with money than to buy money with goods" (Smith 1976, p. 438).

As Morishima (1977, pp. 123–24) emphasized, there is a third function of money, the store of value, in addition to the two functions considered, the measure of value and the medium of exchange. Those who, like Patinkin (1956), discussed the classical dichotomy may be criticized for having failed to pay due attention to the store of value function of money in the Walrasian system. One might be able to point out the similarity between the Walrasian concept of *encaisse désirée* and the Keynesian concept of liquidity preference. Even if we take the store of value function of money into consideration by introducing money not into the model of exchange or that of production but into the model of credit and capital formation, as Walras himself did, however, we cannot get rid of the dichotomy and neutrality provided that we still retain the *tâtonnement* assumption. Relative prices including the rate of interest and the allocation of resources that are fully employed are not changed by the introduction of money, whose function includes the store of value, into the model of credit and capital formation. Morishima skillfully utilized the neutrality of money to prove the existence of a general equilibrium in the model of circulation and money on the basis of a general equilibrium in the model of credit and capital formation (Morishima et al. 1973, p. 130; Morishima 1977, pp. 171, 184). Even if preference for liquidity is recognized, Walrasian equilibrium in the model of circulation and money is quite different from Keynesian equilibrium, since prices are flexible and resources are fully employed in the former whereas prices are rigid and resources may not be fully employed in the latter. Liquidity preference itself is generally not responsible for the demand deficiency unless it is coupled with price rigidity, which is explained elsewhere (Negishi 1979a, chs. 7, 8), only in the non-*tâtonnement* process, where individuals have to take into consideration the effects of price change and marketing difficulty.

Marshall's monetary theory of trade cycle

Keynes argued in his contribution to a Festschrift for Spiethoff, titled "A monetary theory of production," which played an important role in Keynes's movement from *Treatise* to *General theory*, that

the main reason why the problem of crises is unsolved, or at any rate why this theory is so unsatisfactory, is to be found in the lack of what might be termed a *monetary theory of production*. . . . An economy, which uses money but uses it merely as a neutral link between transactions in real things and real assets and does not allow it to enter into motives or decisions, might be called a *real-exchange economy*. The theory which I desiderate would deal, in contradiction to this, with an economy in which money plays a part of its own and affects motives and decisions and is, in short, one of the operative factors in the situation, so that the course of events cannot be predicted, either in the long period or in the short, without a knowledge of the behaviour of money between the first state and the last. And it is this which we ought to mean when we speak of a *monetary economy*. . . . it is my belief that the far-reaching and in some respects fundamental differences between the conclusions of a monetary economy and those of the more simplified real-exchange economy have been greatly underestimated by the exponents of the traditional economics; with the result that machinery of thought with which real-exchange economics has equipped the minds of practitioneers in the world of affairs, and also of economists themselves, has led in practice to many erroneous conclusions and policies. . . . I am saying that booms and depressions are phenomena peculiar to an economy in which money is not neutral. (Keynes 1973, pp. 408–11)

It should be noted that money, though it is neutral, does exist in the real-exchange economy in the sense of Keynes, which is therefore different from an abstract, moneyless subsystem of dichotomized Walrasian economics.

It is clear that Walrasian theory as a whole, dichotomized into real and monetary subsystems, is a typical theory of a real-exchange economy in the sense of Keynes. While money is introduced after relative prices are determined in a Walrasian system, in a Marshallian system money does exist from the beginning, but its purchasing power is assumed constant when relative prices are considered. Keynes argued that

Marshall's *Principles of economics* is avowedly concerned with a real-exchange economy. . . . Marshall expressly states (*Principles*, pp. 61, 62) that he is dealing with *relative* exchange values. The proposition that the prices of a ton of lead and a ton of tin are £15 and £90 means no more to him in this context than that the value of a ton of tin in terms of lead is six tons. "We may throughout this volume," he explains, "neglect possible changes in the general purchasing power of money. Thus the price of anything will be taken as representative of its exchange value relative to *things* in general." . . . In short, though money is present and is made use of for convenience, it may be concerned to cancel out for the purposes of most of the general conclusions of the *Principles*. . . . Now the conditions required for the "neutrality" of money, in the sense in which this is assumed in Marshall's *Principles of economics*, are I suspect, precisely the same as those which still insure that crises *do not occur*.[3] (Keynes 1973, pp. 409–11)

Since the trade cycle is given an explicit and extensive treatment by Marshall (Hansen 1951, 270–76; Wolfe 1956; Eshag 1963, pp. 72–110), however, it is somewhat unfair, as far as Marshall is concerned, to conclude that "most treaties on principles of economics are concerned mainly, if not entirely, with a real exchange economy, and – which is more peculiar – the same thing is also largely true of most treatises on the theory of money" (Keynes 1973, p. 409). Marshall's theory of the trade cycle was first developed in *Economics of industry* (jointly with his wife). He made use of it in his testimony before the Depression of Trade and Industry Commission, reproduced it in *Principles of economics*, and repeated it in *Money, credit and commerce*.[4] Although the general purchasing power of money is assumed constant in Marshall's *Principles of economics*, even there we can find the following argument.

When we come to discuss the causes of alternating periods of inflation and depression of commercial activity, we shall find that they are intimately connected with those variations in the real rate of interest which are caused by changes in the purchasing power of money. For when prices are likely to rise, people rush to borrow money and buy goods and thus help prices to rise; business is inflated and is managed recklessly and wastefully; those working on borrowed capital pay back less real capital than they borrowed, and enrich themselves at the expense of the community. When afterwards credit is shaken and prices begin to fall, everyone wants to get rid of commodities, and get hold of money which is rapidly rising in value; this makes price fall all the faster, and the further fall makes credit shrink even more, and thus for a long time prices fall because prices have fallen. (Marshall 1961, pp. 594–95)

Thus Marshall's economics consists of two parts. The first is that of a real-exchange economy in the sense of Keynes, where the general purchasing power of money is assumed to be constant, money is neutral, and crises do not occur. The second is that of a monetary economy in the sense of Keynes, where the general purchasing power of money changes, money is not neutral, and crises do occur. Because Marshall's economics as a whole is the economics of monetary economy in the sense of Keynes, it has to be able to explain changes in aggregate output and employment, as Keynes argued that "the divergence between the real-exchange economics and my desired monetary economics is, however, most marked and perhaps most important when we come to the discussion of the rate of interest and to the relation between the volume of output and amount of expenditure" (1973, p. 410). Though Marshall considered the trade cycle as changes in purchasing power of money, he was, of course, aware of a suspension of industry and unemployment induced by changes in prices.

The connection between a fall of prices and a suspension of industry requires to be worked out.... when prices are rising, the rise in the price of the finished commodity is generally more rapid than that in the price of the raw material, always more rapid than that in the price of labour; and when prices are falling, the fall in the price of the finished commodity is generally more rapid than that in the price of the raw material, always more rapid than that in the price of labour. And therefore when prices are falling the manufacturer's receipts are sometimes scarcely sufficient even to repay him for his outlay on raw material, wages, and other forms of Circulating capital; they seldom give him in addition enough to pay interest on his Fixed capital and Earnings of Management for himself.... We conclude, then, that manufacturing cannot be carried on, except at a low rate of profit or at a loss, when the prices of finished goods are low relatively to those of labour and raw material, or prices are falling (Marshall 1879, pp. 155–56; 1926, pp. 7–8; 1961, vol. II, pp. 714–16).

I agree with the general opinion that a steady upward tendency in general prices conduces a little more to the general well-being than does a tendency downwards, because it keeps industry somewhat better employed.... people of all classes, and especially of the working classes, spend their income more wisely when prices and money-wages are falling, and they think themselves worse off than they are, than when a rise of prices and money-wage leads them to exaggerate their real incomes and to be careless about their expenditure. (Marshall 1926, p. 9)

Marshall explained changes in aggregate output and employment by changes in relative prices which are induced by changes in the purchasing power of money. In Keynesian economics, price changes are largely ignored or, if considered at all, said to be induced by changes in output. Marshall's theory to explain the trade cycle cannot, therefore, be a foundation to Keynesian economics. It is, however, rather isomorphic to recent monetarist explanations of employment. Friedman (1968) describes the effects of decrease in the rate of money growth in a long-run equilibrium where prices have been stable. Prices of products respond to an unanticipated decrease in nominal demand faster than prices of factors of production (as the supply of labor is temporarily decreased by the reduction in wages to below the anticipated normal level). Therefore real wages received go up, though real wages anticipated by employees go down since at first they tend to evaluate the wages offered at the unchanged price level. This simultaneous rise *ex post* in real wages to employers and fall *ex ante* in real wages to employees enable unemployment to increase. The former effect is clearly the one emphasized by Marshall when he wrote, "the prices of finished goods are low relatively to those of labor" while Marshall also grasped somewhat vaguely the latter effect when he commented that employees "think themselves worse off than they are."[5]

Marshall's non-*tâtonnement* theory of market

Though Marshallian theory of the trade cycle with variable purchasing power of money is different from Keynesian macroeconomics, it is somewhat ironic that Marshallian price theory with constant purchasing power of money, which is a real-exchange economics in the sense of Keynes, can be a microeconomic foundation of Keynesian macroeconomics. The reason is that, unlike Walrasian price theory, it is a non-*tâtonnement* theory, made possible by fact that money does exist in Marshallian economic system even when relative prices and allocation of real resources are considered.

Let us first consider the temporary equilibrium to the Marshallian corn market (Marshall 1961, p. 332). Demand and supply schedules are given as follows.

At the price	Holders will be willing to sell	Buyers will be willing to buy
37s.	1,000 quarters	600 quarters
36s.	700	700
35s.	600	900

The price of 36 shillings is, of course, the Walrasian equilibrium price that is established by *tâtonnement* and announced by the auctioneer to individual dealers. Marshall considered, however, a non-*tâtonnement* market where actual transactions are carried out at disequilibrium price among dealers without perfect knowledge.

It is not indeed necessary for our argument that any dealers should have a thorough knowledge of the circumstances of the market. Many of the buyers may perhaps underrate the willingness of the sellers to sell, with the effect that for some time the price rules at the highest level at which any buyers can be found; and thus 500 quarters may be sold before the price sinks below 37s. But afterwards the price must begin to fall and the result will still probably be that 200 more quarters will be sold, and the market will close on a price of about 36s. For when 700 quarters have been sold, no seller will be anxious to dispose of any more except at a higher price than 36s., and no buyer will be anxious to purchase any more except at a lower price than 36s. In the same way if the sellers had underrated the willingness of the buyers to pay high price, some of them might begin to sell at the lowest price they would take, rather than their corn left on their hands, and in this case much corn might be sold at a price of 35s.; but the market would probably close on a price of 36s. and a total sale of 700 quarters. (Marshall 1961, p. 334)

Why is the same price of 36s. reached by *tâtonnement* as well as non-*tâtonnement* process? Why is price considered as independent of how transactions of disequilibria are carried out? The reason is the Marshallian assumption of constant marginal utility of money.

We tacitly assumed that the sum which purchasers were willing to pay, and which sellers were willing to take, for the seven hundredth quarter would not be affected by the question whether the earlier bargains had been made at a high or a low rate. We allowed for the diminution in the buyers' need of corn (its marginal utility to them) as the amount bought increased. But we did not allow for any appreciable change in their unwillingness to part with money (its marginal utility); we assumed that that would be practically the same whether the early payment had been at a high or a low rate. (Marshall 1961, pp. 334–35)

In the Marshallian temporary equilibrium, the level of output is constant, and therefore the total gross supply of corn is constant. As was pointed out by Hicks (1946, pp. 127–29), the assumption of constant marginal utility of money implies no income effect on demand for corn, with the result that the total gross demand for corn, including reservation demand for suppliers, is independent of the transactions carried out at disequilibria. It is clear, then, that the final equilibrium price reached by any non-*tâtonnement* process is identical to the one established by *tâtonnement*. Strictly speaking, however, there is no reason, contrary to what Marshall thought, that the cumulated volume of transactions in any non-*tâtonnement* process would also equal 700 quarters, since, as was emphasized by Walker (1969), individual net demands and supplies are not independent of the disequilibrium transactions.

Let us next consider the Marshallian short-run situation. Unlike in Walrasian *tâtonnement*, a firm in the Marshallian market is not informed by auctioneer the equilibrium price at which it can sell whatever amount of its output it likes. Since price is uncertain, the Marshallian market is, even though competitive, not homogeneous and very imperfect. Marshall's broad picture of competitive markets in the economic world of his day is as follows.

Everyone buys, and nearly every producer sells, to some extent, in a "*general*" market, in which he is on about the same footing with others around him. But nearly everyone has also some "*particular*" market; that is, some people or groups of people with whom he is in somewhat close touch; mutual knowledge and trust lead him to approach them, and them to approach him, in preference to strangers. A producer, a wholesale dealer, or a shopkeeper, who has built up a strong connexion among purchasers of his goods has a valuable property. He does not generally expect to get better prices from his clients than from others. But he expects to sell easily to them because they know and trust him; and he does not sell at low prices in order to call attention to his business, as he often does in a market where he is little known. (Marshall 1921, p. 182)

Particularly when the cost of production is diminishing, the problem of marketing and the downward sloping individual demand curve are emphasized by Marshall (Hollander, 1961).

There are many trades in which an individual producer could secure much increased "internal" economies by a great increase of his output; and there are many in which he could market that output easily; yet there are few in which he could do both. And this is not an accidental, but almost a necessary result. For in most of those trades in which the economies of production in a large scale are of first-rate importance, marketing is difficult. (Marshall 1961, p. 286)

When we are considering an individual producer, we must couple his supply curve – not with the general demand curve for his commodity in a wide market, but with the particular demand curve of his own special market. And this particular demand curve will generally be very steep; perhaps as steep as his own supply curve is likely to be, even when an increased output will given him an important increase of internal economies. (p. 458)

When the cost of production is diminishing, firms are facing demand deficiency in the sense that they wish to supply a larger amount at the unchanging price or slightly lower price. The passages just quoted therefore strongly suggest how the microeconomic foundation of Keynesian economics should be developed, since, as in the definition of Keynesian involuntary unemployment, suppliers wish to supply more at the current price or slightly lower price in Keynesian situation of demand deficiency (Keynes 1936, p. 15). The downward sloping demand curve for an individual producer considered by Marshall should, furthermore, be kinked at the current price and current sale in the sense argued in Chapter 2. It is very steep for a quantity larger than the current sale, since the producer has to sell not only in his own special or particular market but also in a wide general market, "a market where he is little known," and has to "sell at low prices in order to call attention to his business." For a quantity not larger than the current sale, on the other hand, demand is very elastic at the level of the current price, since the producer in his own particular market "does not generally expect to get better prices from his clients than from others" in the general market.

A kinked demand curve is also suggested in the model of an imperfectly competitive firm of Sraffa (1926), who in a sense still belongs to Marshallian tradition of the theory of non-*tâtonnement* process in an imperfect and nonhomogeneous, though competitive, market.

It is not easy, in times of normal activity, to find an undertaking which systematically restricts its own production to an amount less than that which it could sell at the current price, and which at the same time is prevented by competition from exceeding that price. Businessmen, who regard themselves as being subject to competitive conditions, ... The chief obstacle against which they have to contend when they want gradually to increase production does not lie in the cost of production but in the difficulty of selling the larger quantity of goods without reducing the price, or without having to face increasing market expenses. (Sraffa 1926, p. 543)

A firm in Sraffa's model has to face a kinked demand curve that is perfectly elastic at the level of current price for a quantity not larger then the current sale, since it is "prevented by competition from exceeding that price," and imperfectly elastic (downward sloping), for a quantity larger than the current sale, since the only price changes considered are price reductions due to "the difficulty of selling the larger quantity of goods without reducing the price."[6]

Our model of a competitive firm in a Keynesian situation is, at least in some formal aspects, very much like the Sweezy's (1939) model of oligopoly, though the kink in the demand curve is due to the asymmetric reaction of rival firms in the latter but due to the asymmetric reaction of customers in the former (see the Chapter 2 section, titled "Demand deficiency and increasing returns"). Sweezy's model has been criticized from the Walrasian point of view because it cannot locate the point of kink theoretically; Sweezy argued that it is the starting point of the model which is historically determined. In our case the point of kink is considered to be determined partly by price expectations historically given and partly by the level of aggregate demand, when short-run expectations are realized – that is, when current realized sale and planned level of output are equal, which is the original assumption made by Keynes in the *General theory* (Keynes 1936, pp. 50–51; Negishi 1979a, pp. 28–29).

Suppose that the starting point of a competitive firm is given as $(\bar{p}, \bar{y})$, where $\bar{p}$ denotes the current market price of the product and $\bar{y}$ denotes the current sales of the product. The firm perceives a demand curve through the starting point or a demand function, $p = p(y, \bar{p}, \bar{y})$ such that $\bar{p} = p(\bar{y}, \bar{p}, \bar{y})$ and $p = \bar{p}$ for $y \leq \bar{y}$ and $(\partial p/\partial y) < 0$ for $y > \bar{y}$, where y is the possible level of output and p is the price at which the firm expects that y can be sold. If the short-run production function of the firm is $y = F(k)$, where k denotes the input of labor service, the profit of the firm to be maximized is given as $p(y, \bar{p}, \bar{y})F(k) - wk$, where w denotes the money wage rate. When the short-term expectation is realized ($y = \bar{y}$, and therefore $p = \bar{p}$), the condition for the maximization is $p(1 + e)F'(k) \leq w$ and $pF'(k) \geq w$, at (p, y), where e is the right-hand-side elasticity of p with respect to y at $y = \bar{y}$ and $F' = (dF/dk)$. The corresponding left-hand-side elasticity of p with respect to y is zero. While $\bar{y}$ is related to the level of aggregate effective demend, $\bar{p}$ can be explained by the equilibrium price in the previous period modified by changes in the price expectation.[7]

It is clear that our microeconomic foundation of Keynesian economics is very Marshallian. Our condition for the equilibrium of the firm is "an optimality condition fulfilled ex post for the representative firm in equilibrium" (Leijonhufvud 1974), since we have abstracted from the distribution of limited demand among firms and the equilibria of firms and of markets cannot be separated. When the conditions are satisfied with strict inequalities, firms operate involuntarily under capacity because they wish to supply more at the current price or the price slightly lower.[8] An increase in $\bar{y}$, unless it is very large, is absorbed in the increase in y, without any changes in p, to explain which is the aim of microeconomic foundation of Keynesian economics.

Unlike the case of monetarism, no established standard theory of microeconomic foundation has yet been developed in the case of Keynesian microeconomics. There is, however, a growing literature and some interesting, though still fragmentary, ideas and suggestions have been offered.[9] Together with some of these, the theory of a kinked demand curve can be, I believe, an important cornerstone of the microeconomic foundation of Keynesian macroeconomics to be established in the near future.

Notes

1. Anti-neoclassical or non-Walrasian economic theories

1 For the significance of astronomy to Adam Smith, see Smith (1967, pp. 768–69), for the analogy Smith drew between natural philosophy (science) and moral philosophy (social science). See also Schumpeter (1954, pp. 182, 185); Thomson (1965) and Jaffé (1977).

2 The fact that Copernicus had studied and been influenced by the ancient theories of astronomy is confirmed in the letter that he prefixed to the *De Revolutionibus* (see Kuhn 1957, pp. 140–41). See also Kuhn 1957, p. 143, where Kuhn added that Copernicus even refers, in his earlier manuscript, to Aristarchus, whose sun-centered universe very closely resembles his own.

3 There is also a problem whether unemployment in the mercantilist era was similar in character to unemployment recurring in industrialized economies. See Heckscher (1955, pp. 340–58, especially pp. 354–56), and see Hutchison (1978, p. 130).

4 Pythagorean and Aristarchan theories of the world system made a progressive comeback in the Copernican revolution after 2,000 years of seemingly permanent defeat. Similarly, mercantilist and Malthusian ideas have been revived in the Keynesian revolution after a hundred years of classical and neoclassical economics, which had treated them as imbecile, while the quantity theory of money returned as monetarism with a new theory to explain changes in employment which pre-Keynesian quantity theory had not.

5 "For Walras, capital consisted narrowly of fixed capital; i.e., goods which enter production but are not used up in a single time period. Prior accumulation of the commodities which constituted variable capital was thus no longer required by economic theory. Accordingly, the responsibility formerly assigned the capitalist class dropped from sight and received no further attention beyond the Austrian school" (Eagly 1974, pp. 7–8).

2. Adam Smith and increasing returns in a competitive situation

1 It is so even if Smith had not a very complete theory of the firm. See Hollander (1973, p. 143).

2 In other words, the effectual demand is the demand at the natural price (natural price is defined subsequently).

3 In other words, it cannot be all sold at the natural price.

4 Hollander (1973, p. 143) argued that Smith simply takes for granted that the

size of the average productive unit will rise along with the expansion of the industry.

5 We may consider that both the long-run average cost and the short-run average cost curves pass through point E in Figure 2.1, because the natural price is the long-run normal cost.

6 In other words, a firm with an internal economy of scale is always faced with demand deficiency. See Weddenpohl (1978).

7 The capacity of, say, a pipeline can be quadrupled by doubling its diameter; costs are more nearly related to diameter than is capacity, however. This space principle applies equally to nondurable items like plastic containers or paper bags no less than to durable equipment like steel pipes.

3. A reconstruction of Smith's doctrine on the natural order of investment

1 See the General Introduction of Smith (1976, p. 32). As for the role of the division of labor in Adam Smith's *The wealth of nations*, see the introductory section of Chapter 2 of this book. The significance of Smith's rudimentary equilibrium theory was emphasized by Schumpeter, but it seems to me that it lies not so much in general equilibrium as in the recognition of positive profit in equilibrium. See Schumpeter (1954, p. 189), Kobayashi (1977, p. 151), and the introductory section of Chapter 5.

2 See Bowley (1975). For the division of labor and capital accumulation we owe to Professor Hirotaka Kato of Soka University valuable suggestions.

3 Productive labor is the labor employed by the capital that advances the wage costs. In other words, it is used in the production of goods where the period of production is not negligible. See Chapter 7 of this book and Smith (1976, pp. 330–32).

4 Even if input coefficients and relative preference on two goods remain unchanged, allocation of labor may be changed, since labor productivities are changed by the division of labor.

5 The progressive division of industries and specialization of firms in industries is an essential part of the process by which increasing returns are realized. There is a strong resemblance between this concept of process and the later development of the theory of the capitalistic process of production by Böhm-Bawerk (Young 1928; Bowley 1975). To the division of labor and the number of specialized subindustries of the former corresponds the roundabout production and the length of the period of production of the latter.

6 Since capital of traders replaces the capital of producers, required capital may be accumulated in the hands of traders.

7 For other notations, see the explanation of Equations (3.1) to (3.3). Equations (3.4) to (3.7) describe the situation with international division of labor, where the first (second) country is specialized in the production of the first (second) good and imports the second (first) good for materials and provisions for laborers from the second (first) country. International distribution of surplus goods is not specified.

4. The possibility of a falling rate of profit under diminishing cost

1 See Shibata (1934; 1935, pp. 236–42; 1939), Okishio (1961; 1965, pp. 111–48, especially pp. 111–14, 142–48; and 1977, pp. 250–52). Organic composition corresponds roughly to the capital–labor ratio of neoclassical economics and is defined as the ratio of constant capital (materials, depreciation of fixed capital, etc.) and variable capital (advance of wages), and the rate of profit is defined as the ratio of profit to the sum of constant and variable capitals.

2 See Shaikh (1978) and Okishio (1965, pp. 139–142). Nakatani (1980) argued that rising real wage is expected as an effect of lower prices caused by adoption of a technique with higher organic composition. Even so, for a single capitalist firm whose contribution to this effect is negligible, rising real wage is a cause and higher organic composition is its effect.

3 Shibata claimed that a simplified version of the general-equilibrium system of Lausanne school is very useful for studying economic theories. See Shibata (1935, introduction).

4 I owe to Professor Yasuhiro Sakai of Tsukuba University the suggestion that a Marxist economic system should not be considered as a system of constant returns to scale. For dd and DD curves, see Chamberlin (1948, pp. 90–91). See also the section titled Dynamics of the rate of profit, later in this chapter.

5 For Japanese literature for Marx on competition, see Hirase (1967, pp. 22, 102) and Hishiyama (1965).

6 See also Hishiyama (1965), though he considered not merely internal scale economy, but rather a U-shaped cost curve.

7 For the extension of the case of multiple goods in general, see this chapter's final section.

8 If p and q are increased proportionally, G is also increased proportionally. Since p is constant, however, G increases less than proportionally. This is because G is an increasing function of p. Since r is reduced, furthermore, t must be increased so as to increase G further and to keep Equation (4.2) satisfied.

9 For the durability aspect of the fixed capital with respect to the Shibata–Okishio theorem, see Kamisato (1963), Nakatani (1980), Okishio (1965, pp. 142–43), and Shaikh (1978).

10 I identify fixed capital with constant capital and I identify circulating capital with variable capital, to make the story simple.

11 It is interesting to see that relative price also increases for a good in the production of which a new technique has been introduced; see Salvadori's (1981) numerical example of the falling rate of profit under the assumptions of joint production and constant returns to scale.

12 See Morishima (1964, pp. 195–215), where the Frobenius theorem itself is also given fully. In the following discussion, to keep the story simple, a weaker version of Morishima's result is given.

5. Rehabilitation of Marshall's life-cycle theory to explain diminishing cost

1 Discussion with Messrs. Toshihide Mizuno and Michihiro Kandori of the

University of Tokyo was useful for this chapter, particularly for the section titled "Stationary state and balanced growth."

2 It was in the sixth edition of *Principles* (1910) that Marshall first added a reservation clause on joint-stock companies. See Marshall (1961, vol. II, p. 343).

3 See Whitaker (1975 vol. II, pp. 305–16), for Marshall's unpublished notes on the theory of economic growth, in which changes in the art of production are taken into consideration. Unfortunately, Marshall did not inquire "into the qualitative properties of solutions for secular growth paths: indeed the models as they stand are much too complex and unrestricted to lend themselves readily to such analysis."

4 While Marshall considers here the growth with both population and wealth growing but technology unchanged, we are going to consider the growth of physical wealth with technical progress and unchanged population.

6. Conditions for the wages fund doctrine and Mill's recantation of it

1 For the wages fund doctrine in general and Mill's recantation in particular, see Mill, J.S. "Thornton on Labour and Its Claims" (1869), pp. 631–68 in Mill (1967), Taussig (1896, pp. 215–65); Schumpeter (1954, pp. 662–71), and Blaug (1978, pp. 193–96). The literature to be discussed here includes Hollander (1968); Schwartz (1972, pp. 90–101); Ekelund (1976).

2 The concept of the capital left idle temporarily is not foreign to Mill. "Capital may be temporarily unemployed, as in the case of unsold goods, or funds that have not yet found an investment: during this interval it does not set in motion any industry" (Mill 1965, p. 65).

3 Therefore, longer run effects do not start. For the boomerang effect, see Schwartz (1972, p. 79).

4 Alternatively, we can construct a two-period budget equation from (6.6) and (6.7) and maximize the utility, being subject to it, to obtain (6.9).

7. Marx and exploitations in production and in circulation

1 Interest here implies *Kapitalzins*, which is a real rate of interest and not a monetary rate of interest, and is comparable to the Marxist rate of surplus value (exploitation) or rate of profit. See Chapter 9 and Negishi (1980).

2 See Hilferding (1975), Okishio (1965, pp. 22–24), Morishima (1973, pp. 190–93), Itoh (1981, pp. 216–27), and Fujimori (1982, pp. 75–116).

3 See Wicksteed "The Marxian Theory of Value" (1884), reprinted in Wicksteed (1934, pp. 705–733). I owe this reference to Professor Yoshihiro Takasuka of Hitotsubashi University.

4 Böhm-Bawerk's *Karl Marx and the close of his system* was first published in 1896, under the title *Zum Abschluss des Marxschen Systems*, while Marx's *Theorien über den Mehrwert* was published in 1905–1910. See, however, Blaug (1978, p. 291).

5 This argument is a nice criticism against the so-called historical transformation problem, which Hilferding himself, very ironically, accepted (Morishima and Catephores 1978, p. 180).

6 See Chapter 9 for the case where laborers can save and become capitalists and the rate of interest can be positive in a stationary state.

7 I exclude the case where present and future goods are perfect or intrinsic complements so that an indifference curve is L shaped with a kink at S in Figure 7.1. I owe this qualification to Professor Eiji Ohyano of Saga University.

8 Some Marxist economists argue that physically identical goods are also identical socially and economically in a balanced growth economy. This argument is impossible, however, if we take into consideration the existence of an industrial reserve army in the Marxist system, let alone the existence of land.

9 I owe this conclusion to Professor Massayuki Iwata of Chiba University.

10 The quotation within the quotation from Marx is from Petty.

11 Itoh warned, very cleverly as a Marxist economist, not to overvaluate the importance of the problem of skilled labor. Not only the different rate of exploitation for different types of labor, which Morishima pointed out, but also the fact that laborers advance capital for the reproduction of labor power are embarrassing to Marxist theory of capitalistic exploitation.

12 For a non-Marxist emphasis of the role of an industrial reserve army in a capitalist society, see Beveridge (1945, p. 194).

13 See the quotation from Marx following. In a Marxist system of price of production as well as in the classical system of natural price, equalization of profit rates and equality of demand and supply are consistent, in spite of the notoriously misleading argument that "either there may be a tendency towards uniformity of wages and the rate of profit in different lines of production, or prices may be governed by supply and demand, but not both. Where supply and demand rule, there is no room for uniform levels of wages and the rate of profits" (Robinson 1961).

14 For an argument for exploitation based on an industrial reserve army not in a competitive economy but in a world of monopolies, see Kühne (1979, p. 181).

8. Marx's dichotomy between exploitation and redistribution of surplus products

1 In other words, only the relative price is determined. In Marx's transformation of value to price, absolute prices are determined by arbitrary assumptions that "the sum of the prices of production of all commodities produced in society is equal to the sum of their values" (Marx 1959, pp. 159–60) and "surplus-value and profit are identical from the stand point of their mass" (p. 167).

2 It should be emphasized that this conclusion depends on the assumption of the constant returns to scale. If Marx's consideration of increasing returns to scale is to be emphasized (as was done in Chapter 4), the dichotomy does not work even between theory of value and theory of price of production.

3 Since Equation (8.14) is obtained only for the marginal product and input coefficients are increasing function of the level of output, there exists, strictly speaking, differential rent for intramarginal units of product. Its role is limited, however, because of the assumption of the given unchanged level of output, and

we disregard its existence in this section.

4 Equation (8.16) is also obtained from (8.13)–(8.15) by eliminating prices and wage through substitutions.

5 Since the output of the first good is given, from (8.4)–(8.8), net output of two goods are also given. Prices are changed so that demands are equalized to these given supplies.

6 Differential rent I is concerned with extensive margin while differential rent II is concerned with intensive margin. See, however, Blaug (1978, p. 299).

7 Liubimov (1930, ch. 40), on the other hand, criticized Bulgakov and followers and proposed the so-called production theory of differential rent, according to which differential rent is a part of surplus value created in agriculture. If we follow this theory, the total value created is no longer L, but larger than L by the differential rent expressed in value terms, though the conclusion of this section remains unchanged.

8 I am grateful to Professor Hanjiro Haga of Tohoku University for several useful comments.

9. Böhm-Bawerk and the positive rate of interest in a stationary state

1 Schumpeter's argument on the ralation between the second cause and other causes is confused, however. Nor is his assertion that "Böhm-Bawerk himself tried to show that the first two reasons will not necessarily produce a premium without the third" warranted.

2 See Böhm-Bawerk's numerical example of the third cause (1959b, pp. 351–65) and Wicksell (1977, pp. 172–84). See also Lutz (1956, pp. 25–36, 186–87).

3 See Lutz (1956, pp. 34–36), Hirshleifer (1967), Pasinetti (1979), and Sandelin (1980). I am grateful to Mr. Toshihide Mizuno of University of Tokyo for calling my attention to Hirshleifer (1967).

4 It is true that the first cause is introduced implicitly along with the second cause in Bernholz, Faber, and Reiss (1978). In the case of a stationary state where net investment is zero, however, the positive rate of interest is still explained by the second cause. See also Faber (1979, pp. 111–30).

5 I am indebted to Professor G.O. Orosel for the suggestion that the life-cycle model should be used, while I owe to Professor M. Faber the reference to Arvidsson (1956), an important article that discusses the mutual relations among Böhm-Bawerk's three causes of interest.

6 Kuenne (1963, p. 282) was right here to point out the role of capital scarcity to assure that $f(t)$ is increasing. His argument was, however, confusing, since he did not make clear distinction between the first and second causes. See also Faber (1979, p. 133).

7 This corresponds to Yasui's (1936) correction of the Walrasian system. See also Garegnani (1960, part 2, ch. 2). Even if one considers subsistence fund and makes capital homogeneous ($K = aWLt/2$), furthermore, one has to explain endogenously why such an amount of fund is maintained, – in other words, why it is neither accumulated further nor consumed away.

8 As for comments on Sandelin (1980), see Samuelson (1982) and Negishi (1982d). Samuelson (1983), furthermore, argued that the model will be over-determined if it includes both a saving function (as I shall explain) and a nonconstant returns production function and that this overdetermination can be avoided by allowing the number of firms in the market to be variable.

9 Professor Orosel pointed out that this assumption can be dropped if the period of production is shorter by more than one period than the life span of the individual person.

10 Although we have mainly followed Negishi (1982c) so far, the rest of this chapter is different from the corresponding part of it, since the latter is quite unsatisfactory. I am grateful, for their useful comments, to Mr. Kiminori Matsuyama of University of Tokyo and Mr. Shinji Yoshimoto, formerly of the Japanese Ministry of Finance.

11 Discussion with Professor Makoto Yano of Cornell University was very useful in this respect.

10. The role of exporters and importers in classical and Keynesian theories

1 Dornbusch, Fisher, and Samuelson (1976) considered the case with infinitely many goods.

2 For the more general neoclassical case, see Anderson and Takayama (1977).

3 See Dornbusch and Mussa (1975), where such a behavior of expenditure is explained by intertemporal optimization.

4 See Chipman (1965a), which explains this assumption as the generalization of numerical example considered by Mill (1965).

5 Numerical values of a in (10.4) and (10.5) are different from those in (10.1) and (10.2).

6 This interpretation of Ricardo that the terms of trade are one-to-one is due to Yukizawa (1974).

7 So far this section is largely dependent on a part of Negishi (1982b) while the rest of this section discusses the same problem differently from the corres-ponding part of (1982b), though it arrives at the identical conclusion.

8 The rest of this section is largely based on Negishi (1979b). I am grateful to Professor Michihiro Ohyama of Keio University who corrected errors in an earlier version of it.

9 Note that the domestic price of the importables is constant in terms of the home currency.

10 B is defined in terms of foreign currency. What the home country receives from foreign importers for the export of M^* is given in terms of the home currency and what the home country pays through its importers for the import M is given in terms of foreign currency.

11 When trade balances, the foreign exchange market is unstable, since the stabilizing effects of changes in export and import are overtaken by the destabilizing effect of changes in exchange rate, given export.

12 Note that what the home country receives through its exporters for M^* is given

in terms of foreign currency while what the country pays to foreign exporters for M is given in terms of home currency.

13 When trade balances, the foreign exchange market is stable, since the destabilizing effects of changes in export and import are overtaken by the stabilizing effect of changes in exchange rate, given import.

14 In this case, both of what the home country receives for M^* and what it pays for M are given in terms of foreign currency.

11. Ricardo, the natural wage, and international unequal exchange

1 See also Helpman and Razin (1978, pp. 5–12), and Takayama (1972, pp. 109–29). According to interpretations in the recently growing literature of the neo-Ricardians, however, labor is not the only factor requiring remuneration and wage is given independently of productivity. See, for example, Steedman and Metcalfe (1979).

2 Hollander (1979, pp. 463–64) noted that wage in Portugal must be lower relative to labor productivity in the Ricardian system where the rate of profit is lower in England.

3 Strictly speaking, labor productivity in each country might be changed before and after trade because of the changes in population and capital in each country. We ignore this possibility by assuming that marginal productivity of labor does not change continuously, but changes in stepwise fashion, and remains unchanged for the changes in population and capital under consideration.

4 This section depends largely on Negishi (1982b), though more emphasis is placed on the possible difference among countries in natural wage.

5 The rate of profit is, of course, the ratio of profit to the total capital, the sum of advancement of wage cost and other forms of capital.

6 Input coefficient of wage good implies the input coefficient of labor multiplied by the input coefficient of wage good in the reproduction of labor power.

7 Trivial corrections are made. See Japanese translation of S. Amin, *L'échange inégal et la loi de la valeur*, i.e., *Futokakokan to Kachihosoku*, translated by K. Hanasaki (Tokyo: Aki Shobo, 1979), p. 133.

8 It should be noted that wage cost is not advanced by capitalists in Saigal's model.

9 Similar results are obtained also in the case where country $A(B)$ is specialized in good II (I). See Saigal (1973, pp. 121–28).

10 Similar arguments can be made to the case where country $A(B)$ is specialized in good II (I). See Saigal's exercise 3, where the condition for unequal exchange is $P_e < P_e^B < P_e^A$.

11 Emmanuel (1972, p. xiii), argued with respect to the Ricardian example of comparative advantage as follows. "It is clear that this specialization constitutes only a relative optimum. The absolute optimum would be, not for Portugal to specialize in wine and England in cloth, but for the English to move to Portugal with their capital in order to produce both wine and cloth.... But such an absolute condition would be neither possible nor

desirable.... Man is hardest to transport." Whether desirable or not, however, English capital alone, without the English, will move to Portugal to make
a larger profit.

12 Evans (1981b, p. 125) suggested the possibility of the same result for the case of
complete equalization of rate of profit and suitably different technologies.

13 Of course, Saigal's argument can also be refuted similarly if we assume that
country $A(B)$ is specialized in good II (I). This can be seen simply by
exchanging the role of two countries, since the proof of the nonexistence of
unequal exchange in the text is independent of the conditions $W^A > W^B$ and
$q > 1$.

12. Jevons, Edgeworth, and the competitive equilibrium of exchange

1 See Jaffé (1976). See also Walras (1954, pp. 205–206). For the assessment of
Jevons by recent historians of economic thought, see Howey (1960, pp. 39–60),
Black et al. (1973, pp. 98–139), Jaffé (1976), and Blaug (1978, pp. 324–32).

2 We may perhaps say that the infinitesimal divisibility of trade plays in this
chapter the role that the infinite number of traders does in the Edgeworth game
of exchange. Professor Kotaro Suzumura of Hitotsubashi University kindly
pointed out the possible relation to his unpublished work based on the concept
of F-blocking in the theory of games.

3 See Chipman (1965b, pp. 690–98), where conditions for the existence of social
indifference curves are discussed. For example, homothetic utility functions are
sufficient for Jevons's example given below.

4 Except for the case of bilateral monopoly, however, we shall see that Jevons was
right.

5 For the original argument of Edgeworth, to which this paragraph is a simplified
close substitute, see (Edgeworth 1881, pp. 34–42). See also Hildenbrand and
Kirman (1976, pp. 18–23).

6 I owe this remark to an anonymous referee of the *Manchester School* for Negishi
(1982e).

7 Otherwise, that is, if A_1 (A_2) has transaction CK with B_1 (B_2) and transaction
KH with B_2 (B_1), similar arbitrage is also possible where each trader tries to
replace an unfavorable transaction with a favorable one. For the general
definition of arbitrage, see Boulding (1955, p. 73).

8 See Akashi (1981) for a closely related and more rigorous demonstration.

13. Menger's *Absatzfähigkeit*, a non-Walrasian theory of markets and money

1 See Streissler (1973a). See also Borch (1973), however, for a somewhat
different interpretation.

2 This chapter is based on a paper that was read before the forty-fifth annual
meeting of Japanese Society for the History of Economic Thought in 1981.
Comments of Professor Kiichiro Yagi of Okayama University were useful for
the revision of the paper into this chapter.

3 See Menger (1892), where *Absatzfähigkeit* is translated into salableness. See also Menger (1950, p. 242), where *Absatzfähig* is translated into liquid and *Absatzfähigkeit* into marketability.

4 Referring to Menger, however, Fujino (1982) argued more strongly that the salability of commodities are always limited, irrespective of the existence of excess supply or excess demand. See Negishi (1984) for further references to this highly interesting argument.

5 Mr. Kiminori Matsuyama of the University of Tokyo pointed that casual suppliers can sell to regular suppliers only at the price equal to or less than the marginal cost of the latter.

6 This example is given by Professor Takatoshi Ito of University of Minnesota. See Negishi (1979a, pp. 21–23).

7 A rule closely related to that of voluntary exchange is the so-called Edgeworth's rule that transactions are carried out so that utility of individual commodity stock holding is always nondiminishing, which is a rule for direct exchange and rules out the possibility of indirect exchange. See Uzawa (1962).

8 The last assumption is plausible. We often have more money than we wanted to keep ultimately, temporarily after the sale and before purchase.

9 For this chapter of the *General theory* itself, see Lerner (1952) and Turvey (1965).

14. The Marshallian foundation of macroeconomic theories

1 For a typical example of such a quantity theory of money before Keynes, see Fisher (1918, pp. 55–73).

2 This section is largely dependent on Negishi (1979a, ch. 2). For the classical dichotomy in general, see (Negishi 1972, ch. 16).

3 Keynes (1973, pp. 409–11). For the references to Marshall, see Marshall (1961, pp. 61–62).

4 See Marshall (1879, pp. 150–67; 1961, pp. 710–11; 1923, Book IV; and 1926, pp. 1–16). See also Hansen (1951, pp. 270, 275), Hayasaka (1979), and Wolfe (1956).

5 For recent literature on microeconomic foundations to equilibrium macro-economics or quantity theory after Keynes, see Grossman (1973) and articles by Alchian, Holt, Phelps, Mortensen, Lucas, and Rapping in Phelps et al. (1971).

6 See Negishi (1979a, p. 36). It is also plausible that marketing cost function has a kink at the current sale point and the following argument can also be done in terms of marketing cost. See Negishi (1979a, ch. 8).

7 See Figure 2.2. See also Negishi (1979a, chs. 7 and 10).

8 This denies the first postulate of classical economics, which is assumed in Keynes (1936). See Negishi (1979a, p. 33).

9 For a good survey of recent literature on microeconomic foundations of Keynesian or disequilibrium macroeconomics, see Drazen (1980). Clower (1975) discusses the so-called neo-Marshallian models. See also the Chapter 2, section titled "Demand deficiency and increasing returns" for some recent literature based on the kinked demand curve.

References

Akashi, S. 1981. "Price Competition and Competitive Equilibrium in an Economy with a Finite Number of Agents." Unpublished paper. Hitotsubashi University.

Allen, R.G.D. 1967. *Macro-Economic Theory*. London: Macmillan Press.

Amin, S. 1976. *Unequal Development*, translated by B. Pearce. New York: Monthly Review Press.

Anderson, R.K., and A. Takayama. 1977. "Devaluation, the Specie Flow Mechanism and the Steady State." *Review of Economic Studies* 44: 347–61.

Arrow, K.J. "The Division of Labor in the Economy, the Polity and Society." In G.P. O'Driscoll, ed., *Adam Smith and Modern Political Economy*, Ames: Iowa State University Press, pp. 153–64.

Arrow, K.J., and F.H. Hahn, 1971. *General Competitive Analysis*. San Francisco: Holden-Day.

Arvidsson, G. 1956. "On the Reasons for a Rate of Interest." *International Economic Papers* 6: 23–33.

Benassy, J.P. 1978. "A Neo-Keynesian Model of Price and Quantity Determination in Disequilibrium." In G. Schwödiauer, ed., *Equilibrium and Disequilibrium in Economic Theory*. Dordrecht, Holland: D. Reidel, pp. 511–44.

Bernholz, P. 1971. "Superiority of Roundabout Processes and Positive Rate of Interest; A Simple Model of Capital and Growth." *Kyklos* 24: 687–721.

Bernholz, P., M. Faber, and W. Reiss. 1978. "A Neo-Austrian Two Period Multi-Sector Model of Capital." *Journal of Economic Theory* 17: 38–50.

Beveridge, W.H. 1954. *Full Employment in a Free Society*. New York: Norton.

Black, R.D.C., et al. 1973. *The Marginal Revolutions in Economics*. Durham, N.C.: Duke University Press.

Bladen, V. 1974. *From Adam Smith to Maynard Keynes*. Toronto: University of Toronto Press.

Blaug, M. 1978. *Economic Theory in Retrospect*. Cambridge: Cambridge University Press.

1980. *The Methodology of Economics*, Cambridge: Cambridge University Press.

Bloomfield, A.I. 1975. "Adam Smith and the Theory of International Trade." In A.S. Skinner and T. Wilson, eds., *Essays on Adam Smith*, London: Oxford University Press, pp. 153–64.

Böhm-Bawerk, E.V. 1959a. *Capital and Interest. The History and Critique of Interest Theories*, translated by G.D. Huncke and H.F. Sennholz. South Holland, Ill.: Libertarian Press.

1959b. *Capital and Interest. Positive Theory of Capital*, translated by G.D. Huncke and H.F. Sennholz. South Holland, Ill.: Libertarian Press.

192

References

193

1959c. *Capital and Interest. Further Essays on Capital and Interest*, translated by H.F. Sennholz. South Holland, Ill.: Libertarian Press.

Böhm-Bawerk, E.V., and R. Hilferding, 1975. *Karl Marx and the Close of His System*, and *Böhm-Bawerk's Marx-Kritik*, edited by P.M. Sweezy, London: Merlin.

Borch, K. 1973. "The Place of Uncertainty in the Theories of the Austrian School." In J.R. Hicks and W. Weber, eds., *Carl Menger and the Austrian School of Economics*. London: Oxford University Press, pp. 61–74.

Bortkiewicz, L.V. 1911. "Die Rodbertus'sche Grundrententheorie und die Marx'sche Lehre von der absoluten Grundrente." Zweiter Artikel. *Archiv für die Geschichte des Sozialismus und der Arbeiterbewegung* 1: 389–434.

Boudin, L.B. 1907. *The Theoretical System of Karl Marx* Chicago: Kerr.

Boulding, K.E. 1955. *Economic Analysis*. New York: Harper & Row.

Bowley, M. 1975. "Some Aspects of the Treatment of Capital in *The Wealth of Nations*." In A.S. Skinner and T. Wilson, eds., *Essays on Adam Smith*. London: Oxford University Press, pp. 361–76.

Bronfenbrenner, M. 1971. "The Structure of Revolutions in Economic Thought." *History of Political Economy* 3: 136–51.

Caves, R.E., and R.W. Jones 1973. *World Trade and Payments*. Boston: Little, Brown.

Cesarano, F. 1983. "On the Role of the History of Economic Analysis." *History of Political Economy* 15: 63–82.

Chamberlin, E.H. 1948. *The Theory of Monopolistic Competition*. Cambridge, Mass.: Harvard University Press.

Chipman, J.S. 1965a. "A Survey of the Theory of International Trade, 1." *Econometrica* 33: 477–519.

1965b. "A Survey of the Theory of International Trade, 2." *Econometrica* 33: 685–760.

Clower, R. 1975. "Reflections on the Keynesian Perplex." *Zeitschrift für Nationalökonomie* 35: 1–24.

Corden, W.M. 1974. *Trade Policy and Economic Welfare*. London: Oxford University Press.

Dornbusch, R., S. Fisher, and P.A. Samuelson. 1976. "Comparative Advantage, Trade and Payments in a Ricardian Model with a Continuum of Goods." *American Economic Review* 67: 823–39.

Dornbusch, R., and M. Mussa. 1975. "Consumption, Real Balances and the Hoarding Function." *International Economic Review* 16: 415–21.

Drazen, A. 1980. "Recent Developments in Macroeconomic Disequilibrium Theory." *Econometrica* 48: 283–306.

Eagly, R.V. 1974. *The Structure of Classical Economic Theory*. New York: Oxford University Press.

Easlea, B. 1973. *Liberation and the Aims of Science*. London: Sussex University Press.

Edgeworth, F.Y. 1881. *Mathematical Psychics*. London: Kegan Paul.

Ekelund, R.B. 1976. "A Short-Run Classical Model of Capital and Wages: Mill's Recantation of Wages Fund." *Oxford Economic Papers* 28: 66–85.

Emmanuel, A. 1972. *Unequal Exchange*, translated by B. Pearce. New York: Monthly Review Press.

194   References

Eshag, E. 1963. *From Marshall to Keynes.* Oxford: Basil Blackwell.

Evans, H.D. 1981a. "Trade, Production and Self-Reliance." In D. Seers, ed., *Dependency Theory: A Critical Assessment.* London: Frances Pinter, pp. 119–34.

1981b. "Unequal Exchange and Economic Policies: Some Implications of the Neo-Ricardian Critique of the Theory of Comparative Advantage." In I. Livingson, ed., *Development Economics and Policy: Readings.* London: George Allen and Unwin, pp. 117–28.

Faber, M. 1979. *Introduction to Modern Austrian Capital Theory.* Berlin: Springer.

Fisher, I. 1918. *The Purchasing Power of Money.* New York: Macmillan.

Friedman, M. 1968. "The Role of Monetary Policy." *American Economic Review* 58: 1–17.

Frisch, R. 1950. "Alfred Marshall's Theory of Value." *Quarterly Journal of Economics* 64: 495–524.

Fujimori, Y. 1982. *Modern Analysis of Value Theory.* Berlin: Springer.

Fujino, S. 1982. Book Review of Negishi 1979a. *The Economic Review* 33: 94–96.

Garegnani, P. 1960. *Il Capitale nelle Teorie della Destribuzione.* Milan: Giuffrè.

Goodwin, C.D. 1980. "Toward a Theory of the History of Economics." *History of Political Economy* 12: 610–19.

Grossman, H.I. 1973. "Aggregate Demand, Job Search, and Employment." *Journal of Political Economy* 81: 1353–69.

Hague, D.C. 1958. "Alfred Marshall and the Competitive Firm." *Economic Journal* 68: 673–90.

Hahn, F.H., and T. Negishi, 1962. "A Theorem on Non-Tâtonnement Stability." *Econometrica* 30: 463–69.

Hansen, A.H. 1951. *Business Cycles and National Income.* New York: Norton.

Harris, J.R. and M.P. Todaro 1970. "Migration, Unemployment and Development." *American Economic Review* 60: 126–42.

Hayasaka, T. 1979. "Marshall Keizaigaku niokeru Shijokozo [The Market Structue in Marshall's Economics], 2." *Gaikokugokakenkyukiyo* [The Proceedings of the Department of Foreign Languages and Literatures, College of General Education, University of Tokyo] 27(3): 1–38.

Hayek, F.A. 1973. "The Place of Menger's *Grundsätze* in the History of Economic Thought." In J.R. Hicks and W. Weber, eds., *Carl Menger and the Austrian School of Economics.* London: Oxford University Press, pp. 1–14.

Heckscher, E.F. 1955. *Mercantilism,* edited by E.F. Söderland. London: George Allen and Unwin.

Helpman, E., and A. Razin. 1978. *A Theory of International Trade under Uncertainty.* New York: Academic Press.

Hicks, J.R. 1946. *Value and Capital.* London: Oxford University Press.

1977. *Economic Perspectives.* London: Oxford University Press.

Hildenbrand, W., and A.P. Kirman. 1976. *Introduction to Equilibrium Analysis.* Amsterdam: North-Holland.

Hilferding, R. 1975. See Böhm-Bawerk and Hilferding 1975.

Hirase, M. 1967. *Keizaigaku Yottsu no Miketsu Mondai* [Four Unsettled Questions in Economics] Tokyo: Miraisha.

Hirshleifer, J. 1967. "A Note on the Böhm-Bawerk/Wicksell Theory of Interest."

Review of Economic Studies 34: 191–99.

Hishiyama, I. 1965. "Daikiboseisan to Shijokinko [Large Scale Production and Market Equilibrium]." In Committee on Festschrift for Dr. S. Kishimoto, eds., *Keizaigaku niokeru Koten to Gendai* [Classics and Moderns in Economics]. Tokyo: Nihon-Hyoron.

Hollander, S. 1961. "The Representative Firm and Imperfect Competition." *Canadian Journal of Economics and Political Science* 27: 236–41.

1968. "The Role of Fixed Technical Coefficients in the Evolution of the Wages Fund Controversy." *Oxford Economic Papers* 20: 320–41.

1973. *The Economics of Adam Smith*. Toronto: University of Toronto Press.

1979. *The Economics of David Ricardo*. Toronto: University of Toronto Press.

Howey, R.S. 1960. *The Rise of the Marginal Utility School*. Lawrence: University of Kansas Press.

Hume, D. 1955. *Writings on Economics*, edited by E. Rotwein. Edinburgh: Nelson.

Hurwicz, L. 1972. "On Informationally Decentralized Systems." In C.B. McGuire and R. Radner, eds., *Decisions and Organization*, Amsterdam: North-Holland.

Hutchison, T.W. 1978. *On Revolutions and Progress in Economic Knowledge*. Cambridge: Cambridge University Press.

Itoh, Makoto 1981. *Kachi to Shihon no Riron* [Theory of Value and Capital]. Tokyo: Iwanami.

Jaffé, W. 1976. "Menger, Jevons and Walras De-Homogenized." *Economic Inquiry* 14: 511–24.

1977. "A Centenarian on a Bicentenarian, Leon Walras's *Elements* on Adam Smith's *Wealth of Nations*." *Canadian Journal of Economics* 10: 19–33.

Jevons, W.S. 1888. *The Theory of Political Economy*. London: Macmillan Press.

Kaldor, N. 1972. "The Irrelevance of Equilibrium Economics." *Economic Journal* 82: 1237–55.

Kamisato, K. 1963. "Rijunritsu, Jitshitsu-chinginritsu, Gijutsushinpo [Rate of Profit, Real Wage, Technical Progress]." *Toyo University Keizaikeieironshu* 32: 52–79.

Karni, E. 1973. "Transaction Costs and the Demand for Medium of Exchange." *Western Economic Journal* 11: 71–80.

Kemp, M.C. 1964. *The Pure Theory of International Trade*. Englewood Cliffs, N.J.: Prentice-Hall.

Keynes, J.M. 1936. *The General Theory of Employment, Interest and Money*, London: Macmillan Press.

1972. *Collected Writings, X, Essays in Biography*. London: Macmillan Press.

1973. *Collected Writings, XIII, The General Theory and After*. Part I. London: Macmillan Press.

Kobayashi, N. 1977. *Kokufurontaikei no Seiritsu* [Formation of the System of *Wealth of Nations*]. Tokyo: Miraisha.

Kojima, K. 1952. *Kokusaikeizairiron no Kenkyu* [Studies in the Theory of International Economics]. Tokyo: Toyokeizai.

1971. *Japan and a Pacific Free Trade Area*. London: Macmillan Press.

Kuenne, R.E. 1963. *The Theory of General Economic Equilibrium*. Princeton, N.J.: Princeton University Press.

Kuhn, T.S. 1957. *The Copernican Revolution*. Cambridge, Mass.: Harvard University Press.

1970. *The Structure of Scientific Revolutions*, 2nd ed. Chicago: University of Chicago Press.

Kühne, K. 1979. *Economics and Marxism*, vol. I, translated by R. Shaw. London: Macmillan Press.

Lakatos, I. 1970. "Falsification and the Methodology of Scientific Research Programmes." In I. Lakatos and A. Musgrave, eds., *Criticism and the Growth of Knowledge*. London: Cambridge University Press.

Latsis, S., ed. 1976. *Method and Appraisal in Economics*. Cambridge: Cambridge University Press.

Leijonhufvud, A. 1974. "The Varieties of Price Theory." Unpublished paper, University of California, Los Angeles.

Lerner, A.P. 1952. "The Essential Properties of Interest and Money." *Quarterly Journal of Economics* 66: 172–93.

Liubimov, L. 1930. *Ocherki teorii zemelinoi renty*. Moscow: National Publishing House.

Lutz, F.A. 1956. *Zinstheorie*. Tübingen: Mohr.

McCulloch, J.R., ed. 1954. *Early English Tracts on Commerce*. Cambridge: Cambridge University Press.

Malinvaud, E. 1977. *Theory of Unemployment Reconsidered*. Oxford: Blackwell.

Marshall, A. 1921. *Industry and Trade*. London: Macmillan Press.

1923. *Money, Credit and Commerce*. London: Macmillan Press.

1926. *Official Papers*. London: Macmillan Press.

1961. *Principles of Economics*. London: Macmillan Press.

Marshall, A., and M.P. Marshall, 1879. *The Economics of Industry*. London: Macmillan Press.

Marx, K. 1920. *The Poverty of Philosophy*, translated by H. Quelch. Chicago: Kerr.

1954. *Capital*, vol. I. Moscow: Progress Publishers.

1959. *Capital*, vol. III, Moscow: Progress Publishers.

1963. *Theories of Surplus Value*, vol. I. Moscow: Foreign Language Publishing House.

1968. *Theories of Surplus Value*, vol. II. Moscow: Progress Publishers.

Mehta, G. 1977. *The Structure of the Keynesian Revolution*. London: Martin Robertson.

Menger, C. 1892. "On the Origin of Money." *Economic Journal* 2: 239–55.

1950. *Principles of Economics*, translated by J. Dingwall and B.F. Hoselitz. Glencoe, Ill.: Free Press.

Mill, J.S. 1965. *Principles of Political Economy*. Toronto: University of Toronto Press.

1967. *Essays on Economics and Society*. Toronto: University of Toronto Press.

Morishima, M. 1964. *Equilibrium Stability and Growth*. London: Oxford University Press.

1973. *Marx's Economics*. London: Cambridge University Press.

1977. *Walras's Economics*. Cambridge: Cambridge University Press.

Morishima, M., and G. Catephores. 1978. *Value Exploitation and Growth*. London: McGraw-Hill.

Morishima, M., and M. Majumdar. 1978. "The Cournot–Walras Arbitrage,

Resource Consuming Exchange, and Competitive Equilibrium." *Hommage à F. Perroux.* Grenoble: Presse Universitaires de Grenoble, pp. 501–14.

Morishima, M., et al. 1973. *Theory of Demand.* London: Oxford University Press.

Morita, K. 1977. "Kotenha Kokusaibungyoron Saiko [The Classical Theory of International Division of Labor: A Reappraisal]." *Keizaigakuronshu* [University of Tokyo Journal of Economics] 43(3): 2–20.

Nagatani, K. 1978. *Monetary Theory.* Amsterdam: North-Holland.

Nakatani, T. 1980. "The Law of Falling Rate of Profit and the Competitive Battle; Comment on Shaikh." *Cambridge Journal of Economics* 4: 65–68.

Negishi, T. 1962. "The Stability of a Competitive Economy, A Survey Article." *Econometrica* 30: 635–69.

1972. *General Equilibrium Theory and International Trade.* Amsterdam: North-Holland.

1979a. *Microeconomic Foundations of Keynesian Macroeconomics.* Amsterdam: North-Holland.

1979b. "Foreign Exchange Gains in a Keynesian Model of International Trade." *Économie Appliquée* 32: 623–33.

1980. "Marx and Böhm-Bawerk in the Theory of Interest." *Économies et Sociétés* 14: 287–304.

1982a. "From Samuelson's Stability Analysis to Non-Walrasian Economics." In J.R. Feiwel, ed., *Samuelson and Neoclassical Economics.* Boston: Kluwer-Nijhoff, pp. 119–25.

1982b. "The Labor Theory of Value in the Ricardian Theory of International Trade." *History of Political Economy* 14: 199–210.

1982c. "Wicksell's Missing Equation and Böhm-Bawerk's Three Causes of Interest in a Stationary State." *Zeitschrift für Nationalökonomie* 42: 161–74.

1982d. "Wicksell's Missing Equation: A Comment." *History of Political Economy* 14: 310–11.

1982e. "A Note on Jevons's Law of Indifference and Competitive Equilibrium." *Manchester School* 50: 220–30.

1985. "Non-Walrasian Foundations of Macroeconomics." In J.R. Feiwel, ed., *Issues in Contemporary Macroeconomics and Distribution.* New York: Macmillan.

Newman, P. 1960. "The Erosion of Marshall's Theory of Value." *Quarterly Journal of Economics* 74: 587–600.

Newman, P., and J.N. Wolfe. 1961. "A Model for the Long-Run Theory of Value." *Review of Economic Studies* 29: 51–61.

Niehans, J. 1971. "Money and Barter in General Equilibrium with Transaction Costs." *American Economic Review* 61: 773–83.

1978. *The Theory of Money.* Baltimore: Johns Hopkins University Press.

Okishio, N. 1961. "Technical Changes and the Rate of Profit." *Kobe University Economic Review* 7: 85–99.

1965. *Shihonseikeizai no Kisoriron* [Basic Theory of Capitalist Economy]. Tokyo: Sobunsha.

1977. *Marx Keizaigaku* [Marxian Economics]. Tokyo: Chikuma.

Orosel, G.O. 1981. "Faber's Modern Austrian Capital Theory: A Critical Survey." *Zeitschrift für Nationalökonomie* 41: 141–55.

198   References

Ouchi, T. 1958. *Jidai to Tochishoyu* [Rent and Landownership]. Tokyo: University of Tokyo Press.

Pasinetti, L.L. 1974. *Growth and Income Distribution*. Cambridge: Cambridge University Press.

1979. "Wicksell Effects and Reswitchings of Technique in Capital Theory." In S. Strom and B. Thalberg, eds., *The Theoretical Contributions of Knut Wicksell*. London: Macmillan Press, pp. 53–61.

Patinkin, D. 1956. *Money Interest and Prices*. Evanston, Ill.: Row, Peterson.

Phelps, E.S., et al. 1971. *Microeconomic Foundations of Employment and Inflation Theory*. London: Macmillan Press.

Popper, K.R. 1959. *The Logic of Scientific Discovery*. London: Hutchinson.

Reid, G.C. 1981. *The Kinked Demand Curve Analysis of Oligopoly*. Edinburgh: Edinburgh University Press.

Ricardo, D. 1951. *On the Principles of Political Economy and Taxation*. Cambridge: Cambridge University Press.

Richardson, G.B. 1975. "Adam Smith on Competition and Increasing Returns." In A.S. Skinner and T. Wilson, eds., *Essays on Adam Smith*. London: Oxford University Press.

Roberts, D.J., and A. Postlewaite. 1976. "The Incentives for Price-Taking Behavior in Large Exchange Economies." *Econometrica* 44: 115–27.

Robertson, D.H. 1930. "The Trees of the Forest." *Economic Journal* 40: 80–89.

Robinson, J. 1933. *The Economics of Imperfect Competition*. London: Macmillan.

1961. "Prelude to a Critique of Economic Theory." *Oxford Economic Papers* 13: 7–14.

Rodbertus, J.C. 1851. *Sociale Briefe an von Kirchmann*. Dritter Brief. Widerlegung der Ricardo'schen Lehre von der Grundrente und Begrundung einer neuen Rententheorie. Berlin: Allegemeine Deutche Verlags-Anstalt.

Saigal, J.C. 1973. "Réflexions sur la théorie de 'l'échange inégal'." In S. Amin, *L'échange inégal et la loi de la valeur*. Paris: Éditions Anthropos.

Sakisaka, I. 1977. *Jidairon Kenkyu* [Studies in the Theory of Rent]. Tokyo: Shakaishugikyokai.

Salvadori, N. 1981. "Falling Rate of Profit with a Constant Real Wage, An Example." *Cambridge Journal of Economics* 5: 59–66.

Samuelson, L. 1982. "On Wicksell's Missing Equation." *History of Political Economy* 14: 301–307.

1983. "Returns to Scale and Wicksell's Missing Equation." Unpublished paper. Pennsylvania State University.

Samuelson, P.A. 1966. *Collected Scientific Papers*, vol. I. Cambridge, Mass.: MIT Press.

1972. *Collected Scientific Papers*, vol. III. Cambridge, Mass.: MIT Press.

1977a. "A Modern Theorist's Vindication of Adam Smith." *American Economic Review* 67: 42–49.

1977b. *Collected Scientific Papers*, vol. IV. Cambridge, Mass.: MIT Press.

Sandelin, B. 1980. "Wicksell's Missing Equation, the Production Function, and the Wicksell Effect." *History of Political Economy* 12: 29–40.

Schmitt, H.O. 1979. "Mercantilism: A Modern Argument." *Manchester School* 47: 93–111.

Schumpeter, J.A. 1926. *Theorie der Wirtschaftlichen Entwicklung.* Munich: Dunker and Humblot.

1954. *History of Economic Analysis.* New York: Oxford University Press.

Schwartz, P. 1972. *The New Political Economy of J.S. Mill.* Durham, N.C.: Duke University Press.

Scitovsky, T. 1978. "Asymmetries in Economics." *Scottish Journal of Political Economy* 25: 227–37.

Shaikh, A. 1978. "Political Economy and Capitalism: Notes on Dobb's Theory of Crisis." *Cambridge Journal of Economics* 2: 233–51.

Shibata, K. 1934. "On the Law of Decline in the Rate of Profit." *Kyoto University Economic Review* 9(1): 61–75.

1935. *Riron Keizaigaku* [Economic Theory], vol. I. Tokyo: Kobundo.

1939. "On the General Profit Rate." *Kyoto University Economic Review* 14(1): 40–66.

Shove, G.F. 1930. "The Representative Firm and Increasing Returns." *Economic Journal* 40: 94–116.

1942. "The Place of Marshall's *Principles* in the Development of Economic Theory." *Economic Journal* 52: 294–329.

Smith, A. 1967. *The Early Writings of Adam Smith*, edited by J.R. Lindgren. Fairfield, N.J.: Kelley.

1973. *The Wealth of Nations*, edited with an introduction, notes, marginal summary and an enlarged index by E. Cannan. New York: Modern Library.

1976. *An Inquiry into the Nature and Causes of the Wealth of Nations.* London: Oxford University Press.

1978. *Lectures on Jurisprudence.* London: Oxford University Press.

Sraffa, P. 1926. "The Law of Returns under Competitive Conditions." *Economic Journal* 36: 535–50.

Steedman, I. 1977. *Marx after Sraffa.* London: NBL.

Steedman, I., and J.S. Metcalfe. "On Foreign Trade." In I. Steedman, ed., *Fundamental Issues in Trade Theory.* London: Macmillan Press, pp. 99–109.

Stigler, G.J. 1965. *Essays in the History of Economics.* Chicago: University of Chicago Press.

Stiglitz, J. 1979. "Equilibrium in Product Markets with Imperfect Information." *American Economic Review* 119: 339–45.

Streissler, E. 1973a. "Menger's Theory of Money and Uncertainty." In J.R. Hicks and W. Weber, eds., *Carl Menger and the Austrian School of Economics.* London: Oxford University Press, pp. 164–89.

1973b. "To What Extent was the Austrian School Marginalist?" In R.D. Collison Black, A.W. Coats, and C.D.W. Goodwin, eds., *The Marginal Revolution in Economics.* Durham, N.C.: Duke University Press, pp. 160–72.

Sweezy, P.M. 1939. "Demand under Conditions of Oligopoly." *Journal of Political Economy* 47: 568–73.

1942. *The Theory of Capitalist Development.* New York: Oxford University Press.

Sylos-Labini, P. 1976. "Competition: The Product Markets." In T. Wilson and A.S. Skinner, eds., *The Market and the State.* London: Oxford University Press, pp. 200–32.

Takayama, A. 1972. *International Trade.* New York: Holt, Rinehart and Winston.

200   References

Taussig, F.W. 1896. *Wages and Capital*. New York: Appleton.

Thomson, H.F. 1965. "Adam Smith's Philosophy of Science." *Quarterly Journal of Economics* 79: 213–33.

Turvey, R. 1965. "Does the Rate of Interest Rule the Roost?" In F.H. Hahn and F.P.R. Brechling, eds., *The Theory of Interest Rates*. London: Macmillan Press, pp. 164–72.

Uzawa, H. 1962. "On the Stability of Edgeworth's Barter Process." *International Economic Review* 3: 218–32.

Viner, J. 1937. *Studies in the Theory of International Trade*. New York: Harper.

Walker, D.A. 1969. "Marshall's Theory of Competitive Exchange." *Canadian Journal of Economics* 2: 590–98.

Walras, L. 1954. *Elements of Pure Economics*, translated by W. Jaffé. Homewood, Ill.: Irwin.

     1965. *Correspondence of Leon Walras and Related Papers*, vol. I, edited by W. Jaffé. Amsterdam: North-Holland.

Weber, W., and E. Streissler. 1973. "The Menger Tradition." In J.R. Hicks and W. Weber, eds., *Carl Menger and the Austrian School of Economics*. London: Oxford University Press, pp. 226–32.

Weddenpohl, C. 1978. "Increasing Returns and Fixed Market Shares." *International Economic Review* 19: 405–14.

Weizsäcker, C.C. 1973. "Modern Capital Theory and the Concept of Exploitation." *Kyklos* 26: 245–81.

Whitaker, J.K. 1975. *The Early Economic Writings of Alfred Marshall, 1867–1890*. London: Macmillan Press.

Wicksell, K. 1977. *Lectures on Political Economy*, vol. I, translated by E. Classen. Fairfield, N.J.: Kelley.

Wicksteed, P.H. 1934. *The Common Sense of Political Economy*, vol. II. London: Routledge.

Wolfe, J.N. 1954. "The Representative Firm." *Economic Journal* 64: 337–49.

     1956. "Marshall and the Trade Cycle." *Oxford Economic Papers* 8: 90–101.

Woglom, G. 1982. "Underemployment Equilibrium with Rational Expectations." *Quarterly Journal of Economics* 96: 89–107.

Yasui, T. 1936. "Jikanyoso to Shihonrishi [Time Element and Interest]" *Keizaigakuronshu* [University of Tokyo Journal of Economics] 6: pp. 1332–82.

Young, A.A. 1928. "Increasing Returns and Economic Progress." *Economic Journal* 38: 527–42.

Yukizawa, K. 1974. "Ricardo Hikakuseisanhisetsu no Genkeirikai to Henkeirikai [Ricardo's Comparative Cost Theory as It Was]" *Shogakuronsan* [Chuo University Journal of Commerce] 15(6): 25–51.

Zawadzki, W. 1914. *Les Mathématiques appliquées à l'économie politique*. Paris: Rivière.

Author index

Subject index